Also publ

ROUT... **ckburn**
Edited by ... ...ier,
Nick Hostettle... ...

Transcendence
Critical realism and God

Margaret S. Archer, Andrew Collier
and Douglas V. Porpora

Routledge
Taylor & Francis Group

LONDON AND NEW YORK

First published 2004
by Routledge
11 New Fetter Lane, London EC4P 4EE

Simultaneously published in the USA and Canada
by Routledge
29 West 35th Street, New York, NY 10001

Routledge is an imprint of the Taylor & Francis Group

© 2004 Margaret S. Archer, Andrew Collier and Douglas V. Porpora

Typeset in Garamond by
Keystroke, Jacaranda Lodge, Wolverhampton

British Library Cataloguing in Publication Data
A catalogue record for this book is available from the British Library

Library of Congress Cataloging in Publication Data
A catalog record for this book has been requested

ISBN: 978-0-41533-617-8

CRITICAL REALISM: INTERVENTIONS
Edited by Margaret S. Archer, Roy Bhaskar, Andrew Collier,
Nick Hostettler, Tony Lawson and Alan Norrie

Critical realism is one of the most influential new developments in the
philosophy of science and in the social sciences, providing a powerful alternative to positivism and postmodernism. This series will explore the critical
realist position in philosophy and across the social sciences.

Transcendence

Atheism as a belief does not have to present intellectual credentials within academia. Yet to hold beliefs means giving reasons for doing so – ones which may be found wanting. Instead, atheism is the automatic default setting within the academic world.

Conversely, religious belief confronts a double standard. Religious believers are not permitted to make 'truth' claims but are instead forced to present their beliefs as part of one language game among many. Religious truth claims are expected to satisfy empiricist criteria of evidence but when they fail – as they must – religious belief becomes subject to the hermeneutics of suspicion.

Transcendence explores religious experience as a justifiable reason for religious belief. It uniquely demonstrates that the three pillars of critical realism – ontological intransitivity, epistemic relativity and judgemental rationality – can be applied to religion as to any other belief or theory.

The three authors are critical realists by philosophical position. They seek to establish a level playing field between religion and secular ideas, which has not existed in the academic world for several generations, in order for reasoned debate to be conducted.

Margaret S. Archer is Professor of Sociology at the University of Warwick. Her previous books include *Culture and Agency*, *Realist Social Theory*, *Being Human* and *Structure, Agency and the Internal Conversation*. She is a former editor of *Current Sociology* and the only woman to have been President of the International Sociological Association. She is a member of the Pontifical Academy of Social Sciences and a Trustee of the Centre for Critical Realism. **Andrew Collier** is Professor of Philosophy at the University of Southampton and has previously lectured at Warwick, Sussex and Bangor universities. His recent publications include *Being and Worth*, which extends realism to ethics, and *Christianity and Marxism*, which aims to reconcile these two world-views. **Douglas V. Porpora** is Professor of Sociology and Head of the Department of Culture and Communication at Drexel University, Philadelphia. He is an active member of NETWORK, a national social justice lobby. His previous works include *How Holocausts Happen: the United States in central America* and *Landscapes of the Soul: the loss of moral meaning in American life*. He is one of the leading exponents of critical realism in the USA.

Contents

Preface

The authors of this book have several things in common. We are all critical realists by philosophical position. We had all until recently written purely secular and in some cases secularist books, but had arrived at religious positions (more specifically, Christian ones) about which we wanted to go public. We were brought together by Roy Bhaskar, who was then making his own re-evaluation of religion in his book *From East to West*. The present book was conceived in a series of long and intensive discussions which we had with Roy at his house in Suffolk. It would never have come into being without Roy's inspiration, and the hospitality of Roy and his friends. Nevertheless, he would not necessarily agree with all our various conclusions, and has indeed since moved towards a more immanent conception of transcendence (if that is not an oxymoron), in his book *Reflections on Meta-Reality*. Also, it will be obvious that there is a degree of diversity as well as agreement between the three of us. Margaret Archer has a greater involvement with the Catholic mystics, Andrew Collier with Protestant theology, and Doug Porpora with process theology.

We all hope to open up the debate of religious issues within critical realism, an opening which has already begun with Roy's *From East to West*, and also with Doug's *Landscapes of the Soul*, Andrew's *Christianity and Marxism*, and Maggie's *Work and Human Fulfilment*. If critical realists and others in philosophy and the human sciences can be persuaded that religious issues are live issues at all, we will feel that we have succeeded.

We also hope that we may have shown that critical realism can be of value for theology and religious studies, although we ourselves are amateurs in these areas, being trained rather in sociology, philosophy or both.

The first two chapters appear under the signatures of all three of us, and their contents are agreed by us all, though naturally there was some division of labour in the actual writing, with Doug contributing the largest share. The remaining essays have been read and discussed by all of us, but the opinions are in each case the individual author's. Nevertheless, there is a considerable community of ideas and themes running through the book. First, there is the criticism of the idea that atheism is obvious, and that the onus is on any departure from it to justify itself. We try to establish a level playing field between religious and secular ideas, which has not existed in the academic world for some generations. Second, there is a common orientation to religious experience as the basis of religious knowledge. There is no engagement with the ontological or cosmological arguments for the existence of God; there is some discussion of design arguments by Doug, but it is assumed that all theistic arguments worthy of consideration are *a posteriori*. A religious epistemology, like any other epistemology, will have to broach questions about the relations between theory, experience, practical reality-testing, and so forth. In accordance with critical realism, it will need to articulate ontological realism, epistemic relativity and fallibilism, together with judgemental rationality. Consequently, third, we share a critique of the sort of relativism that treats religious beliefs as making no truth claims, and hence not up for rational argument. Finally, since we believe that there is a truth to be found out, that we are fallible in our pursuit of it, and that we can argue rationally about it, we value debate about religious matters highly. There should be genuine inter-faith dialogue, in which participants defend their positions and are open to criticisms of them, rather than either the crossed monologues that dogmatism generates, or the attitude that all positions are equally 'valid', and, by the same token, equally unfounded.

Margaret S. Archer, Andrew Collier and Douglas V. Porpora

1 Introduction

Margaret S. Archer, Andrew Collier and Douglas V. Porpora

Does God exist? More specifically, does God exist as a reality independent of our human belief in God? Certainly, we cannot answer this question on the same kinds of grounds as we can answer questions about the existence of, say, magnetism, electricity or radiation. Actually, in this book, our aim is not even to answer this question definitively.

Our aim is more modest. We wish merely to establish three preliminary points about the question from a critical realist perspective.[1] Critical realism is a philosophy of science that stands midway between a positivism that has failed and a more current postmodernism, which, from a critical realist perspective, is equally flawed. Indeed, from the standpoint of critical realism, postmodernism is much more akin to positivism than its proponents allow. For example, in both positivism and postmodernism the question of God's existence is not legitimately admissible to rational debate.

Reflecting our critical realist perspective, the first point we want to make is that the question of God's existence is indeed susceptible of rational debate. It is not a pseudo-question; nor is it a category mistake to ask it. Furthermore, the question, we maintain, has an ontologically objective answer – even if we cannot say definitively what the answer is.

For many today, it will already be startling for us to assert that God may exist even if we cannot know for certain that God exists. Yet, one of the premises of critical realism is ontological realism. Ontological realism asserts the ontologically objective existence of reality, independent of our beliefs about it. It follows that something may belong to reality even if we remain mistaken about it or even completely ignorant of it. The existence or non-existence of God is a paradigm case.

Ontological realism rescues ontology from absorption into epistemology. Widely fashionable today is an error that critical realists call the 'epistemic fallacy'. We commit the epistemic fallacy when we allow epistemology completely to swallow up ontology. Since the downfall of positivism, it has become almost universally acknowledged that there is no such thing as objective knowledge, knowledge that is in any sense value-free or theory-neutral. Along with almost everyone else today, we agree that all knowledge is value-laden and theory-laden.

Critical realism does not deny the value and theory ladenness of knowledge. What it does is to counter the epistemic fallacy. The epistemic fallacy involves the fallacious inference that because there is no epistemologically objective view of the world, there is also no objective world ontologically. Such an inference leads to the extravagant and relativist claim that, to the extent that we embrace different world-views, we inhabit objectively different worlds.

The problem with such relativism is readily apparent. It implies that when people discovered that the earth revolves around the sun and changed their opinions accordingly, then the objective world they inhabited actually changed. Before, say, Galileo, the sun revolved around the earth and then suddenly did not. For better or worse, critical realists believe that the world cannot be altered just by altering our beliefs about it.

Clearly, the mistake involved in the epistemic fallacy is the failure to distinguish epistemology from ontology and, specifically, epistemological objectivity from ontological objectivity. Even if we can know the world only in epistemically partisan ways, it hardly follows that there is no ontologically objective world there to be known. It may be that, epistemically, we can only know the world through concepts of our own making, but within our own concepts, we must always make an ontological distinction between what we believe exists independently of us, and what does not. Otherwise, we simply conclude that the universe is coterminous with our knowledge of it. To avoid this conflation, critical realism insists on an epistemological distinction between what it calls the transitive dimension (our beliefs or knowledge claims about the world), and the intransitive dimension (what the world is actually like apart from us).

Many readers will be prepared to go with us this far. Indeed, after the famous hoax that the physicist Alan Sokal played on the postmodernist journal, *Social Text*, even many who identify with postmodernism now claim that they have never denied an ontologically objective world. What they tend to persist in denying is that we can know anything about this world.

In contrast, a second premise of critical realism is the ever present possibility for 'judgemental rationality' about the world. Judgemental rationality means that we can publicly discuss our claims about reality, as we think it is, and marshal better or worse arguments on behalf of those claims. By comparatively evaluating the existing arguments, we can arrive at reasoned, though provisional, judgements about what reality is objectively like: about what belongs to that reality and what does not.

Epistemologically, all such judgements remain provisional, subject to new information or re-evaluation. Yet, we often reach a point where the arguments for certain claims are so strong that we are ready to consider the case as being virtually settled. In such cases, we consider ourselves to have arrived at what critical realists call alethia or alethic truth, the truth of reality as such.[2] Although we remain open to new arguments should they appear, we do not expect any to turn up. Among the alethic truths that most people hold today are the roundness of the earth, the law of gravity, and the existence of microbes. It is not that absolutely everyone accepts these putative truths, but that among those who do the remaining arguments of the dissenters fail even to be intellectually challenging. Further, intellectually challenging arguments to the contrary do not even appear on the horizon. On matters such as these, those familiar with the arguments are fairly sure that they have got reality right.

Of course, there are also a great many issues for which the alethic truth continues to remain elusive. It is not that judgemental rationality does not apply to such cases but that judgemental rationality has not yet completed its task. Component arguments are still raised and debated, accepted or rejected. Positions become refined and more nuanced. Even so, the public argument remains inconclusive and the ultimate truth indeterminate. Individually, we may each have our own hunches, perhaps even convictions, about what the truth will turn out to be. Yet, each of us recognises an inability to mount an argument that would convince even ourselves, had we intuitions different from what they are. At such a stage in public debate, it might be equally rational to hold either of two contradictory views, even though, ultimately, one must or both may eventually turn out to be mistaken.

The second point we wish to make in this book is that the question of God's existence is amenable to the judgemental rationality just described. We can publicly discuss the existence of God and debate it. There are arguments, both conceptual and empirical, which we can pose that address at least part of the issue, and we ourselves can often be rationally persuaded that even a position we have advanced is insufficient, faulty or completely untenable.

Saying that judgemental rationality applies to the question of God's existence hardly means that the question can be definitively answered. At the moment, although there certainly are irrational reasons to believe or disbelieve in God, there are also rational grounds both for belief and disbelief. In this book, the equal rationality of belief and disbelief is all we wish to establish about the question of God's existence.

If the objective arguments for and against God's existence are equally strong, or weak, why do some people choose to believe and others not? A third basic premise of critical realism is what is called 'epistemic relativism'. Despite the name, epistemic relativism does not connote judgemental relativism, a relativism that regards all judgements as equally valid. As we have seen, critical realism is committed to the opposite view, i.e. judgemental rationality, which holds some judgements to be objectively better than others.

What epistemic relativism does mean is that all our judgements are socially and historically situated. Our judgements are conditioned by our circumstances, by what we know at the time and by the prevailing criteria of evaluation. For this reason among others, our judgements are always fallible. Epistemic relativism further means that we are each positioned to see the world somewhat differently. Our experiences of the world vary.

Our experiences clearly vary with respect to religion. Many people report experiences of transcendence or even of specific, transcendent realities. Integral to such experiences are emotional reactions to what is experienced and, in many cases, emotional attachments to the objects of such experience. All such experiences come to us already partially interpreted. Although some mystical experiences are partly ineffable relative to existing concepts, some level of interpretation is always an ingredient of any experience. At least, we cannot say what it is we have experienced apart from one or another conceptual scheme.

As religious conceptual schemes vary from culture to culture and from one historical epoch to another, religious experience confronts us as something plural. In this plurality of religious experience, there are also inevitably elements of mutual contradiction. The veracity of each view is called into question by mutually exclusive others. The plural, fallible, socio-historically situated nature of religious experience is part of what is encompassed by epistemic relativism.

The quality of epistemic relativism extends even to atheists and agnostics. Their absence of religious experience is itself a kind of experience. The absence of religious experience is epistemically relative too, subject to prevailing norms, circumstances and conceptual schemes. It is subject even to such factors of personal biography as resistances, prejudices and preferences. Perhaps, for whatever reason, atheists and agnostics are just not situated so as to experience transcendent reality. Perhaps they experience it but fail to attend to it. Perhaps they experience transcendent reality and attend to it but interpret it in more mundane ways. In any case, the purported experience of absence is no less corrigible than the experience of presence.

In terms of epistemic relativism, we can now offer one reason why different people are disposed to believe or disbelieve in transcendent realities like God. Simply put, for whatever reason, some people personally experience such transcendent realities and interpret them as such; others do not.

Prima facie, unless and until there are compelling reasons to discount it, each of us is inclined to trust our own personal experience. Moreover, it is perfectly rational for us to do so. True, our experience often leads us astray. We experience the world as flat, but it is not. Quite often, we misperceive, hallucinate or engage in wish fulfilment. Still, we are material creatures whose very survival depends on our ability to navigate our way in the world. We could not do so effectively if, as a whole, the beliefs based on our experience were routinely incorrect. Thus, although we can be sure that individual beliefs or even entire sections of our belief system might be wrong, we do well to trust in our belief system as a whole.[3] It follows that unless we have compelling grounds to discount a particular experience, our first impulse rationally is to trust it.

Given the presumptive trust that each of us places in our own experience, the objective evidence on transcendent reality is approached asymmetrically by those with and those without personal experience of transcendent reality. For each of us, the burden of proof falls on the side counter to our own experience.[4] It is a burden that can be and often is met. We come to realise that, in many ways, we all see only in part as through a glass darkly. Thus, if we are self-critical about our own experiences, we may come to revise our original interpretations of our experiences or, in some cases even, to abandon those interpretations altogether.

Our argumentative situation with regard to God's existence is really no different from any other issue. As Caroline New has observed, all theoretical debates originate in differing standpoints of experience.[5] In other words, our theories differ, in part, because our experiences differ. Our different experiences, however, are not the end of the story. They do not remain impervious to adjudication and correction. Instead, we come together in conversation to reason about them.

What makes religion seem different is the legacy of the enlightenment. It is an unexamined legacy of the enlightenment that we privilege atheism as the intellectual baseline and make religious belief alone something which is to be explained or defended.

If postmodernism has done anything positive, it has made us all more alert to such implicit structures of discursive privilege. Thus, against the prevailing enlightenment assumption, it is only a rather modest position we seek to defend; whereas the religious and non-religious approach the objective data asymmetrically, the rationality and validity of their respective beliefs must be treated symmetrically. If religious belief is partly to be explained socially, then so is religious disbelief. If, given an atheist's experienced absence of the transcendent, it is rational for the atheist to disbelieve in transcendent reality, then, similarly, given the religious person's experience of transcendence, it is equally rational for the religious person to believe in transcendent reality. Although, ontologically, at least one of these positions is mistaken, not every mistake is attributable to irrationality. At the moment, we cannot say which of these two views is mistaken. At the moment, therefore, there are rational reasons to subscribe to either. The foregoing points can all be summarised in a single proposition, a proposition that underlies this book. That proposition is as follows:

Ontological realism about God in the intransitive dimension is consistent with epistemic or experiential relativism in the transitive dimension.

It is compatible with the view that God manifests himself and is accessible in a variety of different ways experientially.

Essentially, our modest claim here is that ontological realism about God is consistent with, although not required by, critical realism generally. The authors of this book are realist about God in two senses. First, we think that talk about God should be interpreted realistically so that statements about God, like most statements in science and everyday life, must be treated as either true or false. Second, the authors are committed to the further view that God, as understood and explicated here, does in fact exist. Although we do not attempt a deductive proof of God's existence (and probably no such proof is possible), we are trying to enhance the plausibility of belief in God as a matter open to rational discussion. As we expect even our modest position to meet with substantial resistance, we need to consider more closely the sub-points expressed in the above proposition.

Ontological realism about God

Does God exist? There are philosophers today who debate this question. Nevertheless, in many quarters of the academy, especially on the left, the question will be judged highly peculiar. It is those quarters we want to address. We want to address them because we, ourselves, come from them. The three of us are all academics. One of us is a philosopher, and two are sociologists. Similarly, we are all associated with the political left, the economic or Marxian left particularly. A strange place perhaps from which to expect a defence of religion! Yet, we are all religious too. Two of us are Roman Catholics and one is a Protestant.

Within the left, it may no longer be surprising that some comrades are religious, but our religiosity is still regarded as something of an anomaly, at best a charming eccentricity. Because in academic circles particularly, the intellectual baseline is atheism, it is an eccentricity that we often keep to ourselves. When we cease keeping it to ourselves, we suddenly find that there are a surprising number of us. Whether it is the new millennium or a final exhaustion with the postmodern exhaustion of meaning, many academics, including leftist academics, are coming out of the religious closet. The time is apt, therefore, to recover the legitimacy of ultimate questions and of our efforts to answer them.

Does God exist? It is an ultimate question but one that it is widely considered illegitimate to raise. Ironically, it is not the common or garden variety of atheist who judges it so. On the contrary, those who do judge the question illicit are often religious themselves or at least endeavouring to be sympathetic to religion.

Whether or not God exists is a question that common or garden variety atheists themselves ask. They may declare God non-real, but they definitely are realists about the question. Thus, as Andrew Collier observes in Chapter 3, common or garden variety atheists extend a certain respect to their theistic partners in conversation. However mistaken atheists may judge theists to be, atheists at least allow that theists, too, are serious players in the same game: the game in which truth claims are made about a common world. Such atheists recognise that if theists are right, then theists are saying something not just about themselves but about this common reality.

Accordingly, the theist claim imposes a demand for consideration even on those who do not share the theist form of life.

In contrast, the old positivist philosophy of science considered the theistic affirmation of God not to be mistaken but as vacuous. Positivism tried to move all metaphysics out of bounds. As part of this project, it held what was called the 'verification theory' of meaning. According to the verification theory, the meaning of a claim is determined by the concrete, empirical criteria by which the claim is to be verified. Claims that could not be so verified were neither true nor false but, rather, meaningless. So it was with the claim that God exists. It sounds as if it is saying something, but so does the claim that 'the slithy toves did gyre and gimble in the wabe'. On inspection, both claims turn out to be gibberish.

Positivism, thus, went beyond common or garden variety atheism in barring any discussion of God before it could even get off the ground. Until it were specified how any claims about God could be empirically verified, one meaningfully could neither assert nor deny the existence of God. The issue itself was illicit. Ludwig Wittgenstein once counselled silence concerning anything about which we cannot speak. According to positivism, God was one matter about which silence was definitely in order.

The positivist judgement on the (ir)rationality of God-talk was one with which atheists could at least live. On their own, atheists were not inclined to speak of God anyway. But what about theists? To the extent that they still went on talking about God, they did so under suspicion that they were not saying anything meaningful. They were literally spouting nonsense.

Of course, there was an embarrassing secret about the verification theory of meaning. By its own criterion, it, too, was meaningless. If it is claimed that the meanings of propositions consist in the criteria by which they are verified, how is this claim itself to be verified? It cannot be.

There were efforts to save the verification theory, but by that time positivism was in deep trouble on other fronts. The same Wittgenstein who did so much to develop it, subsequently returned to initiate its demolition. By the end of the 1960s, positivism was dead in philosophy, although it continued to be hegemonic in the social sciences until well into the 1980s. Even today its legacy remains strong. Among positivism's current remains, however, the verification theory is not to be found. The verification theory, at least, remains buried.

On the other hand, in relation to religion, one of the most popular replacements for the verification theory has been a certain Trojan horse. It is a Trojan horse proffered by the followers of the later Wittgenstein, many of whom have themselves been religious. According to the post-Wittgensteinians, language performs multiple functions in various, self-contained language games. Each language game is but the discursive component of an entire form of life, from which the language game derives its sense.

From this perspective, it is a mistake to impose the criteria of one language game and form of life on a wholly different language game and form of life.

According to the post-Wittgensteinians, this was the mistake that the positivists made with respect to religion. The positivists applied to the religious form of life the criteria of sense and meaning appropriate to the scientific form of life.

The two forms of life, however, are different, as are the language games they play. Specifically, in contrast with scientific language, religious language putatively is not being employed to make assertions about reality, independent of the believing community. Instead, religious language is invoked to orient or mobilise the believing community in certain spiritual directions. Religious language thus serves an exclusively performative function that is not served by scientific language. When religious people pray to God together, it matters not whether God is or is not really there. What matters is that those praying are ritually reconsolidating themselves and their values as a religious community.

The post-Wittgensteinian approach to religion has been particularly well received by anthropologists and sociologists. In his classic work, *The Elementary Forms of the Religious Life*, Emile Durkheim suggested that the experience of God is the experience of group feeling and that in worshipping God, society essentially is worshipping itself. Ever since, anthropologists and sociologists have been inclined to approach religion as an expression of community. The theological question – whether or not God actually exists – is considered to be beyond the compass of social science. Consequently, the post-Wittgensteinian perspective offers anthropology and sociology a way of studying religion that does not require their taking any stand on the reality of the referents of religious language. Does God exist? Well, in some religious language games, God does exist, and in non-religious and even some religious language games, God does not exist. That is all there is to the matter.

As theology has become increasingly influenced by anthropology and sociology, and as it strives to be more ecumenical in orientation, many theologians too find the post-Wittgensteinian perspective congenial. Its attractions are multiple. First, whatever religious language may appear to be saying about external reality, if it really refers exclusively to human experience, religion need fight no losing battles against science. The creation story in Genesis, for example, may be regarded as a metaphor for the contingency of human existence and not as a rival account of astrophysics. Similarly, if it is not the Jesus of history who concerns the Church but only the Christ story proclaimed by the community of Christian faithful, there need be no anxiety over anything turned up by contemporary Biblical criticism.

The post-Wittgensteinian perspective is also theologically attractive from an ecumenical perspective. The different religions no longer need be opposed by their mutually exclusive claims to the truth. In reality, none of them is making truth claims at all. They are all just expressing the different stories by which their respective communities live. As such, the stories are just sources for different social identities that can each be enjoyed and appreciated together.

Finally, the post-Wittgensteinian perspective allows the religious to go on being religious in a safe, unobjectionable way. The religious are no longer asserting anything to which even a hard-nosed atheist might object; their statements relate only to the building of community. Religion, from this perspective, is but a collective form of poetry.

We have called the post-Wittgensteinian perspective a Trojan horse for theology, and such is what we do think it is. That is not to say there is nothing valid about the perspective. Certainly, religion and science are two different forms of life, and language functions differently in each. Certainly, many religious formulations that do appear to be making claims about history or cosmology or biology are more aptly understood as existential metaphors for human experience.

Certainly, too, we share the objective of ecumenism, of respect for one another's differing religious traditions. We just need to ask whether we genuinely extend such respect by endorsing a mutual suicide pact that declares everything any of us are saying as being equally untrue. Such an understanding may render religion inoffensive, but it also removes all bite from religion. The religion that survives is little more than atheism in disguise.

True religion may be partly poetry but it is not just poetry. Mainline Protestantism and Reform Judaism may each have heroically demythologised their religious content to an extent that no other religion has dared. It is no accident, however, that these are each also denominational forms in decline.

The fact is that vibrant religious communities do not understand themselves as just telling stories about community. They understand themselves as telling stories that in some sense and to some degree also express truths about the wider cosmos that we all commonly inhabit. The creation story in Genesis may be metaphorical, but it is not merely a metaphor about the contingency of human life; it is a metaphor about the contingency of creation on a God who created it. Similarly, if the Christ of faith is to have any substance at all, that Christ cannot be utterly divorced from the historical life of the Jesus who actually lived. Truth claims of one sort or another are part and parcel of the whole that religion is.

In the end, the post-Wittgensteinian perspective still leaves us asking whether or not, apart from the stories we tell ourselves, God really exists. This question cannot simply be legislated out of existence. The question goes on being asked with definite sense. If this sense cannot be captured by post-Wittgensteinian philosophy, then so much the worse for post-Wittgensteinian philosophy.

Of course, today it is not only post-Wittgensteinian philosophy that would entirely rule out of court the question of God's existence. Does God exist? If, today, this is a peculiar question to ask, it is largely because today we find ourselves pressed by a scepticism that is even more basic. Forget about whether or not God exists. Does anything exist? If nothing – not even tables and chairs – exists apart from our cultural beliefs, certainly it is pure folly to ask about the existence of God.

Today, under the sway of postmodernist philosophy, this level of scepticism is widely fashionable in academic circles, particularly in circles of the academic left. For postmodernism, not even the most solid results of science are objectively real. All reality is just a social construction and as such is riven with the exercise of unequal power. In the words of French philosopher, Jacques Derrida, one of postmodernism's founding thinkers, 'there is nothing outside the text.'

Whatever Derrida meant by this claim, and he has since equivocated on what he did mean, there is no question about how this pronouncement was heard by many within the academic community – who subsequently went on to become heralds of the new postmodernist movement. It was heard as a declaration that there is no objective reality beyond our own, individual, cultural interpretations. If reality exists anywhere, it exists only in our cultural texts and discourses. As these vary, so does reality itself. Thus, once again, it becomes illicit to ask about God's existence in itself, apart from any cultural context. As with post-Wittgensteinian philosophy with which it is closely aligned, with postmodernism too we can only ask whether God exists in this or that discourse or social text.

Heard as such, Derrida's declaration is, from a critical realist perspective, merely a consecration of the epistemic fallacy, the complete reduction of ontology to epistemology. Much has been written from a critical realist perspective challenging, or 'contesting', the postmodernist viewpoint. Those arguments will not be rehearsed here. Instead, it may suffice to say that like the positivist verification theory of meaning, the postmodernist position is self-refuting. For it to be at all intelligible, the denial of anything outside the text must be understood as the very kind of abstract truth claim that the declaration itself disallows. From the perspective of critical realism, any theory is immediately suspect that cannot even be advanced without committing a performative contradiction. As a philosophical position, postmodernism, like the verification theory of meaning, falls into this category.

We thus arrive at the critical realist affirmation of ontological realism. Does God exist? From the standpoint of ontological realism, the question is legitimate. The question has both sense and possible answers. From the standpoint of ontological realism, reality in general exists quite apart from our knowledge of it. There is, then, nothing inappropriate about asking whether or not that reality includes God.

God, transcendence and epistemic relativism

Epistemic relativism means that our knowledge or beliefs about reality are always socially and historically conditioned. The criteria we use to decide upon the truth, and the concepts by which we express it, are all fallible. Moreover, we arrive at truth – when we arrive at all – without foundations, without fail-safe methods that can be determined in advance of enquiry.

The only methodological *a priori* is continued openness to dialogue, dialogue especially with those with whom we disagree. In contrast with postmodernism, the critical realist stance towards oppositional others is neither respectful silence, nor the uncritical eclecticism of pastiche, but a Socratic openness that takes the other's viewpoint seriously enough to allow it the possibility of altering our own.

For both post-Wittgensteinian philosophy and postmodernism, there is no commensurability between paradigms or language games, no basis for common adjudication of truth. But then post-Wittgensteinian philosophy and postmodernism are both closer to positivism than they appear. Like positivism, both de-privilege metaphysics and portray empirical evidence as the only argumentative consideration there is.

Naturally, what counts as evidence for one language game may not count as such for another. Hence, the stalemate, the relativist incommensurability across paradigms. Overlooked, however, are the deeper, philosophical questions that we can pose, even across paradigms, about what counts as evidence. To pose such questions, of course, is to enter the terrain of metaphysical debate, sacred ground from which positivism, post-Wittgensteinian philosophy and postmodernism all shrink. In contrast with these philosophies, critical realism is at home on this terrain. In the humanities and social sciences, it is not in normal science, conducted within a paradigm, where the most vital questions arise, but in inter-paradigm dialogue. It is in its countenancing of inter-paradigm dialogue and argument that critical realism offers its most distinctive contribution.

Inter-paradigm argument is certainly at issue where religion is concerned. When it comes to religion, the one decisive fact that confronts us all is plurality; the plurality of experience and the plurality of interpretation, even of similar experiences. Plurality is a descriptive fact. It only becomes relativism when we conclude *a priori* from that plurality that all experiences and all interpretations are equally valid. As relativism secures this equality among all, by offering as sacrifice the truth claims of each, this equality is one that critical realism declines. Instead, critical realism follows the more difficult and daring path of seeking the coherent, alethic truth behind each. Implicit in that quest for alethic truth is the assumption, made respectfully, that each religious tradition – including our own – may be partly or even wholly wrong.

It is the fact of plurality, however, that immediately confronts us. To begin with, the experience of transcendent reality is not singular. It comes in great variety even within the confines of a single religious tradition. There are both episodic visions and more continuous intimations of what is transcendent. There is the feeling of creature-consciousness identified by Friedrich Schleiermacher; the experience of the numinous or holy as identified by Rudolf Otto; the sense of the transcendent address expressed by Martin Buber; and the experience of self-engulfment and cosmic union described by the Western mystical tradition but particularly associated with the Eastern religions.[6]

There is the experience of one god, many gods and no god at all. Even when God is experienced and experienced as a singular reality, the plurality of experience makes us question whether this god is the highest reality yet. Perhaps the Tao or some other reality is higher still.

There is the matter not just of the object of experience but the variety of ways in which even the same object is experienced. What, for example, distinguishes Christians from those who are not, is less the Jesus encountered than the emotional reaction to that encounter. For many Christians, Jesus inspires feelings of the numinous, of the wholly other, the feeling, in short, of encountering that which is transcendent. The theological question about Jesus, then, has in part to do with the cognitive content of this emotional reaction, with whether or not it is apt. Epistemic relativism relates not only to differences in how the transcendent manifests itself but also to differences in how such manifestations are epistemically received.

The brute fact of plurality cuts two ways. On one cut – the atheistic cut – the salient observation is that so many people believe and experience so many different, mutually contradictory things, and that what is believed and experienced seems to vary systematically with that which one was religiously socialised to believe and experience. It can all seem like so many different social constructions.

There is power to such observation, and it needs to be taken seriously. Yet, the atheistic cut to religious plurality is not the only cut there is. On a religious cut, a different observation becomes salient: so many from so many different cultures all independently report some experience of transcendent reality. Is there not some reality behind it all? Can all be similarly mistaken about the category of the transcendent and are all just mistaking group consciousness for the divine? There are no simple answers, but this observation, too, carries its own power.

Up to now in academic circles, the atheist has occupied a privileged position in all this plurality. Refraining from any beliefs about transcendent reality, atheism has appeared to be the position of value-neutrality in this arena, the rational default category against which all other beliefs are measured. Yet, not even atheism is immune from epistemic relativism. Atheism, as we indicated, reflects its own experience, the experience of the transcendent absent. It cannot then be held, as it so often has been, especially in anthropology and sociology, that religion alone is something to be explained and not atheism as well.

Admittedly, in anthropology and sociology today, social scientists approach religion with caution. They do not want to embroil themselves in theological issues. That, they think, would compromise their status as scientists. It is partly for this reason that social scientists prefer the post-Wittgensteinian and postmodern approaches to religion. An exclusive focus on religious practices, discourses and texts allows social scientists to bracket method-ologically any question about the truth of the putative realities to which they refer. Instead, social scientists can examine the exclusively social contribution to religion.[7]

The problem, however, with this methodological approach to religion is the same as when it is applied to science. In both science and religion, our beliefs are actually in dialogue with the world. Thus, methodologically to bracket the world is in essence to break apart a dialectical process and to examine only one element – the social element – in isolation. In both cases, the world's contribution is thereby rendered illicit by an *a priori* method-ological principle. Such a methodology renders it impossible from the start to understand either science or religion as anything other than a social construction. The social is the only token allowed on the board.

It is not only any independent reality that is lost or bracketed out of analysis by an exclusive focus on practices, discourses and texts. The indi-vidual subject is bracketed out of existence as well. As a result, what is lost is the very category of experience. Practices, discourses and texts do not experience. Only individual subjects do; and what individual subjects experience, when they experience, is reality. Individuals and reality are the twin end-points connected by practices, discourses and texts. It is through practices, discourses and texts that individuals experience reality and express the reality they experience. Thus, to try to understand practices, discourses and texts, without their end-points, is like trying to understand the insti-tution of marriage while bracketing out husbands and wives. To the extent that the plurality of stances toward the transcendent originates in the plural ways that the transcendent is experienced (or not), our approach to the transcendent must readmit the category of experience.[8]

It may appear as if the category of experience has never left, because anthropologists and sociologists do speak endlessly of different group experiences. Yet the category of experience is not present just because the word is used. Too often, anthropologists and sociologists conflate experience with perspective. Thus, for them, to speak of a group's experience is to speak of its perspective. A perspective, however, is only the result of experience and not the experience itself.[9]

Experience consists of three elements: the experiencing subject, the content of experience and the object of experience. Clearly, however much anthropologists and sociologists invoke the word, experience is not present in their discourse when two of its three elements are methodologically absented. In any true experience, the object of experience contributes some-thing to the content of experience. If a putative object of experience contributes nothing to the content of experience, the putative experience is not a genuine experience at all, but only the illusion of one. Thus, by methodologically absenting the object of experience, social constructionism – in both science and religion – ends up losing altogether the very category of experience. To make progress, this discursive absence must itself be absented.

Critical realist readers may be surprised by the affirmative emphasis given here to the category of experience. After all, critical realism made its mark against positivism by denying positivism's reduction of all reality to what we empirically experience. In contrast with positivism, and postmodernism, critical realism argues that the happenings, which we empirically experience, are only a subset of the 'actual', the set of all happenings – whether we experience them or not. For critical realism, moreover, even the actual is just a subset of the real. Happenings – events – do not exhaust the real. For critical realism, structures and generative mechanisms are real too, including those that in principle are not even directly experienceable.

The position we articulate here marks no retreat from this general critical realist perspective. The real, we continue to affirm, encompasses more – much more than just experience. Yet, that affirmation hardly means that experience is unimportant, and, indeed, critical realism never has denied the importance of experience. As critical realists, we continue to deny that experience trumps everything. Because experiences are corrigible, they themselves may be impugned by considerations arising from reasoned, public debate and scrutiny. To maintain, however, that a relativist impasse between rival experiences is not where we end up, is not necessarily to deny that it is from a plurality of rival experiences that we actually begin. Certainly, not only in the case of religion, but also on so many other matters as well, the manifest fact is that it is from a plurality of experience that we do begin debate.

God, transcendence and judgemental rationality

Can we really apply judgemental rationality to religion and to religious experience? Will the religious themselves really accept the results of such judgements? From the perspective of the secular academy, these questions appear reasonable. Their apparent reasonableness, however, itself reflects the epistemic relativity of all knowledge. The questions appear reasonable only because religion is so marginalised within the academy as to become the academy's Other, on to which all sorts of static and essentialist projections become unremarkable.

The questions above are sometimes asked as a way of precluding rational discussion. Let us immediately put such questioners on the defensive by asking some counter-questions of our own. Can we really apply judgemental rationality to politics or to social theory? Are those who have invested themselves in Marxism, capitalism, postmodernism or positivism really persuadable by rational argument?

The answer to the first question, certainly, is, 'Yes': judgemental rationality can be applied to political and social issues. The honest answer to the second question is a more troubled, 'Well, yes and no . . .'. Some people will and some will not respond to rational argument; yet, it is at least the responsibility of each of us so to respond, and we collectively operate on the assumption that all will take this responsibility seriously.

Exactly the same responses are forthcoming when these questions are applied to religion. Can we really apply judgemental rationality to religion and to religious experience? Without question this is so. Not only can judgemental rationality be applied to religion; both within and across religious traditions, the religious have been applying judgemental rationality for ages. Who is it who applied the most ruthless criteria of Biblical criticism to the life of Jesus? Not predominantly atheistic scholars who, for the most part, could not care less what Jesus actually did or did not say and do. For the past two hundred years, such criticism has issued from Christians themselves, specifically from academically situated Christian scholars. It is many Christians themselves, moreover, who, for reasons deriving from judgemental rationality, resist literalist readings of the Bible; who reject narrow, exclusivist understandings of salvation; who notice that the manifest evil in the world is incompatible with any straightforward understanding of God as both all good and all-powerful.

Given the marginalisation of religion in the academy, it is easy to attribute to religion a static and essentialist nature. Yet, religious traditions are neither monolithic nor static. Christianity was a pluralist movement from the beginning. From the beginning, there were Jewish Christians and Hellenistic Christians. There were Gnostics, and Marcionites, Docetists and Arians. Among all these Christian perspectives, there was conflict and debate. There was debate as well between Christians and Jews; between Christians and Pagans; and between Jews and Pagans. The Christianity we have today is not the same as it was 2,000 years ago. In part, the Christianity we have today has been shaped not just by force but by centuries of debate. Similar debate and historical progression are found in every other religious tradition.

Perhaps it is the concept of faith that renders strange the suggestion that we can apply judgemental rationality to religion. Popularly, the concept of faith is often used by religious believers to privilege their religious convictions, which is to remove those convictions from critical scrutiny. Some beliefs, it is said, just need to be accepted on faith. Faith, it is also said, is a leap taken without evidence. Sometimes faith is even described as believing in something contrary to the evidence. Tertullian famously remarked, 'I believe because it is absurd.' When religious believers deploy the concept of faith this way, they do not incline non-believers to consider them as appropriate partners for debate.

There are, however, appropriate ways to speak of faith, even faith in something contrary to the evidence. We may retain faith in a socialist vision, despite the circumstantial evidence now before us. We may similarly retain faith in someone's good will when confronted with actions that appear the opposite. Even scientists practise faith – in a theory or basic principle – against early findings pointing to the contrary.

In such cases, faith is not based on nothing; nor is it a way to insulate a belief from critical scrutiny. If we retain faith in socialism despite its current failure, it is because we do not consider its current standing to be a conclusive judgement on the intrinsic nature of socialism as a whole. Yet, even about socialism's intrinsic nature, we still remain willing to countenance counter-argument.

Similarly, if we retain faith in a person's integrity despite circumstances that appear damning, this faith likewise is based on our prior knowledge of that person's nature, apart from current appearances. Again, however, we would be foolish to allow no evidence whatsoever to call that person's integrity into question.

Finally, when scientists express their faith in a theory or principle despite counter-evidence, their faith, too, is not blind faith but based on past experience and their knowledge of the nature of the principle or theory. At some point, however, should sufficient evidence accumulate over a long enough period of time, even the scientist's faith may need to be re-examined.

Originally, in a religious context, faith in God had little to do with belief in God's very existence. God's existence itself was taken for granted. The faith called for was trust in God's providence. As in the previous cases, this was a trust based on a prior understanding of the intrinsic nature of God and on past experience with God. It, too, was a faith based on something and that something was still, possibly, corrigible. Indeed, after the Holocaust, many within Judaism concluded that God had forsaken their faith.

To make faith into blind faith, as some religious people do, is not intellectually acceptable. It is not intellectually appropriate to privilege any belief – not even a religious belief – in such a way that it becomes immune to judgemental rationality. If we feel free to privilege our own pet beliefs in this way, why should not racists so privilege their racism or homophobes their homophobia? If, as religious believers, we are still to remain a part of the community of rational dialogue, all our beliefs, including our religious beliefs, must be equally placed on the table.

When religion enters into rational dialogue as an equal, it can ably hold its own. The one qualification is that religion must truly be allowed equal entrance. Religion enters rational dialogue in a de-privileged position when the onus is exclusively on religion to prove its case publicly. Religion cannot do so. But why should the onus not be on atheism to prove its case publicly? Atheism cannot do so any better. To put the burden of proof exclusively on religion, then, is to grant an *a priori* privilege to atheism.

It is, of course, a mainstay of philosophy to debate which side of an issue should bear the burden of proof. The truth, however, is that in many cases the burden of proof is actually asymmetrical, relative to our personal experiences. It is definitely so in the case of religion.

With the element of experience, we introduce another place where we may speak of a legitimate faith. It is in fact a legitimate faith in personal experience that ordinary religious believers may be trying to articulate when they instead make a mistaken appeal to blind faith. Suppose Mary experiences herself as having a personal relationship with God. God, Mary not only believes but feels, is always with her. She not only talks to God but also feels God addressing her. God's presence is not just a belief for Mary but also a continuous sensation.

When Mary meets with her atheistic friend, Thomas, however, Thomas tells her that her belief in God is irrational. Can Mary prove to him, Thomas asks her, that God exists? Mary concedes she cannot. Thomas suggests that Mary's feeling of God's presence is all in her mind. He speaks of Durkheim, Freud, Marx and Feuerbach. Mary is taken aback. She has heard of Freud and Marx, but she has never read the works of any of these thinkers.

Upon receiving Thomas's revelations, what is Mary's epistemically rational response? Should she immediately suspend her belief in God until she can prove to the likes of doubting Thomas that God exists? Should Mary repress her feeling of God's presence because she now must take seriously the suggestion that her feeling of being addressed by God is just a social or psychological construction?

These are not epistemically rational responses if, as we are supposing, Mary's belief in God is important to her. Mary would be more rational to adopt a wait and see approach. In a spirit of self-criticism, she should definitely explore Thomas's suggestions, but until she has convinced herself that Thomas is right, she rationally should continue trusting in the veracity of her own personal experience. Because Mary is quite rational, she provisionally maintains that kind of faith.

By their next meeting, Mary has done a lot of reading; as a by-product, she has even gone out and joined the Socialist Workers' Party. 'You know,' Mary tells Thomas, 'Freud, Marx, Feuerbach and Durkheim – they all explain religion differently. Marx says it is a palliative for social oppression; Freud a kind of infantile regression; Feuerbach suggests it is a mistaken projection of human qualities; and Durkheim a disguised worship of the group.'

'That's right,' Thomas smiles. He sits back and folds his arms, both impressed with and proud of his student.

'But,' Mary goes on, 'well, which is it? The problem is that none of these guys demonstrates that it is his explanation that is correct and not one of the others.'

Thomas sits up. 'Well . . .'

'And to the extent that none of them rules out the others' explanations, they do not really prove their own case, do they? In fact, none of them even bothers to rule out the possibility that people believe in God because there actually is a God that people are experiencing. They all just dismiss that possibility without argument.'

'Well . . .' Thomas coughs. He actually has not read these authors quite so closely.

'So,' Mary sums up, 'although these naturalistic explanations of religious belief are all plausible suggestions, that is all they are – suggestions.'

Thomas nods reluctantly, looks at his watch, and asks Mary if they should go and get some lunch.

'Not yet. There is another point I want to make.' Mary turns a page in her notebook. 'I have also been doing a lot of reading on astrophysics. Are you familiar with the problem associated with the so-called anthropic coincidences?'

Thomas slowly and nervously shakes his head.

'Well,' Mary remarks, 'it turns out this universe we live in is fantastically fine-tuned. It is not just any old universe. The force strengths, the fundamental constants, the initial conditions – if any of a great number of them had been even minutely different, the universe would be fundamentally different from the way it is now – and unlikely to support life.

'Look.' Mary turns her notebook around, showing Thomas a series of quotations from such physicists as Freeman Dyson, Paul Davies, John Barrow and Fred Hoyle. 'All say the universe looks very much – almost inescapably – as if it had been designed to be this way. And if it has been designed . . .'

'Just a minute, Mary.' Thomas can see where this is going. 'None of this proves that God exists.'

Mary looks searchingly into Thomas's eyes. 'Thomas, surely you are not a positivist, are you? Of course, the anthropic coincidences do not prove God's existence, but then nothing empirical can be proven with mathematical certainty.' Mary turns another page in her notebook. 'I've also been reading a lot of Wittgenstein on mathematics . . .'

Although shaken by Mary's arguments, Thomas does not leave the encounter a religious believer. Why not? The answer, surely, is that Thomas has a rational faith of his own, what he would describe as a faith in science.

Thomas's designation of his own faith is a bit misleading. It is not the 'scientific method' Mary has challenged. The new, intellectual Mary is as committed as Thomas to evidence and rational argument. More precisely, Thomas's faith is in naturalism, the belief that everything in life can be explained without appeal to any kind of transcendental reality.

There is no need to impugn Thomas's faith. Given naturalism's history of success and Thomas' own experience of the transcendent absent, Thomas's faith in naturalism is epistemically rational – for him. Our only point is that Mary's opposing faith in her religious experience is equally rational epistemically for her.

We are not left, however, at a relativist impasse, with Mary's and Thomas's rival faiths opposing each other as two immutable objects. Already, in their early discussions, Mary and Thomas are forcing each other to apply judgemental rationality to their own beliefs. Mary has had to concede that her religious experience is corrigible; Thomas that the arguments so far made against Mary's experience are inconclusive. Upon further reading, Thomas also finds himself forced to admit that the universe we inhabit is a fantastically improbable one.

What Mary and Thomas have so far said to each other is just the beginning. Eventually, Thomas comes across the many-universe theory, and Mary is forced to concede that this is equally plausible an explanation for our universe's appearance of design.

It is already evident that Mary has grown intellectually from her discussion with Thomas and that Thomas is growing intellectually as well. As the two discuss further, they become for each other what the Jewish tradition calls Haverim.[10] Haverim are study partners who inspire each other's intellectual growth by lovingly challenging each other's claims to the truth. From a critical realist perspective, it is Haverim that we all ought to be to each other.

The postmodernist philosopher Richard Rorty tells us that truth is not important; what is important is ongoing discussion. Yet, if not the truth, what are Haverim supposed to discuss? The concept of Haverim makes little sense from a postmodernist perspective. If, according to postmodern relativism, all views are equally valid, then the views with which Mary and Thomas begin their discussions are no worse than the ones at which they might arrive by the end. In that case, discussion is rather pointless.

The concept of Haverim presupposes a critical realist ontology. What Haverim discuss is the cogency of truth claims about an objective reality, ontologically independent of the claimant (ontological realism). Discussion is important because claims can be wholly or partly mistaken about that reality and because discussion is the way to reach that conclusion (judgemental rationality). Finally, there is only something to discuss because, owing to our different experiences, our takes on reality are initially different (epistemic relativism). If we all had the same experience and the same take, there would be nothing to discuss. Thus, far from precluding a quest for truth, our diversity is an epistemic asset.

Epistemologically, we arrive at a kind of standpoint theory, where epistemic privilege is only personal rather than public and only presumptive rather than absolute. In feminist standpoint theories and in the older Marxist standpoint theory associated with Lukács, the standpoint of the oppressed is privileged publicly and absolutely. The idea is that because the oppressed are uniquely positioned to experience certain aspects of reality, their standpoint on those matters has a greater claim to truth in public argument.

The current consensus is that no one standpoint can be absolutely privileged in public argument. Yet, there is no need to privilege any one standpoint either absolutely or publicly in order to affirm the grain of truth that standpoint theories were perhaps trying to articulate. If our personal experiences all vary and if it is epistemically rational for each of us to trust our own experience – at least presumptively, then we all approach public argument asymmetrically.

All this means is that when we first come together for discussion, we each will assign the burden of proof to perspectives counter to our own experience. In other words, we each will require more convincing of a position that is counter to, rather than aligned with, our own perspective. The epistemic privilege here is personal or individual rather than public. We each personally accord the privilege to our own standpoint, and it is epistemically rational for us to do so. Just as in science as a whole it would not be epistemically rational to abandon a paradigm at the first anomaly or problem, so, too, is there a rational, inertial tendency associated with our own personal paradigms.

In debate, however, no position is publicly privileged over any other. Nor is the epistemic privilege involved absolute but only presumptive. That we each require more persuasion to surrender views which reflect our own experience or emotional investments hardly means that we cannot be so persuaded. The salutary fact is that when we engage in discussion, we quite often are so persuaded.

Our personal experiences are only our point of entry to rational debate. Our experiences in themselves do not trump all other rational considerations. In particular, our putative religious experiences can be contested from many angles. As we have already seen, a putative experience of God can be challenged as a social or psychological construction. Alternatively, the experience may be regarded as genuine but the object mistaken. All such possibilities need to be entertained.

The interpretative schemes or world-views founded on a religious experience can likewise be contested. Such world-views may contain apparent or real logical inconsistencies. There are, for example, all the famous puzzles about the ability of an omnipotent God to create a square circle or a rock too heavy even for this God to lift. There may be inconsistencies, too, of a more substantial nature. In fundamentalist versions of Christianity, God appears willing to consign billions of people to hell for what is essentially an epistemological mistake. Can such a God simultaneously be affirmed as loving, or even just? The problem of evil, moreover, remains a puzzle for any affirmation of a good and powerful God.

Religious world-views may also be questioned on their compatibility with other, perhaps firmer bodies of knowledge. The famous case, of course, is the incompatibility of a literal reading of Genesis with the theory of evolution. There are, however, many other such issues. Consider, for example, issues relating to philosophical psychology and the mind–body question. At one time, physicalist reductionism and psychological egoism were the prevailing views in several scientific disciplines. Both are incompatible with most of the major religious traditions.

In the cases of physicalist reductionism and psychological egoism, it was the religious rather than the scientific position that was eventually vindicated. Today, physicalist reductionism and psychological egoism have both been widely discredited even by scientists themselves.

True, today's more defensible, non-reductive materialism still poses problems for religious world-views that presuppose a soul as an ontologically distinct, spiritual substance. Yet, then again, religious world-views that traditionally seemed to presuppose such a soul may actually not need to do so. On inspection, it turns out that the concept of a soul is a Greek idea, absent from the Hebrew and Christian scriptures. Even a Hindu belief in reincarnation can be preserved via a dispositional realism as opposed to a dualism of substances.[11] So the dialogue continues, and with it a growth in sophistication on all sides.

Still, it may be asked, what can one say to a Christian fundamentalist? Possibly much. George Eliot began her life as a Christian fundamentalist but ended up as the English translator of Feuerbach. Conversely, perhaps nothing can be said to certain Christian fundamentalists. One cannot say much to certain fundamentalist Marxists or free marketeers either.

Clearly, one cannot say anything to one who will not enter dialogue. Even with such refuseniks in absentia, however, we can still evaluate their views ourselves. It is sometimes mistakenly thought that what we are ultimately after is consensus, so that a single hold-out spoils the whole enterprise. What we are truly after, however, is our own best understanding of a common, ontologically independent reality. Although that judgement is rationally made only in social dialogue with others, if we are truly seeking to be rational about our beliefs, it is each of us, ourselves, whom we are each ultimately trying to convince.

What do we mean by God?

The foregoing made many references to God without saying much about what we might mean by God. What we have said so far probably does not suffer a great deal as a result of our having left readers to imagine their own idea of God as some ultimate, transcendent reality. In fact, we, the three authors of this book, hardly agree completely ourselves on who or what God is.

Nevertheless, it is incumbent on us to say something more. After all, our argument is that, through rational dialogue, we may eventually be able to make certain, warranted statements about God. What sorts of statements? It is reasonable for readers to ask.

Accordingly, for purposes of illustration, we offer in Chapter 2 a possible theology that might be defended on realist grounds. The point is to give readers a picture of the kinds of transcendental statement we think can be rationally debated. The theology offered does not fully reflect what any of the three of us fully thinks of God. From the perspective of any of us, the theology presented is rather minimal. It is a series of statements to which the three of us could give common assent. Certainly, it is a theological position with which we would expect others to disagree. If that disagreement leads to lively argument, then the statement to come will already have served its purpose. It will have initiated an argument on God, thereby showing that such an argument can indeed take place.

Notes

1 The critical realism defended here developed in response to the writings of British philosopher Roy Bhaskar, most importantly *A Realist Theory of Science* (Leeds Books, Leeds, 1975) and *The Possibility of Naturalism: A Philosophical Critique of the Contemporary Human Sciences* (Harvester, Brighton, 1979). For further developments, see the volume edited by Margaret Archer, Roy Bhaskar, Andrew Collier, Tony Lawson and Alan Norrie, *Critical Realism: Essential Readings* (Routledge, London, 1998). A strikingly similar view, also called 'critical realism', has independently been advanced in religion by Ian Barbour (see, for example, *Issues in Science and Religion*, Harper, San Francisco, 1966); and more recently *Religion and Science* (Harper, San Francisco, 1997); and N.T. Wright (see *The New Testament and the People of God* (Fortress Press, Minneapolis, 1992). Now is an opportune time perhaps for these two streams of critical realism to get to know each other.

2 The term 'alethia' was first used in this connection by Roy Bhaskar in *Dialectics: The Pulse of Freedom*, Verso, London, 1996.

3 This argument goes back to Donald Davidson. See 'On the Very Idea of a Conceptual Scheme', *Proceedings of the American Philosophical Association*, 1973/1974 (17): 5–20.

4 See William Alston, *Perceiving God: The Epistemology of Religious Experience*, Cornell University Press, Ithaca, NY, 1991.

5 Caroline New, *Agency, Health, and Social Survival: The Eco-Politics of Rival Psychologies*, Taylor & Francis, London, 1996.

6 See Martin Buber, *I and Thou*, Charles Scribner's, New York, 1970; Mircea Eliade, *The Sacred and the Profane*, Harcourt, Brace & World, New York, 1958; Rudolf Otto, *The Idea of the Holy*, Oxford University Press, Oxford, 1958; Friedrich Schleiermacher, *On Religion: Speeches to Its Cultured Despisers*, Westminster Press, Philadelphia, 1958.

7 See, for example, Peter Berger, *The Heretical Imperative: Contemporary Possibilities of Religious Affirmation*, Anchor, Garden City, NY, 1979; Clifford Geertz, 'Religion as a Cultural System', pp. 1–46 in Michael Banton (ed.), *Anthropological Approaches to the Study of Religion*, Praeger, New York, 1966; Andrew Greeley, *Religion as Poetry*, Transaction, New Brunswick, 1996; and Rodney Stark, 'Micro Foundations of Religion', *Sociological Theory*, 1999, 17 (3): 264–89.

8 Berger, Greeley and Stark, see note 7, are exceptions here. Greeley does speak of religious experience, although he deliberately still avoids speaking of the transcendental object of religious experience. Berger, similarly, although sympathetic to experience, would have us bracket out the object of experience from sociological study. Stark, a rational choice theorist, definitely refers to the individual, although only as *homo economicus*; he thus subordinates the category of experience to instrumental reason.

9 See, for example, Patricia Hill Collins, 'The Social Construction of Black Feminist Thought', *Signs*, 1989, 14 (4): 745–74; and Dorothy Smith, *The Everyday World as Problematic: A Feminist Sociology*, Northeastern University Press, Evanston, 1989.

10 See Clark Williamson, 'Doing Christian Theology with Jews: The Other, Boundaries, Questions', pp. 37–52 in Roger Badham (ed.), *Introduction to Christian Theology*, Oxford University Press, Oxford, 1998.

11 See Roy Bhaskar, *From East to West: Odyssey of a Soul*, Routledge, London, 2000.

2 What do we mean by God?

*Margaret S. Archer, Andrew Collier and
Douglas V. Porpora*

It is incumbent upon us to say something more about what we mean by
God. This is entailed by our previous argument that it is through bold
and reasoned dialogue that collective advance is made towards warranted
statements about God. The difficulty for the three of us is that, in the past,
we have neither been bold, nor dialogical, nor worked collectively on
religious matters. As closet believers within the academy, we each engaged
in the lonely task of working out the answer to this prime question for
ourselves. We are auto-didacts in 'unsystematic' theology. We are people
who, in isolation, puzzled out the connections between the faith we found
irresistible and the academic vocations to which we are committed.
Consequently, we had each developed singular forms of spiritual shorthand,
acquired perhaps idiosyncratic attachments to parts of the vast theological
library, and forged a *modus vivendi* in the world of people and ideas, which
was expressive of our personal understandings of living out the same ultimate
concern.

In coming together, we discovered that our landscapes of the soul had
different topographies, but with these we could familiarise one another.
However, to have entered into each other's 'inscapes', as Hopkins called them,
which are forms of first-person knowledge, would have required more
biographical and experiential familiarity between the three of us than
our snatched weekends allowed. Accordingly, we offer only a minimal consensus upon what we also agree are central matters relating to God. This
chapter cannot capture what any one of us fully thinks about God – it is
far too spare and bare. None of us believes or feels or lives by this minimal
consensus alone. All the same, our minimalism should not be taken as
the lowest common denominator of our accord. Rather it is the highest common denominator that we considered would engage our secular colleagues
and especially secular critical realists – that engagement being the object
of this undertaking.

However minimal we consider our consensus conception of God to be, it
is, nevertheless, a consensus arrived at by three practising Christians. Thus,
it is no surprise that we share some basic understandings. For all of us, God
is the alpha and the omega, the beginning and the end. God is the origin of

the universe and the telos towards which it returns. God not only creates the universe, establishing its ultimate, ontological properties, but also sustains the universe in each moment. God is the ultimate ground or deepest truth of all things and hence of all beings. In God, reality finds its coherent totality. Existentially and essentially, God is the ground of all grounds, the One who makes possible all possibilities.

The grounds for belief in God

From a critical realist perspective, what is real is real even if it does not act or otherwise manifest itself in a way that is observed. That applies to God. God remains independently real even without a world to act on or a humanity to experience God's manifestations.

At the same time, however, we believe that God does act on and in the world and in such a way as can variously be experienced by us. God is real as the alethic truth of the world, the source from which the world originates and its ultimate meaning. When we humans direct ourselves to this ultimate meaning through religious rituals, we experience it as the sacred.

Beyond our direct experience, God also acts in the world, structuring its historical unfolding. In many Western religious traditions, God particularly stands with and acts for the poor and oppressed, ever struggling in the direction of greater justice. Thus, for us, God is not only a Platonic ideal – the God of the philosophers – but a living God who also acts.

It is no surprise that the traditional 'proofs of God's existence' – supposedly deductive proofs from indubitable premises – have not worked; for no part of human knowledge (with the possible exception of formal systems like logic and mathematics) is like that: not physics, not economics and not theology. Of the traditional proofs, the argument from teleology in nature is perhaps the strongest, and that is by no means a conclusive argument, balanced against its opposite, the argument from evil against the existence of God. Some aspects of nature point to God's existence, some make atheism look probable. Indeed, as Hume maintained, an argument from nature, unless coupled with another source of knowledge of God, is unacceptable theologically as it leads only to belief in a god strong and good enough to produce this actually existing world. It could then be maintained that if this world is fallen and alienated from God, a god so proved would be a fallen god.

The primary source of knowledge of God is religious experience. Most strikingly, these include experiences of which God is the direct object. The status of these as evidence for God's existence has been very well theorised philosophically by William Alston, in his book *Perceiving God*[1] and by Richard Swinburne in *The Existence of God*.[2] Also included are experiences of nature as God's creation, of the work of God in human affairs, visions of God incarnate, and so forth.

Like all human experiences, putative religious experiences are fallible. It is always possible for an experience to be misread, for an apparently religious experience to have a purely secular cause, and so on. This fallibility, however, is not unique to religious experience. It is a common feature of all human experience, and does not vitiate religious experience as a source of knowledge, only as a source of infallibility.

It is sometimes argued that there can be no experience of God, since experience of external entities presupposes that they are spatially located and that the subject's sense organ can be directed upon them. We can see a deer in the forest because it is fifty yards to the north-west of us, and we can turn our heads in that direction with our eyes open. It is asked by the sceptic, 'what is the equivalent way of directing experience on God?'. In fact, there are such ways, and they are communicated in religious traditions. They include religious ceremonies, spiritual exercises, public and private prayer, and silent meditation; they also include actions pleasing to God (see, for instance, Deutero-Isaiah's teaching that God will show himself to those who themselves show justice and mercy, and will hide himself from those who oppress the poor – Isaiah 58.2–12). These are all ways in which we can, so to speak, 'turn our heads' to look in the direction of God.

If not everyone has religious experience, that may be partly because many do not turn their heads in the appropriate way. It should be noted that just as one may misinterpret a secular experience as religious, so also may one misinterpret a religious experience as a purely secular aesthetic or moral experience. However, many people, probably the majority of humankind, do have what they take to be religious experiences. For those who do, it is rational to believe in God unless cogent arguments are presented against such belief. Religious experience is like other experience: fallible, conditioned by received opinions, subject to criticism at the bar of reason, suspicion and explanatory critique. In the end, religious experience is the primary motivation for religious belief, and, as such, no more likely to be a total illusion than any other form of experience. Religious experience normally occurs within a tradition of religious teaching and practice (in this too it is like other experience). Yet, in the end, religious experience constitutes the only ground we can have for giving credence to such traditions, or indeed for developing and transforming them.

Reductionism and transcendental experience

Certain qualities of God may be apprehended and described as such after transcendental experiences, even if those qualities are in themselves beyond full apprehension. It is widely held that religious experience is a subjective phenomenon, amenable to psychological explanation, and hence that no cognitive claims derive from it. Sociologically, the manifestations of religious experience are often held to depend upon belonging to a 'form of life', which predisposes towards religious experience or even actively and collectively determines it. Both the non-cognitive content of transcendental experience and its attribution to the operation of social forces are rejected here. Accepting the profound affectivity of such experiences or admitting their grounding in and filtration by traditions of belief does not compromise this rejection.

To begin with, 'transcendence' is a relative term, referring to the human capacity to overcome some existing state or level of consciousness, including knowledge. In such basic terms, transcendence is everywhere and for everyone. Its absence is only a figment of those irrealist philosophies that conflate knowledge with being, denying anything independent to discover about the way reality is apart from how we take it to be. Instead, transcendence is implicit in the basic, critical realist distinction between the intransitive domain of the real and our transitive knowledge of it. Transcendence is always built on, though never reducible to, an immanent ground made up of pre-existing knowledge, including theories, beliefs, tacit knowledge and traditional practices.

Here we can distinguish three forms of transcendence. These are transcendence in relation to things (including ideas), in relation to people, and in relation to God. First, subject–object relations are grounded in the immanence of the existing corpus of knowledge, upon which we clamber to overcome some problem – by acts of creativity. These conjectural breakthroughs sometimes seem to be *de nihilo*, because they are in no sense merely extrapolations or additions. Such creative transcendence is essential to human agency, which cannot be restricted to routinised action, and, therefore, is universal and also has cognitive import in and upon the environment.

Second, subject–subject relations are grounded in the immanent forms and networks of interpersonal relationships, such as friendship, kinship, community and collegiality. Human love, agapic or erotic, transcends normative expectations in its emotionality and commitment, but it is also an extension of cognition through the intimate knowledge of the other that is acquired.

Third, subject–transcendent relations are grounded in a descriptive religious tradition, but transcend it by a personal awareness of God as the ultimate reality, who may be apprehended in a diversity of ways and situations. Generically, such experiences can only be communicated metaphorically and comparatively, but this does not distinguish them from the difficulties of finding words to capture this-worldly experiences – such as love of another person.

Clearly, not all subject–transcendent experiences are authentic, but that is also true of the two earlier forms of transcendence, for we can be mistaken about our creative leaps and also about the ones we love. Conversely, genuinely subject–transcendent experiences may be – and the evidence is that they are – even more widespread than is generally realised because such genuine experiences are frequently mis-recognised, owing to inadequacies in the descriptive tradition or insufficient familiarity with it.

Religious experience is transcendental, not simply because it entails reference to the transcendent, but because it is held to extend our cognition and affectivity beyond conventional reality. It goes beyond the ground of descriptive tradition, the authority of which itself stems from prior experience. We maintain that infinite goodness entails a divine impetus to communicate its nature. Experience of it can be captured within such diverse modes of apprehension of God as prayer, meditation, silence and solitude.

Transcendental experiences are often considered to be intense learning experiences as well as being intensely moving. Sometimes there is a profound experience of clarification, of removal of impurity or opacity, through which transcendent reality becomes more transparent. Whereas received belief can become over-familiar, obscure, distorted or deadened by institutional forms, religious experience is often described as cutting through this detritus to restore the pristine. Thus, there is a huge experiential difference between, for example, acknowledging the historic Jesus and accepting the risen Christ as Lord (a difference which tradition itself attributes to the working of transcendence (1 Corinthians 12.3)).

Some kinds of illumination can only be obtained through experience. Only an acquaintance with the sacred can communicate them. Were we to deny their putative origins *a priori*, we would illegitimately be imposing a re-description upon them. For example, it might be denied that divine love is a transcendental property, and maintained that it is only an extrapolation from human love, to which resort may indeed have to be made for purposes of explication. However, transcendental experience yields a real cognitive and affective difference; the knowledge of, for example, the 'peace of God which passeth understanding' (Philippians 4.7). Moreover, illumination also covers states of knowledge that are without human analogue, as when we become phenomenally aware of what 'sinfulness', as opposed to wrongdoing, is, or what 'redemption', 'fallenness' or 'maya' mean. What can be called the 'personal applicability' of such terms constitutes new knowledge, which exceeds its traditional grounding and yet works forwards upon it.

Unification does not necessarily come last experientially. Indeed, experiences of engulfment may be the beginning that is also the end. Its subjects construe such awareness as the establishment of a transcendental state that itself constitutes the highest human good. Awareness is autopoetic; it may not have originated in prayer, meditation or special religious activity, but its quintessential desirability then fosters religious practice, as the subject defines it. The experience of divine love exceeds any other known love and thus becomes both human telos, or ultimate concern, and also the logos, or reason that unifies our lovings in due order.

Does God transcend the world or is God immanent within it?

In many religious experiences, God is encountered as transcendent Other, indeed as what Otto[3] called 'wholly other', from profane reality. According to what is called 'negative theology', God is so transcendent – so totally other from us – that we are incapable of making any positive statements about God. To do so putatively attempts to capture what is infinite within finite, anthropomorphic language. At most, we can only legitimately speak of God in the negative, alluding to what God is not. Negative theology has a long history. It is associated with the God *ein Sof* of the Kabbalah and, not coincidentally, with the more recent, postmodern approach to God of Jacques Derrida.

At the other end of the theological spectrum is a tendency to understand God as totally immanent in the world, eliminating completely God's transcendence. Such a tendency is also very old. We find it in Stoicism's equation of God with the whole of the natural order. More recently, it is also a tendency in some process theology and eco-theology.

Of course, even if God were totally immanent in the world, experiences of God's transcendence might still be possible. Even as totally immanent, God would remain the alethic truth of the world, its deepest and most sacred meaning. As such, God would be what John A.T. Robinson[4] called the 'depth dimension of reality' and Huston Smith[5] the 'something more' to the world. Thus, even if God were totally immanent, this sacred level of reality would transcend our profane experience and thus still could be experienced as wholly other. Equally, to revert to the first position, even the total otherness of God would not preclude his communicating with us were that his will.

Nevertheless, the three of us resist both extremes of the spectrum, both the total immanence or the total transcendence of God. Instead, we subscribe to a view of God as both transcendent and immanent. While God is immanent in the world, God exceeds the world. God is more than the world itself, even the world as a totality. Conversely, the world is not co-extensive with God, because not all of the world is of God. In our opinion, some of the world is even opposed to God.

Why do we favour this middle position of 'transcendence-with-immanence'? Let us first consider the view of God as totally transcendent. Were God exclusively transcendent to our experience, we would have no means of knowing that he is such or anything else about his nature.

Consider the most radical statement of complete and exclusive transcendence, namely that God is completely perfect but perfectly unknowable. Quite simply, this claim cannot be advanced. If we cannot know anything about God, his nature and will, then we have no grounds for belief even in his existence or for attributing any property whatsoever to him. Assertions to the contrary are incoherent. In addition, they ironically are wholly anthropocentric. For were God perfectly unknowable, any statement about him could only be completely anthropocentric because it would be due to some reason of ours that we wished to posit his existence, nature, etc. Transcendence alone supplies us with no ontological grounds for so doing.

A weaker variant of the above claim entertains transcendence with severely limited immanence. God is asserted to be the ontological 'first cause' alone – that constituting the limits of his knowability.

This view relegates God to mechanism, a physicist's 'supreme mechanism', perhaps, but a mechanism nonetheless. The problem is that it is hard to think of any physical mechanism as also being supremely good. Once again, God's circumscription comes from humanity, but here the anthropocentric limitations do not stem from the longings of humankind, as in the first case, but concern the limitations of human knowledge. It is we who have imposed the 'mechanistic model' upon God. Furthermore, God could hardly be supremely good were he utterly indifferent to the act of creation. If he were supremely good, he would not withhold all knowledge of his goodness from creation, since such total ignorance cannot be good for human beings. The conclusion is that if there is a transcendent God, then he cannot be wholly and exclusively so. He must also have some measure of immanence in order also to be supremely good.

Thus, as the Kabbalah ultimately does, a totally negative theology is to be resisted. Even if God has further reaches that humanity can never grasp, God also meets us as the object of our experience. Furthermore, in the Jewish, Christian and Islamic views God also meets us in human history. On all major religious views, from East to West, there also is something of God even in us. Thus, in addition to much we cannot say of God, we can also speak positively about who God is in relation to us. Theology cannot be exclusively negative.

Conversely, radical statements about God's complete and exclusive imma-nence are also ontologically problematic. Complete epistemic immanence, meaning the total accessibility of God, implies that there is nothing about God that is beyond human experience. His properties and powers are then circumscribed to ours by definition. Therefore, we would necessarily deny him supreme goodness on this argument too, because such goodness is indeed beyond human beings *sui generis*, including lying beyond our purely human powers to conceive of it fully. Effectively then, to think in terms of complete immanence also entails anthropocentricism, for we then reduce God's properties and powers to those of our own species-being. Most likely, this also involves the epistemic fallacy, since it confuses knowledge of being with being itself. What we can know about God through experience is illicitly confounded with the full extent of his being.

Even more problematic, if the world itself is divinised as total immanence implies, what are we to make of evil? Is evil also of God? Stoicism maintained that evil is an illusion, that what appears evil to us is, nevertheless, some essential part of a greater, cosmic good. At the extreme, this is the view lampooned by Voltaire's *Candide*, where 'all is for the best in this best of all possible worlds'.

It seems to us, on the contrary, that no greater, cosmic purpose could possibly be blessed that relies on such means as colonialism, Hiroshima or the Holocaust. Thus, it seems sounder to say that although God is in the world, not all in the world is of God. Instead, the world variously resists or even opposes God. There is illusion, error and even wilful sin. In addition to God, the world also contains evil. The conclusion here is that the immanence of God cannot be exhaustive of either God or the world: each must also be partially independent of the other.

In short, assertions about either the exclusive transcendence or the complete immanence of God are both problematic ontological propositions. They also entail unacceptable epistemologies. Full and exclusive transcendence commits us to epistemic inaccessibility, whilst full and exclusive immanence commits the epistemic fallacy. Instead, we maintain that God must possess some degree of both immanence and transcendence for God to reveal anything of his nature and for us to know anything at all about God.

It is for these reasons that we are committed to the ontology of transcendence-with-immanence. Epistemologically, we are committed to a thesis of God's limited knowability, where the limits are entailed by our human limitations and where the knowability is entailed by God's supreme goodness, which of its nature cannot be fully concealed.

Transcendence-with-immanence also applies to the human relationship with God as understood by differing religious traditions. For many religious traditions, there is something special of God – a spark of divinity – within each one of us. On this understanding, God is as close to us as our own selves. At the same time, transcendence-with-immanence again denies that this internal spark of divinity is exhaustive of God. It thereby affirms how in certain religious traditions, God is specifically experienced as a Transcendent Other with whom we establish an I–Thou relation. Thus, transcendence-with-immanence affirms God as both within and beyond us. In other words, the spark of divinity within us does not exhaust God, and nor does that spark of divinity exhaust us. In particular, the spark of divinity within us is over-lain by what the Vedic tradition calls maya or illusion and the Christian tradition sin.

Although, according to many religious traditions, the inner and outer God are in some way to be unified or brought into right relationship, the two are far from unified now. Because God does not exhaust what we are, because we exercise our own, independent, free will, we may also lapse into the various kinds of sin – both individual and structural – wherein we now find ourselves. Whereas God affords and enables, we select. This brings us to the problem of evil.

The question of evil

How we understand the admixture of good and evil in the world depends on our understanding of God's immanence. The three of us share a consensus that what looks like evil in the world is very often exactly that. One immediate question is how we reconcile this evil with a God who is at once both all good and all powerful. We believe that the two cannot be reconciled directly and thus follow certain trends in process theology that abandon belief in God's omnipotence. On this view, the God at work in history is a struggling God who suffers with us. Omnipotence is not challenged by the original divine conference of free will upon humankind, but it is restricted by God's forbearing to rescind our autonomy – and thus bearing with its consequences.

Militant atheists, with whom we have argued, are sometimes taken aback by such abandonment of God's omnipotence. They almost seem to regard it as cheating, as if we who believe must remain committed to the exact conception of God against which they happen to rail. Here, contrary to their evident expectation, we have an example of religious believers responding responsibly to argument. The problem of evil is a real one and as such requires a resolution. Given the choice between God's being all-powerful and all good, many religious believers opt for the latter. After all, we ought to worship goodness rather than power, and God can be plenty powerful without being all-powerful. Such a resolution, moreover, places the ball now in the atheist's court. If the problem of evil is truly why they resist belief in God, that complaint seems to be defused.

There are alternative or complementary ways to reconcile evil with God. As ontologically inherent in but not exhaustive of us, God can be understood as providing only the conditions and possibilities of our activity. God affords or enables, but we select and determine. God, on this view, is consistent with error, evil and sin.

Roy Bhaskar has perhaps gone furthest in exploring how this understanding of God's immanence disconnects God from the manifest evil in the world.[6] In *From East to West*, Bhaskar approaches God's immanence by analogy with realist conceptions of ontological emergence. From a critical realist perspective, reality is a stratified order of different levels, higher levels emerging – both diachronically and synchronically – from lower levels. This anti-reductionist understanding denies that, say, human psychology can be reduced to biology and chemistry or that biology and chemistry can be completely reduced to physics. Although 'higher' levels are always ontologically dependent on 'lower' levels, which inhere in the higher levels, these higher levels also display emergent properties and powers. Although it is composition at a lower level that makes possible the new, emergent properties and powers at a higher level, such properties and powers are foreign to the lower level and, once in existence, exceed its determination.

Bhaskar's suggestion is that a hierarchy of ontological levels offers at least one way to account for evil. As the alethic truth of the world and its ultimate source of being, God provides the categorial structure of reality, including space, time and causality. To the extent that this categorial structure applies to all levels of reality, all are ontologically dependent on it. Yet, within the constraints of this basic, categorial structure, all levels of reality enjoy a range of novel forms and behaviour that the categorial structure itself does not necessitate or determine. This is one way in which God might inhere in all levels of reality without being responsible for all that contingently ensues.

Therefore, if we encounter properties and powers that are in no way (including 'functionally') reducible to our human ones, realists are at least provisionally willing to acknowledge the existence of a different stratum of reality. Were they to do so in respect to God, clearly divine ontology cannot be emergent from the natural world and its human inhabitants. The only alternative would be to accept the divine as an underlying stratum. Such 'downwards' acknowledgement of further and further strata is common practice in physics, in relation to smaller and smaller particles. For believers, to acknowledge the divine as an under-girding stratum could make conceptual sense of 'creation as emergence' and of God's 'sustaining the universe' as the exercise of his causal powers.

What God sustains is not just reality as a whole but also our own special, human being. Western tradition describes us as the image of God. According to Vedic and Hindu traditions in the East, we actually are concrete singularisations of God – if only we knew it. What the Western and Eastern traditions share is the understanding that we have a Godlike essence that we have not yet manifested. What we essentially are, we are now not yet.

What keeps us from manifesting our true essence is not just our own personal resistance, but also the whole, collective, human history and condition that we inherit when we are born. Because there is also within us what is not of God, we are subject to constraining determinations, resulting from exercising the emergent properties and powers of our own free will – both now and over human history.

Again, our alienation from both God and from our own true selves is approached by different traditions in different ways. The East speaks of maya and avidya. Maya is the veil of illusion that makes us mistake ourselves. As a result, we fashion our identities around attachments to objects that are superficial rather than deep. In the process, we further forget who we are. Such a state of false attachment is avidya. The West, in contrast, speaks of sin, which may be either individual or collective. It is a stance in opposition to God and to what we essentially are supposed to be. Christianity labels it a state of fallenness. This is why Christians pray 'Thy Kingdom come, Thy will be done, on earth', in recognition that our world and we ourselves are far from being what they should be.

How do we extricate ourselves from this state of alienation? There is much to be done, for the tasks are collective as well as individual. At the collective level, much needs to be undone. We need to transcend myriad oppressions, exclusions and other 'sinful structures'.

At the individual level, East and West approach the task in different ways, reflecting their differing experiences along the spectrum spanning God's immanence and transcendence. For the East, the characteristic experience is of enlightenment, the visceral experience of free, non-attached consciousness, our true selfhood – or, paradoxically, the abandonment of self. The aim of much Eastern meditation is to reach this state and from there to stabilise it in everyday consciousness and practice.

Although the West also knows the experience of union with God, its more characteristic experience is of repentance. Repentance is literally a change of heart, a reorientation in moral space from what is not toward what is God. Repentance paves the way to redemption; literally, to being bought back by God. Whatever the differences in these experiences, however, enlightenment and repentance share the element of abandoning an alienated selfhood.

Fallenness and alienation

Any view holding that the present world is the creation of a perfectly good creator must also hold one of the following:

1 that the creator has limited power to do good;
2 that the world now is as it should be; or
3 that the world has fallen from the creator's intention.

Although there are philosophers of religion who try to justify God by justifying the evil in the world, none of us can countenance the second view. The first view is that of process theology, which involves the notion of God in struggle.

The third view must actually incorporate the first, if it is to be defensible. For if the third view is correct, there are real limits to what God can do: he cannot, for example, make free creatures act unfreely. Although creaturely autonomy is a condition of the possibility of fallenness, it is not fallenness itself; in itself our autonomy is something good and intended by God.

So if God is limited, the limits are at least partly in God's own nature as a being who respects the autonomy of creatures. In a certain sense, the limits of God's own nature are not pernicious limits for God. Medieval Catholic theology has already recognised that it is no defect in omnipotence to be unable to do what is logically contradictory, so that neither does God's omniscience suffer from an inability to be forgetful or malevolent.

The fallenness of the world is a theme of several religious traditions. One cannot pray 'your kingdom come, your will be done on earth as it is in heaven' without recognising that, for the most part on earth, God's will is not being done, and that much of what is being done on earth is directly contrary to the will of God. The implication is that we are creatures alienated from God, from each other; from our own telos, and from the cosmos.

Still, God remains the creator of the world, not just in the sense of being its originator at some past time, but also as its upholder – on whom the world depends for its existence at all times. Thus, even if the world had existed for all eternity, it would be true to say that it is the creation of God. Even in its fallenness, the world only exists because of God's sustaining love for it.

It follows that we cannot be totally alienated from God. Total alienation would entail our non-existence. Again, God is the one in whom all things cohere. Now in so far as things are alienated from God they do not entirely cohere. They are divided against themselves and against each other; they are destructive and destructible. Yet, not to cohere at all would be the same thing as not to exist; there being nothing without some degree of self-unity. Even in their fallenness and wrong action, worldly beings can only exist and act because of God. Evil is dependent on good whereas good is not dependent on evil. Similarly, fallenness is dependent on createdness whereas created-ness is not dependent on fallenness. The unconditional love of God can outlast any alienation from it. This ontological asymmetry gives grounds for believing that alienation can be neither total nor final.

Even if not entirely so, it is still apt to describe us as alienated from God. One manifestation of this alienation perhaps is the very difficulty so many people have in experiencing God, leading them thus to deny God's very existence. One theological way of explaining the experience of God's absence is to identify the forces of occlusion that block out such awareness. Partly, the problem is intrinsic to perception. It is one of the generative powers of humanity to be able to direct our attention selectively towards different 'layers' of a stratified reality. Thus, it is possible just not to attend to intimations of transcendence.

Nor does the current social world help us to attend. Quite the opposite. A consumer culture positively directs our attention away from transcendence and ultimate matters but towards the object domain. This subordinates being to having, and is thus self-alienating.

This state of alienation, which can only conceive of completeness, satisfaction or fulfilment by object acquisition, also binds itself to an un-requited quest, since desire is frustrated or spawns further unrealised desires. In this process, the person can only relate to fellow alienated subjects in terms of conditional love, whose exacting demands for exact reciprocity effectively commodify human relations. The other person is never a source of concern *en soi*, but only a resource, an instrumental means to an end. Conditional love is motivated by desire, literally of gain, and based upon fear, literally of loss. Desire and fear are mutually implicative and mutually undermining. Fear is a desire to avoid the feared loss and desire is fear of not obtaining desired objectives. In conditional exchanges, desire and fear unleash a chain of exactingness, revindication, resentment and attempts to enhance bargaining positions through threat, force and extortion which undermine the very human relationships in which reciprocal exchange might have been realised. The result is to plunge the alienated subject still further into more superficial forms of conditionality, such as increasingly ephemeral relationships, the quest for temporary instant gratification and an insatiable acquisitiveness. These subjects intensify their alienation since they progressively disable themselves from experiencing what is intrinsically satisfying and their attachments are increasingly to what is extrinsically unsatisfying. In turn, primary occlusion produces other blindfolds.

Unconditional love

In the Christian tradition, God's love for us is – and is experienced as – unconditional. Interestingly, given the traditionally male representation of the Judaeo-Christian God, Eric Fromm argues that unconditional love is more a maternal than paternal way of loving. Paternal love, according to Fromm, is conditional, that is, on performance. In contrast, maternal love abides regardless of outcomes.

However unfair Fromm's characterisation may be of paternal love – at least today – the distinction between conditional and unconditional love is an important one. What is loved unconditionally is loved, as Kant put it, as an end in itself and not as a means to an end. It is loved because it is of intrinsic value. That value remains even if what is loved performs in an unlovable manner. For this reason, the Catholic tradition has always upheld the distinction between sin and sinner. Sins may be vigorously opposed, but whatever they do, sinners, as people, as 'thou's', remain objects of value, which, hence, merit our love.

At the core of Christian tradition – although hardly in its historical and contemporary practice – is that we creatures are to emulate the unconditional love we experience ourselves receiving from God. We are to do so because in so loving us, God reveals to us what we ourselves are truly meant and called to be.

Who or what are we to love unconditionally? In the Christian tradition, we are primarily to love other people, other thou's. Just as we meet God's own love in an I–Thou relation, so are we to extend similar love to the other thou's we encounter. This was one of the major points conveyed by the parable of the good Samaritan. We are not just to foster a love for humanity in general but to respond with love to each concrete thou we encounter, precisely because he or she is a thou.

If unconditional love is intrinsic to spiritual enlightenment, in both Western and Eastern traditions, the requirement to love unconditionally may also be taken beyond humanity and extended to all creation. In the critical realist circles to which we belong, such a universalisation of unconditional love is received with distress. The secular Marxists among us want to know whether they are being enjoined to love the capitalist class unconditionally. Others ask whether even viruses are to be loved unconditionally.

So put, the admonition to love unconditionally does seem strange – yet, wisdom often does. Against our secular comrades, we would insist that we can never stop loving any thou's, even oppressors. We may hate and even fight against oppressive behaviour, but not oppressors as persons. Even as we struggle against them, we must love them. If this is not to be an entirely fatuous admonition, then it is profoundly difficult to follow. Yet not to do so is to fall into a vicious circle in which would-be liberators in their own turn become the new oppressors.

What about loving viruses? This at least appears too extreme to be taken seriously. Yet there is a profoundly important element of wisdom here too. Until recently, the Christian tradition has been remiss in confining the admonition to love largely to our own species. The Eastern perspective has always been more encompassing. If what we are to love is other thou's, we all must struggle to experience better the thou-ness in the rest of creation. The Jewish mystic, Martin Buber, who reintroduced the originally Feuerbachian notion of the I–Thou relation, already points the way. He directs us to experience the I–Thou relation we can have even with a tree. Trees are emblematic. They stand for the environment. An admonition to love the environment unconditionally no longer seems so strange.

Perhaps it is not even necessary to see the thou-ness in a tree or a virus to love such things unconditionally. Minimally, to love unconditionally is to regard the other as an end in itself and not just as means to ends of our own – not even the ends of humanity as a whole. The implication then is that nothing in creation can be regarded as only for our own convenience and well-being. Instead, each thing has its own independent status in the cosmos.

In *Being and Worth*,[7] Andrew Collier does still more to extract the wisdom from an admonition to love all unconditionally. Attacking the traditional divide between rationality and emotionality, Collier argues that love is the rationally appropriate orientation to what has intrinsic value. And, according to Collier, being always has intrinsic value. So, then, does all that partakes of being, namely individual beings. Thus, the beingness of all things, including viruses, is to be valued and, therefore, loved.

Most helpful to this discussion, however, are the further implications Collier draws from this perspective. On the one hand, nature is accorded its own intrinsic value independent of its utility to humanity. As only one form of being among many, the claims of humanity are relativised. Nature is to be loved as an end in itself. This result accords with contemporary streams in eco-theology and most particularly what is called 'deep ecology'.

Yet, at the same time, Collier also relativises the perspective of deep ecology, which truly would equate the claims of viruses and persons. While all being is to be valued, says Collier, being is not an all or nothing quality. Arguably, more – or higher – being is possessed by humans than by viruses. Hence, when there is a conflict between their opposing claims, the claims of a higher being must take precedence over the lower. Thus, humans can morally do what they must to control viruses, even if that means killing them. What humans cannot do is come to regard even viruses as if their existence was worthless in its own right. Even the control of viruses must be undertaken with an attitude of reverence for all that is part of the cosmic order. Perhaps were we to cultivate such an attitude towards even viruses, we would treat humans more reverently as well. In any case, Collier's position effectively affirms what is wise in deep ecology without letting it trump all that is necessary to human well-being.

If awareness of God is to experience unconditional love, by definition this is a gift, and we cannot presume to account for its bestowal. However, by focusing upon the gift-relationship, we can say something about the conditions that are pre-dispositional for receiving it. The vicious circle of conditional love and object attachment, together with the commodified relations associated with them, is not self-reversing. The terminus of alienation is simply embitterment. Nevertheless, we can conjecture its reversal in human relationships. The transformative agency necessary is both collective and individual.

At the collective level, counterposed to the notion of 'structural sin' is its opposite, 'structural virtue'. There seems to be no difficulty in demonstrating empirically that the socio-economic institutionalisation of commodified relationships, such as the wage-form, performance indicators, proliferating contractualism and consumerism, preserves and protracts the cycle of occlusive alienation from any source or focus of unconditional love, including that of self. What is much less easy to demonstrate is the proposition that the counter-institutionalisation of society on the basis of civil economy and a normativity of sharing, rather than exchange, would at least cut out some of the present engines generating alienation.

Alone, such measures would be inadequate, as are all secular visions of communism, which rely exclusively upon circumstances changing man. To respond to unconditional love, it is necessary to have experienced it. Thus we cannot make the conditions conducive to its wider diffusion themselves conditional for its manifestation. In human society, such experience can then only be at the individual level.

Every human act of unconditional love foreshadows the reversal of alienation. This is what we understand by witness, leaven or the ethic of engaged and intentional, but unattached, activity in the world. Even though the initial 'fallen' response to unconditional love may well be to take advantage contemptuously, or to repudiate it suspiciously, the repetitious free offer, which is definitional of unconditionality, has its own dispositional dynamics. It will become manifest that its conferral has nothing to do with grasping, negotiation or extortion. Instead, the natural attitude towards abundant giving is gratitude rather than grabbing, appreciation not appropriation, humility not assertion, and trust not contractualism. For all the latter terms yield no greater objective benefit and, instead, penalise by denying the relational good of inter-subjective concourse with the giver. Repeated experiences of receiving such love predispose towards regarding unconditional love as supremely desirable, because it is unconditionally beneficial. This love which heals the divisions of fear, and unifies what conditionality divides, has an expansionist tendency, which points beyond its best human practice to what empowers its practitioners.

However, nothing guarantees that this liberating and unifying power, incarnated in those individuals who have discovered the freedom of unwanting, will be attributed to or lead on to experiencing God by those who begin to know the de-alienating power of unconditional love through them. Yet, those for whom the experience of unconditional love does *not* point towards God, as its origin, are left with the intransigent 'problem of goodness', which is just as problematic for the unbeliever as is the 'problem of evil' for the believer. Unbelievers must at least be willing to entertain the testimony of the saints that there is no good in them, apart from their union with God, as the fountainhead of pure unconditional love. If they have come to accept that conditional and unconditional love have two different tendential powers, the first alienating and the second liberating, it at least becomes open to discussion that while we can very well explain conditionality in naturalistic human terms, the same is not the case for radical, loving unconditionality.

What does the Lord require?

We have seen that God is present in all creation yet distinct from it, and furthermore that this world is not only distinct but alienated from God. The work of God in this world – a work that involves human agents – is in the first place a work of undoing this alienation by making God's presence manifest in all things. But we can go further and say that it is the purpose of God, without abolishing the distinction between God and creatures, to take up these creatures into God's own self so that they can participate in the divine nature and God can be all in all.

To join in this work is the highest goal of humankind. It involves in the first place our own union with God; but it also involves the redemption of creation. Work that human agents can do, such as art, science, care for the oppressed and for nature are part of this purpose, which we are called to carry out creatively. Human society too, while it can never be identical with the reign of God, can be an icon of that reign if it is based on justice, mercy, fellowship and freedom from oppression.

To say that this is the telos of humankind is not just to say that it is God's purpose; it is also immanent in humankind, whether or not we recognise it. The ineradicable tendency in human beings to be creative in art and life, to love nature and seek to understand it, to develop forms of fellowship that are an end in themselves, to project societies exemplifying freedom, equality and fellowship, is at rock bottom a tendency to realise the 'restoration of all things' to God, whether or not we recognise it as such. For this reason, even purely secular and indeed secularist thinkers, like Marx and William Morris, can (despite themselves) be prophets of God in so far as they speak for the realisation of this tendency.

It can be said that everything in creation has some potential for union with the Creator. However, as rational beings humans have an active tendency for this union, and for participation in the work of uniting all things with God. This tendency can be more or less conscious, more or less repressed and denied. The realisation of this tendency is the ultimate fulfilment of human nature.

Notes

1 William Alston, *Perceiving God: The Epistemology of Religious Experience*, Cornell University Press, Ithaca, NY and London, 1991.
2 Richard Swinburne, *The Existence of God*, Oxford University Press, Oxford, 1979.
3 Rudolf Otto, *The Idea of the Holy*, Oxford University Press, New York, 1958.
4 John A.T. Robinson, *Honest to God*, Westminster Press, Philadelphia, 1963.
5 Huston Smith, *Why Religion Matters: The Fate of the Human Spirit in an Age of Disbelief*, Harper, San Francisco, 2001.
6 Roy Bhaskar, *From East to West: Odyssey of a Soul*, Routledge, London, 2000.
7 Andrew Collier, *Being and Worth*, Routledge, London, 1999.

3 Realism, relativism and reason in religious belief

Andrew Collier

When I come to mark the essays for my Philosophy of Religion course, I am struck by an almost unanimous refrain with which they end. After a capable marshalling of the arguments for and against the proof of God from teleology in nature, or the proof of atheism from evil in nature, almost every student will end by saying that the arguments don't really count – it's all down to 'faith' or 'personal belief'. Hardly ever do students think that there is any need to analyse what could possibly be meant by 'faith' or 'personal belief' in these contexts. In secular contexts, belief does not cause too many problems: if you believe that there are foxes in that wood, you will answer 'yes' to the question 'are there any foxes in that wood', and if someone says that there aren't any, you will disagree and perhaps give evidence that there are. If challenged to justify your belief, you will say 'I've tripped over in one's hole' or 'my mate has seen one' or 'I've smelt them'. There is no doubt that your belief is a claim about what there is, contradicting incompatible claims, and that it can be argued for and against; or that the nature of what is claimed determines what evidence is relevant to the claim. Yet these are exactly the things that are being denied when religious beliefs are said to be 'personal beliefs', or 'faith'.

'Faith', of course, is one of the key words in the Christian tradition, but it has not normally had the sense it is made to carry here. In the New Testament and the writings of the Protestant reformers, it does not mean belief at all, it means trust. Of course, in order to trust someone (for example, God), one must first believe that they exist and are trustworthy. This trust cannot be made the ground for that belief, it presupposes it. In medieval Catholicism it has another meaning: belief about God was divided into two kinds – knowledge derived from reason, and faith derived from the authority of the Church. On the face of it, this may look a bit more like the faith-as-opposed-to-proof to which my students appeal, but actually it is not so. For the Catholic, the Church is a rational authority on matters of religious belief, just as the scientific community is a rational authority on beliefs about the mechanisms of nature. So believing that Christ is of one substance with the Father because a council of the Church has said so is not a leap in the dark, any more than believing that there are quarks because my *Penguin Dictionary of Physics* says so, and I assume that it represents the consensus of the scientific community. This sense of 'faith' retains its connection with the notion of trust, because it is believing someone (or some institution) because one trusts them. Yet this does not mean that all argument has to stop, because there are arguments for (and, of course, against) the trustworthiness of the Church. Indeed one kind of such argument concerns whether the pronouncements of the Church are credible or incredible on independent grounds. For myself, as a Protestant, I do not believe that any Church is necessarily reliable, even in its most authoritative pronouncements. However, I recognise that for Catholics, as for myself, belief is amenable to rational arguments and evidence for and against, and that it would be irrational (in a bad sense) to hold beliefs contrary to the weight of evidence.

So the references – referred to at the beginning – to 'faith' and 'personal belief' are talking about something unlike that which most Christians have meant by those words, and unlike what they mean in secular contexts. It is at least clear that they are used with the implication that one cannot judge rationally between two different personal beliefs, for it is precisely to rule out such judgement that appeal is made to these concepts. It is clear too that there is some form of relativism in the offing, probably of the extreme sort which says that something can be true for me but not true for you. Further, if the relativism really is of this extreme form, it looks as though realism – the idea that religious beliefs can tell you something about reality – is also being denied. What account of religious belief could one hold on these terms? I shall first discuss the extreme view that grasps the nettle and accepts a non-realist account of religious belief; then I shall look at the position that accepts realism but rejects rational judgement between beliefs. Finally, I shall compare different sorts of relativism and their motivations, before outlining the sort of realist alternative that I hold. For brevity I shall discuss positions without reference to texts, but I think that the positions that I discuss have all been held by reputable thinkers.[1]

On the face of it, religious beliefs are about beings that exist and events that have happened: God the Father created the heavens and the earth, his only son became a man as the son of Mary, was crucified but is now alive, and so on. Yet this is also true of fictions: Karenin didn't love his wife, she had an affair with Vronsky, and so on. But fictions make no claim to truth, nor do they conflict with other fictions. One cannot choose between *Anna Karenina* and *The Brothers Karamazov* as to truth, since neither claims truth; one may choose between them in other ways. I may say '*Anna Karenina* is just a moralistic tract; *The Brothers Karamazov*, that's something else, that plumbs the depths of the human soul', and so on. Notoriously, the world is divided into Tolstoyans and Dostoevskyans; but their differences are not over beliefs about who lived in nineteenth-century Russia. A non-realist view of religious belief would present the differences between Christians and Buddhists in the same terms: one lot tell stories about Jesus, the other lot tell stories about Buddha, and each thinks that their stories are profoundly expressive of a right attitude to life. Whether either Buddha or Jesus existed is irrelevant. It can even be said in defence of this view that it has roots in a practice essential to Christianity and to some other religions: the telling of parables. But for this view it is not only the good Samaritan that is a parable, the Carpenter of Nazareth is too.

The kind of view of life described in this account – making a story play a major role in inspiring one's attitudes and actions – is a possible one. The story may be a novel, an episode from secular history, or a religious one. Marx, for instance, regularly read the story of Prometheus, in Greek, and drew inspiration from it. Yet this is surely distinct from religious belief; it did not make Marx a Greek pagan, and had he drawn similar inspiration from the New Testament, that would not have made him a Christian. For the definitive Christian attitude is not imagination or even emulation, though both have their place, but trust and love. You can imagine or imitate a fictional being, but you cannot trust one or love one. Any non-realist version of Christianity (I do not speak for other religions) has to relinquish the ideas that Christianity is about love of God issuing in love of neighbours, not just love of neighbours by itself; and that the love of God is a response to his having first loved us, and shown this in the person of Christ.

It is possible to accept realism – to say that faith means nothing unless it is faith in a Being who pre-existed our faith and exists independently of it – yet still to hold that faith is without grounds, i.e. that there is no *reason* to believe that God exists in this way. Although this view has been held, it is very odd. If we accept fictionalism, it seems to make some sort of sense to say that whatever the fictionalist calls 'faith' could exist without grounds. The preacher is simply saying 'here is our story – you can take it or leave it'. Even so, more could be said, as more could be, and has been, between Tolstoyans and Dostoevskyans. However, if someone says 'there are no grounds – I just prefer to stick with Dostoevsky (or the Gospel) rather than Tolstoy (or Buddha)', one would not think that they were saying anything paradoxical. On the other hand, if someone said 'there is a God who died for us', and in response to the question 'why do you think that?' said 'no reason, I just do', we would be left wondering whether they really thought so at all, or whether they were not misdescribing something closer to the fictionalist kind of 'belief'. For I would suggest that it is not only contradictory to say 'I believe that, but it is not true', it is also contradictory to say 'I believe that, but there is no reason to do so'. Indeed if there is a God, as opposed to a story about a God, it would be very strange if he or she had not left some traces of his or her existence, whether in nature or in special revelation. These are the sort of thing that could constitute evidence, just as the fox leaves evidence in the form of holes or spoor or sightings. So a realist view about religious ontology – the being and nature and acts of God – normally leads to a 'rationalist' position about religious judgement – the view, that is, that there can be rational grounds for deciding between different religious beliefs.

In the realist philosophy of knowledge generally, the position has been advanced (by Roy Bhaskar) that we should accept a judgemental rationalism, within an epistemic relativism, within an ontological realism. So far I have defended the ontological realism and the judgemental rationalism, but what of the epistemic relativism?

The first position that I have been criticising – groundless 'personal belief' – is certainly relativism of a kind. However, if it is the kind that licenses phrases like 'true for me', it is a kind which is incompatible with both ontological realism and judgemental rationalism. It is worth speculating why this relativism has become the 'common sense' of the present time. I suspect that it is to do with the teaching of controversial subjects like religion in schools. Obviously the teachers cannot tell a multi-cultural class which religion is right. What they could do is examine the truth claims of several religions, and try to get a tolerant, respectful argument going between the adherents of these different claims. That would be difficult. What is much easier is to present all religious beliefs as, so to speak, cordoned off by quotation marks: this is what Buddhists have as their 'personal beliefs', this is what Muslims have, this is what Christians have, and so on. All the beliefs can be inspected, but since none is taken seriously as a truth claim, but is seen rather as the mark of identity of a different group, no discussion gets going between them. I even suspect that this is part of the spontaneous ideology of the teaching profession, and goes beyond matters of religious beliefs. My colleague who teaches aesthetics reports the ubiquity of the same judgemental relativism there. If I have no statistical survey of teachers' attitudes, at least I have an anecdote about a completely different matter which can be a straw to show which way the wind blows. My wife and I were invited to a meeting at our son's school to learn about the possibilities for his studying a second language. German, Spanish and Latin were offered. We expected some account of the attractions and advantages of learning each of these languages but, with the exception of the Latin teacher, no one gave us anything of the kind, which made us feel that we were wasting our time at the meeting. I asked if the teachers could give us such information and was told that it would not be proper to try to persuade us to opt for one language rather than another. 'The decision was ours' – in other words, we would not be given the information necessary for making a wise decision, we could 'take it or leave it', and that was presented as somehow respecting our freedom more than if we had been told what we needed to know! 'Relativism' is presented as respecting people's freedom, but what it actually is, is treating that freedom as a matter of arbitrary taste rather than rational deliberation which requires grounds for decisions.

Now at least in the case of languages, treating the choice between them as groundless leads to no worse evil than the wasting of parents' time; in the case of religions it leads to the insulting refusal to take their truth claims seriously. To argue for the falsehood of a religious belief is to take its truth claim seriously, thus showing it due respect; to present it along with other such (incompatible) beliefs as all 'equally valid personal beliefs' is to insult the believer with a tangential response. For, of course, it is not possible to affirm all religious beliefs and deny none, any more than to affirm that there are foxes in the wood without denying that it is fox free. If Christianity is right that God is personal, then Taoism cannot be right that the highest reality is impersonal; if Islam is right that God is neither begotten nor begets, then Christianity cannot be right that Jesus was the son of God, and so on. To deny their mutual contradictions is to deny all their truth claims – not by saying that all are false (which again takes their truth claims seriously) but by saying that none even rises to the height of making truth claims.

But there is another kind of relativism, if indeed we want to call it that, which does not insult the various contending beliefs, and is compatible both with ontological realism and judgemental rationalism. This is the recognition that any body of beliefs, including one's own, is likely to contain its quota of false beliefs. This applies to all beliefs, not just religious ones, but it applies to these too. Hence, even if one's own body of beliefs is closer to the truth than someone else's, it may well contain false beliefs about particular issues on which the other person has true beliefs. Thus conversation between believers in different religious positions will certainly be a matter of rational persuasion, but also a matter of listening to the other person to see what one can learn from them. Even if one religion is true, any given person's or any given culture's or any given epoch's presentation of it is likely to be one-sided and to be able to learn from others. The Hebrew prophets undoubtedly had a more advanced sense of social justice than did the Taoist masters; but the Taoist masters had a better sense of the fact that conscious striving to put things right is not always the best way of securing good relations between people. To give an example from within the New Testament, which covers almost the same issues as this last one: James has clearly misunderstood Paul's teaching on faith and works when he snipes at it in his epistle, and Paul has in fact a profounder understanding of how a good life is brought about than James has; yet James has a much more trenchant social ethic (not to say socialist ethic) which, while not entirely absent from Paul (see his comments on equality as the aim of aid in 2 Corinthians 8.13–14), is certainly given a low profile in his writings.[2] From James and Paul – or from Taoism and Judaism – together, we can learn more than from one in isolation, despite the fact that one cannot have both God and the Tao as one's conception of ultimate reality (or both faith and works as one's means of salvation). One may even be able, from within the Judaeo-Christian tradition, to learn something about the way God works by reading what Lao Tzu says about the way the Tao works.

Now let us start from this position which might be called *de facto* relativism, and ask how realism makes possible rational judgements about religious belief. By '*de facto* relativism' I mean first of all the (uncontentious) recognition that there are many different views about religion, and second the (only slightly contentious) view that many of the determinants of any individual's beliefs about religion are not in themselves reasons for holding those beliefs. In the first place they may be merely historical or geographical. One is more likely to be a Muslim if one is born in western Asia or a Buddhist if one is born in eastern Asia, or – until very recently – a Christian if one was born in Europe. (The proportion of Christian families in England and France now is probably smaller than that in India, China or sub-Saharan Africa.) But there are more interesting non-rational reasons why one may adhere to a particular religious or non-religious position. Constitutional pessimism may incline one to Buddhism, or desire for an afterlife to Christianity, or unwillingness to let anything get in the way of the pursuit of profits to secularism. A sociology and psychology, perhaps even a physiology, of religious belief are possible. Nevertheless, one could not give as a reason for being a Buddhist 'I live in Thailand', or for being a Christian 'I want to live after my death' or for being a secularist 'money is all I care about'. If one accepted a fictionalist account of religious belief, one could do so. However, these beliefs make claims about how things are. Buddhism involves the claim that all existence is misery, Christianity involves the claim that the universe depends for its existence on a personal being, secularism involves the belief that the world perceived by the five senses is the only world there is. One can imagine a world populated by adherents of fictionalist religions, but it is not this world: the fact that religions make truth claims is as much a fact about our world as the fact that there are many religions.

When one makes a truth claim, one can work out from what is claimed what sort of evidence would count for and against it. This does not mean that there is necessarily any conclusive evidence. One may know good reasons why there is never likely to be, as with various hypotheses about pre-historic humankind. Nevertheless, one can judge what sort of evidence would be relevant if we had it. If there is a God who cares about us, we might expect three kinds of evidence: traces of the work of God in nature; widespread religious experience among humankind; and self-revelation of God through inspired human teachers. Of course, none of these would be conclusive evidence; other accounts could be given of the same phenomena. In particular, discourses claiming to be divine revelation are not unanimous, and therefore any such discourse requires some kind of authentication. It is difficult to see what that authentication could be (leaving aside the question of its coherence with other known truths), apart from 'by their fruits you shall know them' – in other words, saintly lives on the part of the teachers, plus a long-term beneficial effect of the acceptance of the teaching, could count as evidence for the truth of the teaching. (This presupposes that there is some positive causal relation between instances of truth and of goodness, which I argue elsewhere.)[3]

However, one must not conceive of evidence for a religious outlook in empiricist terms, as building up piecemeal a body of individually well-evidenced beliefs. Rather, we are confronted with a plurality of rich religious traditions, each with an interconnected body of truth claims. While there is no necessity to accept a whole tradition as it stands – one can be critical – it is these we are deciding between, and the question is: which makes most sense of the evidence? Is nature (for instance) most plausibly explained as an accident (secularism), a set of instances of the misery of all existence stemming from desire (Buddhism), an expression of God's will (monistic theism, for example, pantheism, Calvinism, Islam), or God's fallen creation, containing traces both of God's work and of fallenness (non-monistic Christianity)? It should be pointed out here that the consequences of adhering to a religious position may, for a given individual, be grounds for adhering to it. If, for instance, one becomes convinced that marriage is best understood as two people becoming one flesh, rather than as a social institution for the rearing of children or a contract for mutual advantage, that may be a reason for taking Christianity seriously. The irrationalist conception of religious belief that I described at the beginning of the chapter often leads people to think that a person's being (say) a Christian *explains* all their particular Christian beliefs, but it can be the other way around. One may, while still being a non-Christian, think 'Christianity does seem to get a lot of things right: maybe it's true after all.'

Affiliation to a religious position on the grounds that the truth of the truth claims that it makes also makes most sense of the evidence available, is quite unlike the 'personal belief' of the irrationalist. Belief and evidence here mean the same as they do in non-religious contexts, and are accepted on the same sorts of grounds.

In conclusion we may grant, then, that every person's set of religious beliefs (or beliefs about religion, including secularism) is likely to contain some truth and some error, and that the error (and possibly by chance some of the truth) may be explained by determinants which are not good grounds for belief; but the very fact of applying the concepts of truth and error at all, the very claim that religious beliefs are fallible, presupposes that there is a truth from which they might diverge; and because beliefs aim to capture this truth, we will have some idea what sort of thing would count as evidence for or against particular beliefs. So rational discussion of religious beliefs is possible. We have indeed a realist framework, within which we can recognise the relativity of alternative sets of beliefs, between which we can recognise that there is rational debate, and good or bad grounds for judging for one set of beliefs or another.

Notes

1 I think that fictionalism, as I describe it, is recognisably the view of the Cambridge philosopher R.B. Braithwaite in his essay 'The Nature of Religious Belief' (reprinted in Basil Mitchell's *The Philosophy of Religion*, Oxford University Press, Oxford, 1971), and also that of the Anglican clergyman Don Cupitt. The view that accepts realism but denies the rationality of religious judgement was held, if I read him right, by the German theologian Rudolf

Bultmann. Indeed, it is this that makes him so unworried about his own extreme scepticism about the historical evidence in the gospels; for him it is irrelevant to faith. Karl Barth and his followers, while closer to orthodoxy and usually less sceptical than Bultmann, seem to share this conjunction of ontological realism and judgemental irrationalism.

These positions, which I have tried to refute, are among the views criticised at length by Roger Trigg in his book *Rationality and Religion* (Blackwell, Oxford, 1998) – from a position which shares the ontological realism of the present work, though it is not specifically 'critical realist'.

2   This is on the assumption that James wrote his epistle having read those of Paul. It is possible that John A.T. Robinson is right in dating James's epistle in the 40s and Paul's epistles in the 50s of the first century, in which case, of course, James's remarks about faith without works must have another target. (See Robinson's fascinating book *Redating the New Testament*, SCM, London, 1976.)

3   Andrew Collier, *Being and Worth*, Routledge, London, 1999.

4 Judgemental rationality and Jesus

Douglas V. Porpora

My purpose in this chapter is to show how judgemental rationality can be applied to religion and, indeed, how it already has been applied by the religious themselves. My case example is the quest for the historical Jesus. Whereas Christian theology once considered the Christ of faith to be completely separate from the Jesus of history, theology today recognises the need for faith always to be informed by history.[1] Thus, an historically accurate picture of Jesus is very much on the current theological agenda.

Who Jesus actually was is an alethic truth of what critical realists regard as the intransitive object of knowledge, that is, the world. More prosaically, who Jesus actually was is a reality or feature of the world independent of our knowledge.

The discipline that attempts to discover this reality is New Testament Biblical criticism. Among its ranks are many scholars who are Christian. These scholars uncommonly follow Nietzsche's admonition 'to live dangerously', for in their pursuit, they regularly subject to danger their own most cherished beliefs.

What Biblical criticism produces is always what critical realism calls a transitive object of knowledge. It is in other words not the reality itself but only a description of that reality. As such, it is always a human product. If we want, we might refer to it as a social construction.

Calling the results of Biblical criticism social constructions is, however, misleading. Calling them such sounds as if Biblical criticism's transitive objects of knowledge bear no relation to the intransitive objects, that is, as if its descriptions of the world are unrelated to the world itself. That there never is any such relation between transitive and intransitive objects of knowledge is the postmodern view that has come to be called social constructionism. It is particularly prevalent in the sociology of science. Although social constructionism in the sociology of science is quite varied – and often, I must say, quite insightful – the principle of 'methodological relativism' is widely shared: treat the world as if it had no bearing on the results of science.[2]

Methodological relativism is not quite scepticism. It does not actually claim that there is no world. It maintains only that the world does not speak to science in any way that determines scientific conclusions. Scientific conclusions, rather, are entirely determined socially.

If it is misleading to call the results of Biblical criticism social constructions, it is misleading because, contrary to what social constructionism maintains, there is a relation between the results of Biblical criticism and the reality they purport to describe. In fact, when it comes to Biblical criticism, we will see we are misdirected even by the principle of methodological relativism.

Our examination of Biblical criticism will thus do double duty. On the one hand, it will demonstrate that judgemental rationality can be applied very rigorously and systematically to religious beliefs. On the other hand, it will demonstrate that if we listen appropriately, we will hear the world speaking and informing scientific conclusions.

One basic relation that can be shown to hold between transitive and intransitive objects of Biblical knowledge is correspondence. According to the correspondence theory of truth, a claim is true if what is claimed corresponds to the way the world actually is. If the claim fails to correspond, it is false.

Today, the correspondence theory of truth is widely disparaged. Not even all critical realists subscribe to it.[3] I happen to be among those who do. Those of us who continue to subscribe to the correspondence theory do not subscribe to it principally as the criterion of truth but rather as the meaning of truth. In other words, correspondence with reality may be of limited help in determining which claims are true. More importantly, it specifies what we mean when we call certain claims true and others false.

There was a time when I would have said categorically that correspondence is never the criterion but only the meaning of truth. I now think this overstates the case. Correspondence often comes at least close to the criterion we use to determine the truth. It comes close when our criterion is inspection.

We tend to overlook how important and ineluctable inspection is as a criterion of truth. In our daily lives, it is the criterion on which we routinely rely. My wife calls me at home, insisting that a certain phone number is on her desk. I discover that the phone number is not there. How? By inspection. Similarly by inspection, I find the number instead on the coffee table in the living room. I know I have found it in part because I can then immediately employ it by reading it to my wife over the phone.

Inspection plays a similarly ineluctable if overlooked role even in science. It goes too far to say that we determine by inspection whether or not there are, say, gravity waves. For that determination, we need to run complex experiments and debate the results. Whatever we are doing goes well beyond simple inspection. At this point, the correspondence theory definitely breaks down as a criterion of truth. In such cases, we are not in touch with the world as it is in itself, independent of our own observations.

Yet, even here, inspection plays an ineluctable role. Do we even know what our observations are? Yes, we normally do. If our data are equivocal, we at least know what they show. How do we know? By inspection. To the extent that the world speaks to us through our data, it is partly by inspection even in science that we heed its voice.

It is, however, correspondence as the meaning of truth that I especially want to defend. Even here there are worries. If we claim that there are such things as quarks, we may wonder in what way those words correspond to the world. Certainly, no one is maintaining that the words physically resemble quarks. Instead, we mean that the claim is true if, given what we mean by quarks, there is something in the world that answers to that description.

Correspondence as the meaning of truth ought to be less controversial in the human sphere, where we employ it all the time. We accuse a man of murder. If the man actually performed actions answering to our criteria of murder, the accusation corresponds to reality, and we judge it to be true. Otherwise, it is false.

Because Biblical criticism addresses the human sphere, correspondence as the meaning of Biblical truths should similarly be uncontroversial. Suppose, as happens to be the case, Biblical criticism judges Jesus to have announced the reign of God. I see no Kantian problem with saying that this claim either is or is not in correspondence with reality. If the historical Jesus actually did make such an announcement, the claim corresponds to reality and is true. If the historical Jesus never mentioned anything of the kind, the claim fails to correspond to reality and is false.

Contrary then to postmodernist scepticism, there is at least one important relation that holds between the transitive and intransitive objects of Biblical knowledge. The relation of correspondence holds. The transitive and intransitive objects either coincide or they do not.

As important as this point it may be, it is perhaps not the central issue. Even some social constructionists are prepared to concede that transitive and intransitive objects of knowledge may correspond if only by accident.[4] Social constructionism's main point is that the world does not speak in any way that helps science to establish such a correspondence.

Admittedly, the world does not speak in the way social constructionists dictate it must speak if it is to speak at all. For example, on the basis of very rich ethnographic data, Harry Collins shows that scientific conclusions are not generally reached through any kind of algorithm that yields conclusions with the certainty of a deductive proof. Instead, the experimental algorithms regularly break down, at which point scientists must negotiate and argue over rival interpretations of the results.[5]

For Collins, this is enough to show that scientific conclusions are socially constructed. Collins's argument seems to be that if a single, scientific conclusion is not logically necessitated by what the world yields through observation, the world effectively frees us to think in multiple ways. Collins admits that scientists advance arguments on behalf of their interpretations. Nevertheless, he seems to maintain, if none of these arguments deductively proves its conclusion, that any consensus that develops could have been other than it is. Thus, it is the scientific community rather than the world that determines any particular consensus.[6]

There are two basic problems with Collins's argument. First, because Collins tends to hear the world speaking only in the unequivocal results of experimental algorithms, he tends to gloss over the world's other vocalisations. It is hardly the case that the world speaks only in the unequivocal results of experimental algorithms. When experimental results are equivocal, that too is the world speaking. Thus, if, as in one case Collins describes, scientists resist belief in the paranormal, in part because of the inconsistency of findings indicating its existence, scientific resistance is in part also due to what the world has so far told us.[7]

Nor is it only through the results of experimental algorithms that the world speaks. When the algorithms yield equivocal results and the negotiations start, the ensuing scientific arguments are not detached from the the world. Thus, in one of Collins's central cases, many scientists resist believing that Joseph Weber had truly detected gravity waves. One reason is that mathematical calculations indicated that if gravity waves were truly of the amplitude Weber reported, the entire universe would have burned up.[8] Although those mathematical calculations may certainly be wrong, it can hardly be said that the argument based on them had nothing to do with the world.

The second, more serious problem with Collins's argument is that he admits no judgemental rationality other than deductive proof. According to Collins, if no deductive proof is possible, the world equally licenses multiple views, all of which he counts as entirely socially constructed. Yet even in the absence of deductive proof, the world may still not countenance more than one interpretation. The world itself may still render one view more plausible, more likely, or more rational than others. As even the fellow constructionist Andrew Pickering observes, the world resists certain formulations and facilitates others.[9] Besides deductive proof, there is also such a thing as a preponderance of the evidence. If a consensus rests on a preponderance of the evidence, then, even in the absence of deductive proof, that consensus has been determined by the world.

To determine whether a preponderance of the evidence was established, sociological observers must evaluate for themselves the comparative strength of competing arguments. Yet, such evaluation is specifically prohibited by the principle Collins refers to as TRASP, which forbids the sociologist from referring to the truth, rationality, success or progressiveness of scientific formulations.[10]

Unfortunately, Collins cannot have it both ways. He cannot demonstrate that a scientific consensus was not determined by the world without showing that it lacked a preponderance of the evidence; yet he cannot show that the consensus lacked a preponderance of the evidence without violating the principle he calls TRASP. In the end, all Collins succeeds in showing is that scientific conclusions are not infallibly established by deductive proofs.

Critical realists will readily agree with Collins on the absence of deductive proofs yielding absolute certainty. However, they will insist, there are many degrees of certainty short of that by which the world itself may yet constrain us to a single view. This is especially true when the choices before us are binary. For example, the Bible either is or is not the literally true, inerrant word of God. The position of scientific Biblical criticism is that the Bible, whether or not it is ultimately the word of God, is neither always literally true nor inerrant. Is this position just a social construction undetermined by the world? Could this scientific position just as easily have been the opposite?

As anyone who has ever argued with a Christian fundamentalist knows, the Bible's inerrancy cannot be deductively disproven. The Genesis account of creation is dramatically at odds with what we know of evolution and physical cosmology, but fundamentalists are perfectly happy to declare these wrong rather than the Bible.

One can point to what seem to be many contradictions in the Bible. The Bible offers two, very different genealogies for Jesus – one in Matthew and one in Luke. Must not one of them be wrong? Jesus's most famous sermon occurs on a mount in Matthew and on a plain in Luke. Must not one location be wrong? And in that sermon, did Jesus say it was the poor who are blessed (as in Luke) or rather just the poor in spirit (as in Matthew)? In Mark, Jesus curses a fig tree, and Peter finds it withered the next day. In Matthew, Jesus's power is faster acting: the tree withers instantaneously. Finally, among many other such apparent contradictions, who exactly was it who first found Jesus's empty tomb? The gospel accounts diverge widely.

Village atheists who triumphantly think that all they must do is present these contradictions to fundamentalists will find themselves disappointed. Fundamentalists respond that as the Bible's two genealogies evidently disagree, one must belong to Joseph and the other to Mary, even if the latter also, following Jewish custom, is assigned to Joseph. Jesus, similarly, must have presented two very similar sermons, one on a plain and one on a mount. In one he called the poor blessed and in the other the poor in spirit. Perhaps also Jesus cursed two different fig trees or the disciples just failed to notice at first that the tree had withered at once. Finally, one has only to consult the Scofield Bible to learn how the gospels' discrepant discoveries of the empty tomb can all, if torturously, be melded together.

Fundamentalists consider it a victory that all apparent Biblical contradictions can be so resolved. Yet, once we leave behind naive positivism, we should not be surprised. There are no deductive proofs, no simple falsifications. Instead, any anomaly can be saved by suitable auxiliary hypotheses.[11]

Does this mean that the scientific consensus in this case is only a social construction that could as easily have adopted the fundamentalist position instead? Not unless we ignore the world, which, in this case, includes the Biblical texts. In *The Mangle of Practice*, Pickering concedes that our theories often encounter what he calls 'resistances', which reflect the agency of the world.[12] What is resisting the fundamentalist perspective here are the textual contradictions.

Fundamentalists may have ways of resolving what seem to be textual contradictions, but their resolutions all remain conjectural. There is no independent evidence, for example, that one of the New Testament's genealogies is actually Mary's; that the disciples just overlooked an instantaneously withering fig tree; or that the Sermon on the Mount was given again almost identically on a plain. Without independent corroboration, these suggestions are persuasive only if we already assume that, as the inerrant word of God, the Bible cannot contradict itself. This assumption, however, begs the very question at stake.

If we are not to beg the question, then the available evidence – the Biblical contradictions – suggests the normal discrepancies of very human testimony. That conclusion only gains force when we consider that we have no original copies of any of the gospels, but rather multiple versions of each, with some of the earliest only remaining in fragmentary form.[13] We would have to credit King James with a miracle in the seventeenth century, if his version of the Bible had just happened on the right ones. In fact it did not. With the discovery of many, additional Biblical documents, the King James version can only be considered outdated.[14]

We may realise finally that if we abandon the doctrine of Biblical inerrancy, we also recover biological evolution and physical cosmology. Social constructionists themselves acknowledge the principle of inter-theoretical coherence, but they describe it as bringing debate to an end 'by decisions, on the part of experimenters and critics, to preserve the maximum number of prior agreements'.[15] The references to 'decisions' and 'agreements' make it seem as if we have to do here with only the arbitrary mores of a gentlemen's club. Yet, these decisions and agreements are epistemically warranted judgements. To that extent, they reflect what the world itself reveals to us. If there has been prior agreement to accept biological evolution and physical cosmology, it is because of the massive weight of physical evidence behind each. In light of that evidence, it would be epistemically irrational to jettison either easily. That is part of what makes the case against literal Biblical inerrancy so strong.

True, inter-theoretical coherence is a conceptual rather than a strictly empirical consideration. But who said that only empirical considerations are evidential and not conceptual considerations as well? Only the most naive empiricists. Against that target perhaps, social constructionism appears strong. From a critical realist perspective, however, the social constructionists are flogging a dead horse. Once conceptual considerations are also admitted into evidence, then, as even the work of the social constructionists demonstrates, the world much more sharply delimits the epistemically warranted possibilities.[16]

In the end, against literal, Biblical inerrancy, there may be no deductive proofs, but there certainly is a preponderance of the evidence. In fact, the only reason to suppose the Bible is the inerrant word of God is that some people claim to experience it as such. Their reported experience must be respected, but it can also be impugned. After all, many Muslims so experience the Koran and at least some Jews the Talmud.

Perhaps all these people are genuinely experiencing the voice of God, speaking through these respective texts, without God's having specifically dictated any of them verbatim. Such a theological interpretation at least preserves the religious experience involved without sacrifice of judgemental rationality. In any case, the more vaunted claims for each text are untenable, and that judgement is not just a social construction unrelated to the way the world is. Of course, we can only determine that (or its converse) if we exercise judgemental rationality ourselves.

Whether or not science often actually invokes the word truth, it is indispensable to its practice. If scientists are not to remain rehearsing the same issues, they must build on something. What they build on is what they – either collectively or individually – consider to be true or in correspondence with objective reality. Once we accept the Bible as a human creation, there are other truths we can build on that foundation. Many such truths are truths about Jesus. Although some would question even Jesus's historical existence, that is no more warranted than questioning the historical existence of Socrates. Besides the canonical gospels, there are many others that did not make it into the canon. There are in addition some letters, especially those of Paul, which are dated at around the 50s of the first century. Even with the removal of possible Christian interpolation, both Jesus and his brother James are mentioned by the roughly contemporaneous, Jewish historian, Flavius Josephus. Jesus is likewise mentioned as well in the Talmud. Given such documentary evidence, there is more reason than not to suppose that Jesus actually existed.

The canonical gospels, however, remain the primary source of reliable knowledge about Jesus. They are data, largely knowable by inspection. At the same time, the gospels themselves are in their own right intransitive objects of the social world. Thus, when we know their qualities as data, we simultaneously know their qualities as intransitive objects. Some of their objective qualities we know with virtually apodictic certainty. We know, for example, that it is only in the gospel of Luke that Jesus reads from Isaiah and that this occurs early rather than late in the gospel.

The objection may be raised that we can know such intransitive objects with such certainty only because they belong to the subset of the world that is social. I am happy to concede that. The objection, however, seems to concede in turn that truth – even a simple correspondence conception – is applicable at least to the social world. If so, someone should tell the postmodernists. The fact is we have just established that truth and falsity have demonstrable purchase in at least one domain. It cannot be said, then, that the very concept of truth is illicit.

Of course, the kinds of truths to which I just alluded may not be especially interesting. Yet there are more interesting truths that we can know with equal certainty. In particular, we can know, again just by inspection, certain objectively real relations among the intransitive objects we call gospels. About 90 per cent of Mark's material is contained in the gospel of Matthew and about 50 per cent is contained in Luke. The sequence of events is often the same across the three, and when there are divergences, they are between Matthew and Luke. In those cases, the sequence in Mark continues to agree with one against the other. About half the time where the three gospels share common material, they also agree in wording. Where there are discrepancies, rarely do Matthew and Luke agree against Mark.[17]

These objective relations are beyond dispute, but they remain perhaps pretty spare. What, we want to know, do they signify? After long debate, a wide consensus has been achieved on what they do signify. The consensus is that Mark was written first, perhaps just before 70 CE (common era). Matthew and Luke were written later, most likely between 80 and 90. Matthew and Luke, furthermore, were written independently of each other but with definite knowledge of and reliance on Mark.

Is this chronology just a social construction? It depends on what we mean by that. Certainly, the chronology was constructed socially through argument. Just as certainly, it was not constructed by anything like a deductive proof. Yet the chronology is not just a social construction in the sense that it has no relation to the world. As we have already established, in so far as we are speaking of the social world here, there is no Kantian problem that would conceptually preclude us from speaking of a correspondence between phenomenal and noumenal worlds. The actual chronology may have been just as the consensus describes. Nor can we say that the agreed upon chronology was in no way informed by the world. The reliance on the textual features of the gospels as intransitive objects already go a long way towards belying that.

Perhaps by just a social construction we mean that the agreed upon chronology is not absolutely certain. It is fallible. The truth might be otherwise. Indeed, it could be. Critical realists certainly agree that all our knowledge is fallible. After long consideration, however, most Biblical critics have concluded that this is the most likely way it was, and only by the exercise of our own judgemental rationality can we establish anything different.

There is still more. Matthew and Luke each contain material unique to themselves. In addition, however, there are about two hundred verses shared by Matthew and Luke that are not found at all in Mark. These two hundred verses are often so close as to contain the same, grammatically odd constructions.[18] Again, after long discussion, most Biblical critics have concluded that, in addition to Mark, Matthew and Luke independently drew on yet another, early, written source. That source so far has not been found. It is usually designated Q, for the German word *Quelle*, meaning source.

In all, the established chronology is a remarkable, social achievement that provides a kind of scaffold for subsequent work. In their entirety, none of the gospels represents an eye-witness account. Each represents a compilation of tradition passed down by distinct communities within the Christian movement. The chronology thus provides two analytically important elements. First, it identifies distinct community traditions: at the very least, the traditions associated with Paul, Q, Mark, Matthew, Luke and, finally, John, whose gospel is less related to the others. Second, the chronology provides us with actual layers of tradition. We can actually see what happens to stories as they pass from Q or Mark to Matthew or Luke, and see as well in some cases how the communities of Matthew and Luke differentially treat the same essential story.

These are powerful analytical elements that begin to give us criteria for determining what in the Bible actually goes back to the historical Jesus. Let us begin with what is really a derivative criterion, the criterion sometimes called coherence. If we had a bedrock of sayings and actions that we could more reliably attribute to Jesus, we could evaluate others in terms of their coherence with the bedrock. Sayings and actions very incoherent with what we more reliably know about Jesus would seem more likely to have been creations of the early Church.[19]

Of course, the criterion of coherence will work only if we can establish such a more reliable bedrock or beachhead. One criterion that accomplishes this is called the criterion of dissimilarity. Employing this criterion, we are more disposed to consider as authentic to Jesus any statement or action that is discontinuous with both the Judaism of his time and the apparent tendency of the early Church.

A good example is Jesus's prohibition of divorce, which is regarded as authentic by most scholars, including even those associated with the highly sceptical Jesus Seminar. The prohibition on divorce is one reflection of a feminist dimension in Jesus's message as the Judaism of Jesus's time exclusively allowed men to divorce their wives.[20] The prohibition is therefore discontinuous with Jesus's first-century background.

At the same time, even the early Church was uncomfortable with the ban as a categorical prohibition. As it travels from its independent, early citations in both Mark and Q, it becomes softened in Matthew. In Mark, Jesus says, 'Whoever divorces his wife and marries another commits adultery against her.' In Matthew, the text now reads, 'Whoever divorces his wife, except for infidelity, and marries another commits adultery.' Matthew's escape hatch is one that few scholars consider authentic.

In the prohibition of divorce, we evidently have an admonition so discontinuous, both with what came before and what came after, that it very reasonably can be attributed to the historical Jesus. Of course, by itself, the criterion of dissimilarity contains its own dangers. It excludes anything as authentic that might be continuous with either the Judaism of Jesus's time or the early Church. Yet, we would expect that in many ways Jesus's message will also be continuous with these.

This reflection has recently given rise to a further criterion of authenticity, known as the criterion of similarity.[21] This criterion is a reminder that, as Jesus was a Jew, we should expect a thoroughly Jewish Jesus. Most recently, the criterion has been pressed against the Jesus Seminar, some of whose members defend a non-eschatological Jesus in the likeness of a Greek cynic. Although the battle rages on, many scholars regard this as too non-Jewish a Jesus.[22]

The chronology of Christian sources itself implies another two, strong criteria of authenticity: chronological proximity to Jesus and multiple attestation. Chronological proximity refers to the layer of tradition in which a certain saying or action or theme is found. Mark, Q (which many scholars believe predates Mark) and Paul are early, Matthew and Luke later, and John later still. The prohibition of divorce possesses good credentials on this score. It shows up independently in Q, Mark and Paul – that is, throughout the layer comprising our very first written record. For the same reason, the prohibition of divorce is also multiply attested. Multiple attestation refers to inclusion in more than one of the distinct traditions that the chronology identifies. Presumably, if multiple, separate streams of tradition know equally a similar story, one very likely reason is because it happened.

When we consider how the prohibition stands in terms of the criteria of dissimilarity, chronological proximity and multiple attestation, the likelihood is that it brings us face to face with the first-century prophet. Is this an infallible judgement? No, it might be wrong. Is it a good bet? It is by far a better bet than that Jesus said nothing at all about divorce. And, incidentally, if we judge that Jesus truly did issue a prohibition of divorce, we have yet another strong reason for supposing he actually existed.

There is yet another powerful criterion of authenticity that is often invoked. It is the criterion of embarrassment. The reasoning is that as the Church was not likely to have invented any incident it found so embarrassing as to require damage control, the more probable again it is that the incident actually happened. For this reason, no mainstream scholar doubts that Jesus was actually crucified. Throughout the Roman Empire and especially in Palestine, crucifixion was an ignominious way to die. It was not the kind of death to bolster an argument that the one so executed was divine. Thus, if the early Christian tradition says that Jesus was crucified, he most likely was.[23]

For similar reasons, almost all scholars are convinced that Jesus was baptised by John. In fact, the consensus is that the Baptist led a parallel movement of which Jesus was originally a disciple. For a Church that proclaims Jesus God, it is somewhat embarrassing to imagine Jesus, for however brief a time, a disciple of someone else. It is all the more embarrassing when the baptism conferred is symbolic of repentance.

In this case, we can do more than just conjecture. We can actually see the embarrassment at play in the texts. Mark's description of the baptism is simple and straightforward. In contrast, when Matthew's Jesus comes to be baptised, John stops him, protesting that John rather should be baptised by

Jesus. In reply, Jesus essentially says to 'let it go for now' as both need to do what is fitting.[24] Thus does Matthew try to neutralise what had become an embarrassment. If it was an embarrassment, why did Matthew not try to deny it? Why even include a reference to Jesus's baptism? Probably because everyone knew that it had happened, and it needed to be explained away. That, at any rate, is the consensus reasoning on the issue.

Although I hope that I have said much to provoke social constructionists, I probably have not said anything so far to scandalise secular minds. Let me end, therefore, with something more provocative. Let us follow the reasoning we just rehearsed and consider the following incident: Jesus is accused of casting out devils by the power of the demon, Beelzebul. Jesus deftly turns this accusation against his accusers, asking by whom his accusers cast out demons. He goes on to say that if, rather, it is by the 'finger of God' that he casts out demons, then the 'reign of God' is at hand.

The story is found independently in both Mark and Q. It thus has early and double attestation. If we think about it, the story relates a source of embarrassment. Jesus is being accused of witchcraft. Indeed, this accusation persists long enough to appear even in the Talmud.

The consensus view judges authentic both the accusation in general and this particular controversy in particular. But if Jesus was widely accused of witchcraft, he must have been doing something to inspire it. The reasoning we have followed in other cases leads here to a disconcerting conclusion. Among other things, Jesus practised exorcism – and, evidently, with success.

What am I saying? Have I now suddenly gone off the deep end? I do not think so, but that also depends on where one thinks the deep end lies. I am not saying that there are demons. I am saying merely that Jesus seems to have performed healings that his contemporaries considered remarkable.[25]

Were these healings miracles? The word miracle conveys both less and more than we suppose.[26] It conveys less because the miraculous need not imply any pyrotechnics. A miracle can be as prosaic as the birth of a child or the forgiveness of a great offence.

The nineteenth-century quest for the historical Jesus was embarrassed by the miracle stories because it thought they implied violation of natural laws, which scholars then positivistically considered a closed system. With its different understanding of nature as an open system, critical realism does not share this difficulty. Critical realism is thus more open to forces that might be deemed mysterious. The problem for the nineteenth-century quest was that – unlike the so-called nature miracles (walking on water, calming of storms, etc.), which few scholars regard as authentic – references to the healing miracles kept surfacing early in the tradition and are multiply attested.[27] Even an appropriately expurgated Josephus refers to them. Social constructionists sometimes argue that theoretical choices are under-determined by the data.[28] Not in this case. It was not so much that the nineteenth-century quest could not possibly accommodate these data as that *it could not do so reasonably.*

If a miracle may well be less than spectacular, it is also always more than just a supernatural boon. To be a miracle – as opposed to an effect of, say, magic – the boon must also be a manifestation specifically of God. Whether there is a God and a God who chose to be manifest through Jesus's healings is not an historical question.[29] Often it is said to be a question of faith, but I find that word misleading. I would say rather that this determination reflects an emotional reaction to what we make of Jesus as a whole.

To react to Jesus as a whole, we must know Jesus as a whole, the historical Jesus and not some concoction from Sunday School. The concoction is more likely to be known by believers and unbelievers alike. Believers, particularly, however, have an obligation to inform their faith, revise it, and possibly even abandon it in light of knowledge.

That knowledge, I have been arguing, is possible. Indeed, I have been suggesting that contemporary Biblical criticism has already taken us a long way down that road. Do we infallibly know that we are on the right path? No. The criteria of authenticity which we have discussed provide nothing akin to deductive proofs. They offer no algorithms. Biblical scholars heatedly debate the relative stress that should be placed on each criterion and, even when they agree on that, they still disagree on applications. Thus, whereas postmodernists suggest that, in the end, parochial criteria of argument ensure that all truth remains local, in contemporary Biblical criticism we have a case where the criteria themselves are constantly contested.[30] Judgemental rationality, I have argued, can be applied even to religion, and if it can be applied even to religion, wherefore can it not be applied everywhere else?

Notes

1 The separability of the Christ of faith from the Jesus of history reflected the dominating influence of the neo-orthodoxy of Karl Barth and Rudolf Bultmann in the early half of the twentieth century and was in part a reaction to Albert Schweitzer's depressing conclusion to *The Quest of the Historical Jesus* (Macmillan, New York, 1968) that Jesus was a heroic but ultimately deluded prophet.

2 See Harry Collins, *Changing Order*, Sage, London, 1985, pp. 16, 185; 'Stages in the Empirical Programme of Relativism', *Social Studies of Science*, 1981, 11: 3–10.

3 Roy Bhaskar himself seems dismissive of the correspondence theory. See particularly his *Dialectics: The Pulse of Freedom*, Verso, London, 1996, pp. 211–15. Critical realists who continue to subscribe to the correspondence theory include Ruth Groff. See Groff (2000) 'The Truth of the Matter: Roy Bhaskar's Critical Realism and the Concept of Alethic Truth', *Philosophy of the Social Sciences*, 2000, 30 (3): 407–36.

4 See, for example, Peter Berger, *The Heretical Imperative: Contemporary Possibilities of Religious Affirmation*, Anchor, Garden City, NY, 1979.

5 Collins, *Changing Order*.

6 Collins, *Changing Order*. See also Collins, 'A Strong Confirmation of the

Experimenters' Regress', *Studies in the History and Philosophy of Science*, 1994, 25 (3): 493–503.

7 Collins, *Changing Order*.

8 Collins, *Changing Order*. Collins might argue that although the world may be speaking here, it is not speaking unambiguously. All I am pressing at the moment is that if the world is in fact speaking – however ambiguously, scientific arguments based on these vocalisations are related to the way the world is.

9 Andrew Pickering, *The Mangle of Practice: Time, Agency, and Science*, University of Chicago Press, Chicago, 1995.

10 Harry Collins, 'What is TRASP? The Radical Programme as a Methodological Imperative', *Philosophy of the Social Sciences* 1981, 11: 215–24.

11 Imre Lakatos, 'Falsification and the Methodology of Scientific Research Programmes,' in Imre Lakatos and Alan Musgrave (eds), *Criticism and the Growth of Knowledge*, Cambridge University Press, Cambridge, 1970.

12 Pickering, *The Mangle of Practice*.

13 Robert Funk, Roy Hoover and the Jesus Seminar, *The Five Gospels: The Search for the Authentic Words of Jesus*, Macmillan, New York, 1993, pp. 5–6.

14 Robert Funk *et al.*, *The Five Gospels* p. 8.

15 Collins, *Changing Order*, p. 5.

16 See Colin Wight, 'They Shoot Horses Don't They?: Locating Agency in the Agency–Structure Problematique', *European Journal of International Relations*, 1999, 15 (1): 109–42). Ian Hacking in fact argues that the constraints of coherence rather than the world come so to delimit options that this rather than the world makes science seem to progress. See Ian Hacking, *The Social Construction of What?*, Harvard University Press, Cambridge, 1999. The counter-evidence to that is scientific revolutions, several of which have occurred in Biblical criticism.

17 Funk *et al.*, *The Five Gospels*, pp. 10–11.

18 Funk *et al.*, *The Five Gospels*, p. 12.

19 Biblical critics generally begin their analyses by rehearsing these standard criteria and by positioning themselves in relation to them. For three contrasting accounts, see John Dominic Crossan, *The Historical Jesus: The Life of a Mediterranean Jewish Peasant*, Harper, San Francisco, 1991; John P. Meier, *A Marginal Jew: Rethinking the Historical Jesus*, Doubleday, New York, 1991; and N.T. Wright, *The New Testament and the People of God*, Fortress, Minneapolis, 1992.

20 The feminist dimension of Jesus's message is not limited to the proscription against divorce. See Rodney Stark, *The Rise of Christianity*, Princeton University Press, Princeton, 1997.

21 Wright, *The New Testament*. Wright is one of the founders of what is sometimes called the 'Third Quest' for the historical Jesus, which stresses greater continuity with Jesus's first-century Jewish background.

22 Wright, *The New Testament*, is one of the foremost critics of the non-eschatological Jesus as a Greek cynic. See also Wright, *Jesus and the Victory of God*, Fortress Press, Minneapolis, 1996.

23 My own *Landscapes of the Soul*, Oxford University Press, New York, 2001, contains an interview with Hal Taussig, one of the founding scholars of the Jesus Seminar, which, as I have several times suggested, is especially sceptical

about much of the words and deeds attributed to Jesus in the Bible. When I asked Hal what scholars knew about Jesus most certainly, Hal replied, 'That he was crucified.'

24 See Funk *et al.*, *The Five Gospels*, p. 132.
25 This way of putting it is fairly standard for Biblical scholars. See, for example, the classic by Norman Perrin, *Rediscovering the Teaching of Jesus*, Harper & Row, New York, 1967.
26 See John Meier, *A Marginal Jew: Rethinking the Historical Jesus* (Volume II): *Mentor, Message, and Miracles*, Doubleday, New York, 1994, pp. 509–646.
27 It was data like these that ultimately doomed the nineteenth-century quest, especially as they related to an eschatological Jesus, with whom the nineteenth century was as uncomfortable as the twentieth. See Schweitzer, *The Quest*.
28 See, for example, Mary Hesse, *Revolutions and Reconstructions in the Philosophy of Science*, Harvester, Brighton, 1980.
29 This kind of disclaimer is routine among historical Biblical critics. Again, see, for example, Meier, *A Marginal Jew*.
30 See, for example, Steven Seidman, 'The End of Sociological Theory: The Postmodern Hope', *Sociological Theory*, 1991, 9 (2): 131–47.

5 Models of man: the admission of transcendence

Margaret S. Archer

Throughout their history the social sciences have privileged atheism. They are an extended example of the general asymmetry between the need to justify faith, and the assumption that atheism supposedly requires no such justification. Indeed, social science bears much responsibility for enabling atheism to be presented as an epistemologically neutral position, instead of what it is, a commitment to a belief in the absence of religious phenomena. In part, this derived from the personal irreligiosity of the founding fathers; Durkheim and Marx were prominent 'masters of suspicion', whilst Weber declared himself 'religiously unmusical'. In equal part, it can be attributed to the pervasive methodological endorsement of empiricism, which illegitimately confines investigation to observables. At best, empiricists consigned non-observables to the metaphysical realm; at worst, the non-observable was deemed 'nonsense' in logical positivism. In sum, empiricism confirmed the hegemony of sense data over everything that can be known. Since realism has mounted such a remorseless critique upon empiricism, a parallel critique of its bedfellow, atheism, is now overdue.

Until recently, it was commonplace for sociologists to hold that progress in natural science was accountable for the 'God of the Gaps' – namely that divinity only kept a shrinking toehold where scientists had not yet trodden. However, modern scientists themselves are less inclined to view their endeavours in this zero-sum manner. They seem more disposed to admit that their findings do not contradict the majority of theistic beliefs, with the exception of literal fundamentalism. Because nothing in the current enterprise of natural science ultimately hangs upon the presumption of atheism, more of its practitioners endorse the intellectually respectable position of agnosticism, while some actively explore the compatibilities between science and religion (see Porpora in Chapter 11). Conversely, it is not circumstantial that my believing colleagues in sociology can be counted on one's fingers in this country; for much does hang upon atheism in the social sciences, particularly the very concept of the human subject. The less he or she is held to be the product of social forces, then an unwanted modesty is enforced upon these imperialistic disciplines. Thus, Alston appears to be correct in pinpointing the human sciences as the major adversaries of religion, precisely because of their concept of humanity.

I cannot see that there are any contradictions between established scientific results and central Christian doctrines . . . I will not go so far as to maintain that there *can* be no contradiction between scientific results and central tenets of Christianity. *The most obvious possibility concerns the human sciences.* It undoubtedly is crucial for theistic religion that it work with a conception of man as capable of being addressed by God, capable of freely deciding whether or not to follow God's behests, capable of eternal loving communion with God after the death of the body. And some views about human nature do not allow for any such possibilities.[1]

He restricts his case to the examples of behaviourism and psychoanalysis.

I want to go much further than this and to make two additional points. First, the argument will be presented that from the Enlightenment onwards, 'models of man'[2] have systematically precluded the human subject from having transcendental relations, and have assimilated historical and comparative evidence about the extensiveness of religiosity to exclusively social causes. Here, it will be maintained that such conceptions of humanity are defective for social science and for faith alike. Second, the argument will be concerned with how the realist conception of the human being is preferable because it does not assume that all our relations with reality are socially derived, and therefore it does not rule out the possibility of authentic human relations with the divine in advance.

Modernity's Man and Society's Being

To begin with the first point, two defective models of the human being have sequentially dominated social theorising since the Enlightenment. These are mirror images of each other, since the one stresses complete human self-sufficiency, whilst the other emphasises utter social dependency.

In cameo, the Enlightenment had allowed the 'death of God' to issue in titanic Man. Thus, with the secularism of modernity went a progressive humanistic endorsement of human self-determination, of people's powers to come to know the world, master their environment and thus to control their own destiny as the 'measure of all things'. This lies at the heart of secular humanism, a tough anthropocentric doctrine that nothing matters at all except in so far as it matters to man.[3]

Not only does 'Modernity's Man' stand outside nature as its master, he also stands outside history as the lone individual whose relations with other beings and other things are not in any way constitutive of his self, but are merely contingent accretions, detachable from his essence. Thus the modern self is universally pre-given. Because all that is contingent can be stripped from this self, he can step forward as a purely logocentric being whose consciousness, freed from any embedding in historical circumstances, can pellucidly articulate the cosmic story. The metaphysics of modernity thus adduced a model of rational man who could attain his ends in the world by pure logos; this was a disenchanted world made up of natural and social reality alone, for it had been ontologically purged of transcendence.

As the heritage of the Enlightenment tradition, 'Modernity's Man' was a model which had stripped down the human being until he had one property alone, that of instrumental rationality, namely the capacity to maximise his preferences through means–ends relationships and so to optimise his utility. Yet, this model of *homo economicus* could not deal with our normativity or our affectivity, both of which are intentional, that is they are 'about' relations with our environment: natural, practical, social and transcendental. These relationships could not be allowed to be, even partially, constitutive of who we are. Instead, the lone, atomistic and opportunistic bargain-hunter stood forth as the impoverished model of man.

On the one hand, some of the many things social with which this model could not deal were: (i) phenomena like voluntary collective behaviour, leading to the creation of public goods, or (ii) normative behaviour, when *homo economicus* recognised his dependence upon others for his own welfare, and, finally, (iii) his expressive solidarity and willingness to share. All these deficiencies remained, despite tortuous efforts to dismantle the notion of altruism altogether, and thus to reduce seemingly altruistic behaviour to first-order self-interest or to second-order advantages accruing to 'inclusive kin'. On the other hand, one of the most important things with which this model cannot cope is the human capacity to transcend instrumental rationality and to have 'ultimate concerns'. These are concerns that are not a means to anything beyond them, but are commitments that are constitutive of who we are – the expression of our identities. Who we are is a matter of what we care about most. This is what makes us moral beings. It is only in the light of our 'ultimate concerns' that our actions are ultimately intelligible. None of this caring can be impoverished by reducing it to an instrumental means–ends relationship, which is presumed to leave us 'better off' relative to some indeterminate notion of future 'utility'.

However, this was the model of man that was eagerly seized upon by social contract theorists in politics, Utilitarians in ethics and social policy, and liberals in political economy. *Homo economicus* is a survivor. He not only lives on as the anchorman of microeconomics and the hero of neo-liberalism, but he is also a colonial adventurer and, in the hands of rational choice theorists, he bids to conquer social science in general. As Gary Becker outlines this mission, 'The economic approach is a comprehensive one that is applicable to all human behaviour.'[4] True to the Enlightenment tradition, Becker includes human religiosity in this explanandum.[5] The recent burgeoning of rational choice theory in American sociology of religion[6] depends upon the commodification of religion. In the USA, market competition is held to keep the vitality of organised religion high (in contrast to shrinking rates of participation in Europe), as complacent religious organisations cede their positions to the marketeering of thrusting new competitors. Such commodification of religion probably goes some way to explaining the lunar *Landscapes of the Soul* documented by Porpora; we do not find the meaning of life in the conservatories, cruises and consumables that are successfully marketed to us, so why should it be found through denominational marketing?

However, the rise of postmodernism over the last two decades represented a virulent rejection of 'Modernity's Man', which then spilt over into the dissolution of the human subject and a corresponding inflation of the importance of society. Now, in Lyotard's words, 'a *self* does not amount to much',[7] and in Rorty's follow-up, 'Socialisation . . . goes all the way down.'[8] To give humankind this epiphenomenal status necessarily deflects all real interest on to the forces of socialisation, as in every version of social constructionism. People are indeed perfectly uninteresting if they possess no personal powers which can make a difference. Consequently, to Foucault, 'Man would be erased, like a face drawn in sand at the edge of the sea.'[9]

Postmodernism has massively reinforced the anti-realist strand of idealism in social theory and thus given ballast to social constructionism. This is the generic view that there are no emergent properties and powers pertaining to human agents, that is, ones which exist in between human beings as organic parcels of molecules and humankind as generated from a network of social meanings.[10] The model of 'Society's Being' is social constructionism's contribution to the debate, which presents all our human properties and powers, beyond our biological constitution, as the gift of society. From this viewpoint, there is only one flat, unstratified, powerful particular, the human person, who is a site, or a literal point of view. Beyond that, our selfhood is a grammatical fiction, a product of learning to master the first-person pronoun system, and thus quite simply a theory of the self which is appropriated from society. Constructionism thus elides the concept of self with the sense of self; we are nothing beyond what society makes us, and it makes us what we are through our joining society's conversation. Society's Being thus impoverishes humanity, by subtracting from our human powers and accrediting all of them – selfhood, reflexivity, thought, memory, emotionality and belief – to society's discourse.

What makes actors act has now become an urgent question because the answer cannot be given in terms of people themselves, who have neither the human resources to pursue their own aims nor the capacity to find reasons good if they are not in social currency. Effectively, this means that the constructionists' agent can only be moved by reasons *appropriated* from society, and thus is basically a conventionalist, in religion as in everything else. Yet, the objection remains that a real 'self' is still needed as a *focus* for such principles and that an 'over-socialised' self remains inadequate as a *locus* of their origins and their frequent unconventionality. Constructionism is unable to explain why some people seek to replace societies' rules and unwilling to allow that this originates in people themselves, from their own concerns, forged in the space *between* the self and reality as a whole.

Neither of these two models can capture the 'man of faith', who is responsive to sacred revelation or tradition. Thus, 'Modernity's Man' represents an anthropocentric being, incapable as an 'outsider' of sufficient embedding in a sacred tradition such that this helps to constitute his being-in-the-world. He is also closed against revelation by his human self-sufficiency. This means that he will always reduce divinity to the anthropomorphic – ideal typically to the Goddess of Supreme Reason. Conversely, Society's Being is so sociocentric that he is swamped by tradition (form of life, language game, etc.), and thus lacks the wherewithal to elaborate upon it, and is only open to revelation in so far as it is mediated to him by society. Anthropocentric 'Modernity's Man' makes God and his society in his own image. Sociocentric 'over-socialised' man is the product of society, as is his God.

Realism's self

From the realist point of view, the central deficiency of these two models is their basic denial that the *nature of reality* makes any difference to the people that we become, or even to our becoming people. Modernity's Man is pre-formed, and his formation, that is the emergence of his properties and powers, is not dependent upon his experiences of the world. Indeed, the world can only come to him filtered through an instrumental rationality that is shackled to his interests, whose genesis is left mysterious. Preference formation has remained obscure, from the origins of the Humean 'passions' to the goals optimised by the contemporary rational chooser. The model is anthropocentric, because man works on the world, but the world does not work upon man, except by attaching risks and costs to the accomplishment of his pre-formed designs. In short, he is closed against any experience of reality that could make him fundamentally different from what he already is.

Similarly, Society's Being is also a model that forecloses direct interplay with reality. Here the whole of the world comes to people as sieved through one part of it, 'society's conversation'. Their very notion of being selves is merely a theory appropriated from society, and what they make of the world is a matter of permutations upon their appropriations. Once again, this model cuts man off from any experience of reality itself, which could make him fundamentally different from what social discourse makes of him. Society is the gatekeeper of reality and therefore all that we become is society's gift.

What is lost, in both versions, is the crucial notion of direct experience of reality; that the way the world is can affect how we are. This is because both anthropocentricism and sociocentricism are two versions of the 'epistemic fallacy', where what reality is taken to be, courtesy of our instrumental rationality or social discourse, is substituted for what the world really is. Both models condemn humanity to living out this fallacy, because the gatekeepers they have imposed confine us to mediated experiences alone. Realism can never endorse the 'epistemic fallacy' and, in this connection, it must necessarily insist that how the world is has a regulatory effect upon what we make of it and, in turn, what it makes of us. These effects are independent of our discursive penetration, just as gravity influenced us and the projects we could entertain long before we conceptualised it.

In other words, realism opens up a space, which, of course, was never really closed, in which whatever properties and powers pertain to reality can have an unmediated influence upon us, through our experiences of them, which need not be articulated. Primitive man experienced gravity as he fell down inclines and failed to jump over large obstacles, under whatever descriptions, if any, he knew these limitations. Although it is inappropriate to speak of God 'belonging' anywhere, in a purely conceptual sense he 'pertains' to this space, as do other unobservables such as many scientific entities, like gravity. In both religion and science, people can devote their lives to searching for such unobservables and the grounds for their searching are open to rational discussion. What we do know, historically, is that they have neither always been right nor always been wrong. The importance of holding this gap open for reality, which can never be restricted to the known, is that we allow for the possibility of unmediated human experiences which are not *necessarily reducible* to self-referentiality, as in Modernity's Man, or to social constructions, as in Society's Being. Although realists readily allow that all experiences and interpretations are fallible, realism cannot accept any foreclosure which prematurely restricts that which can be experienced, and hence allowed to influence what we become as people.

In fact, because of the 'primacy of practice' in realist accounts of human development, which necessarily eschew the 'linguistic fallacy', unmediated experiences of reality already play a central role. All our typical human properties and powers only exist *in potentia*. Whether or not any of them are realised depends upon our interaction with the world, its properties and powers, which are amenable to our experience, contra the unfolding model of Modernity's Man. Equally, our specific properties and powers as language speakers are dependent upon prior non-linguistic practice in the world. As Merleau-Ponty maintained, the differentiation between self and otherness, then self and object, and finally, self and other subjects, have to be phenomenally acquired before we are capable of making the distinctions which language presupposes. As Piaget's experiments showed, the acquisition of thought and mastery of the principles of identity and non-contradiction, which are indispensable for any communication at all, are acquired in practice. This being the case, language can only be learnt after unmediated practice in the world, and it gains its meaning from its relation to this same independent reality. To consider language to be dependent upon reality, rather than reality upon language, is to lift the linguistic portcullis; what we experience reality to be will determine what we talk about in the public medium, and not vice versa, contra Society's Being.

What the primacy of practice means, in this context, is that the full gamut of reality can enter into our human constitution and development, provided only that we are capable of experiencing it. Of course, we cannot experience everything that is real. Partly this is because of our human limitations. For example, we cannot visit every place in the world or hear the full sound frequencies. Partly it is because of the nature of some real entities or mechanisms, such as distant galaxies or atomic fission.

It will readily be agreed that some of our practices are ineluctable, given the way humans are made, the way the world is, and the necessity of their interaction. This is the case for the natural order, the practical order and the social order, given that we have to navigate our environments, acquire certain practical competencies and also social skills, if we are to survive, flourish and develop the potentials of our species-being. Not all the practices that foster our flourishing are even remotely connected to our survival. Today, survival is perfectly possible without ever having the experience of swimming or horse riding, without being able to drive a car or work a computer, and without belonging to a family or any association. However, the more people are pegged down to survival practices, the more we would judge them to be leading impoverished lives, not because they lack what is physiologically needful, but because they are lacking in that which is humanly enriching.

Now, throughout history, most people have engaged or engage in religious practices. As with every other kind of practitioner, they claim that their experiences are belief-forming; in this case that religious experience justifies, at least in part, their belief in God. Without doubt *all* our belief-forming practices *can* be wrong, because all human knowledge is fallible. Thus some people conclude from their encounters with nature that mice are dangerous, others decide from their own attempts that sewing on a button is beyond them, and most people, most of the time, have believed in erroneous scientific theories. Yet what distinguishes religious beliefs is that they are often deemed to be necessarily false *because* the experiences upon which they are based are automatically discounted. I want to show that making such a distinction is not on for the realist, though it is open to some other philosophies of science: ones which realists have submitted to heavy and sustained critique, especially positivism. The aim is to argue that religious experience is as justi-fiable in theistic belief-formation as are other experiences in their respective domains, before maintaining that it is at least as important as are naturalistic experiences in forming us in our unique personal identities.

The primacy of practice and religious practice

The primacy assigned to practice in making us both distinctively and recognisably human, as well as in the emergence of our concrete singularities, is what is particular to the realist conception of the human subject. If this is the case, we cannot pre-judge which practices contribute to our constitution, although we may eventually succeed in demonstrating that some are more important than others. If this is the case, dismissal of religious practice, as opposed to submitting it to the same rational scrutiny as any other practice that arguably plays a role in making us what we are, represents a performative contradiction. It is so when the justifiability of belief in the transcendental is forced to stand before the bar of sense data, there to be judged inadequate merely because the object to which it points is an unobservable. It is all the more so if certain realists unwarrantedly take features, which are not regarded in realism as being in the least normative for scientific practice, as somehow retaining their vigour for religious practice. The act of dismissal seems to reflect an enduring empiricist stance towards religious practice, which simply involves a category mistake about what kind of practice it is. The awareness of God is not like sense perception, and until we absent this lingering empiricist parallel, it is impossible to show that religious practice is a great deal more like other practices that are regularly admitted to be constitutive of our being-in-the-world.

The performative contradiction, which is committed when realists turn empiricist in relation to religious experience, seems to be rooted in confining realism to academic topics, rather than accepting its thoroughgoing applicability to everyday activities. In short, for many, realism does not 'go all the way down'. Because sense perception does remain of central importance in our quotidian living, it is allowed to exercise an epistemic imperialism that contradicts realist ontology. Inconsistent realists then take their own lack of personal religious awareness as a reason for dismissing its possibility, which becomes decisive when they cannot be so positioned as to experience it. This is domestic Humeanism. It is to adopt, with those like O'Hear, the seemingly 'not unreasonable presumption that if something is objectively real, it will have similar effects on other observers similarly placed'.[11] Yet this is not reasonable at all; it is closed system thinking, which disallows that generative powers can be suspended or occluded, and that one of the prime contingencies responsible is the intervention of the properties and powers of observers themselves. Thus, perfect pitch exists in music, but we do not all have the capacity to hear it, or to know when we do not.

In experience, there are no constant conjunctures between emission and reception, so universal reception cannot define the ontological status of transmission. Yet this is how Gaskin defines experience of any externally existing object, amongst which God would number, namely as an 'experience such that any other person rightly and properly situated with normally functioning *senses*, powers of attention, and a suitable conceptual understanding, will have the same experience'.[12] Since his argument is cast in terms of sense data, he has no difficulty in concluding that religious awareness is not of an externally existing object! Everyday Humeans draw the same conclusion about the source of religious awareness, which is why they are so open to the masters of suspicion (see Collier in Chapter 6). These either internalise religious experience as wish-fulfilment or self-compensation (which is where Nietzsche and Freud display the anthropocentrism of

Modernity's Man), or externalise it as a social product (which is where Marx and Durkheim adhere to the sociocentricism of Society's Being).

Yet why should we accept the imperialism of sense data in religion when we do not in science? In the latter case, we readily accept unobservable entities whose causal effects are not manifested as regularities at the level of events, open to being experienced. Sense data may be crucially important in everyday life, but nevertheless everyday practice does not conform to Gaskin's proposition either. For instance, a wine tasting does not mean that enthusiastic amateurs will 'have the same experience' as a sommelier; but we do not turn our suspiciousness upon him, but rather turn towards educating our palates. So why do we not do the same with religious practice, and betake ourselves to refining our spiritual sensibility? Perhaps this is because we accept that there is a proper set of tests at a *dégustation*, such that if a wine taster detects too much tannin, there are chemical tests for its measurement. However, the *Meilleurs Sommeliers du Monde* did not become such by following analytical chemists around and assimilating their findings into embodied knowledge. Nor is their role confined to such, for they will also evaluate 'balance', 'bouquet', 'heaviness' and 'length', which are *qualitative* assessments. When the lads at the Lagavulin distillery pronounce that the best time to drink this single malt is when it is sixteen years old, they are not making a judgement which can be checked by the analytical chemist; the only test is their agreement which is based upon experience itself.

This is the case for every kind of experience, including sense perception itself, namely that a practice can only be evaluated on the basis of what that practice has taught. Thus we have to rely upon perceptual beliefs to check other perceptual beliefs, on deductive reasoning to test deductive reasoning, and upon memory to evaluate memory claims, and so forth. Any testing involves the same circularity. As Alston puts it, choosing tests is an 'insider job', meaning that 'the practice supplies both the tester and the testee: it grades its own examinations.'[13] Religious practice is in exactly the same position, for it has its own Orders of Contemplatives. To doubt these proficients whilst trusting the lads at Lagavulin or the Association of Analytical Chemists is to employ a double standard. More is demanded of religious practice than other practices can deliver. It has to pass its own insider tests plus those appropriate to sense data reports. The absence of checks from other observers, which are present for sense perception, is held to be an important defect of religious practice and one that prevents religious beliefs, founded upon it, from being epistemologically defensible.

Again this is empiricist imperialism. In general, we do not suppose that beliefs stemming from one practice must be subjected to the same checks as beliefs from a different practice, before the first belief can be accepted as rational. If we did, empiricism would not survive cross-practice testing. Instead, we do in fact conclude that the impossibility of deploying mathematical checks upon perceptual reports is without epistemic significance. Neither, for example, can any item of hermeneutic understanding withstand empiricist cross-checking; its respectability rests upon the intersubjective validation alone of non-observable meanings. This is what is appropriate to religious practice too. Experiential reports are not auto-veridical, but are scutinized against an accumulated tradition of practice by proficients who will be no less inclined to deem a religious report hysterical than would a doctor in a different context. Given that the reliability of all tests is imperfect, this workable degree of intersubjective consensus amongst religious practitioners puts them in a different and possibly superior position compared with those areas of experience from which any intersubjective agreement is ruled out. Yet we still form beliefs about our own conscious states, on the basis of self-awareness, where the checks are internal to the subject and consist largely of her past experience. Indeed, we would be immobilised as reflexive and intentional beings if we did not do so. My being excited or surprised does not depend upon your being so under the same conditions, but neither does this state of affairs question the validity of my feeling this way, or the utility of my recognising it.

What this points to is the existence of plural epistemologies that arise from the irreducible plurality of belief-forming practices. This is why it was maintained that the adoption of an empiricist stance towards religious practice was a category mistake. It accords an unwarranted hegemony to sense data, against which epistemic claims as disparate as those of mathematics, logic, hermeneutics and self-knowledge could not prevail. These are all sovereign spheres of cognition, which necessarily employ different criteria of justification, drawn from their own domains, in a circular process that is the same for sense data too. Nevertheless, it remains interesting to ask to which type of practices religious practice belongs. This is not because a type has to have more than one member, for 'introspection' seems to stand on its own, but rather because of the surprising family resemblances which emerge between religious practice and other practices that do not seem to be found to be problematic.

It belongs to the practical domain, where proficiency requires practice, where acquiring performative competence is a matter of apprenticeship in a tacit skill. What is acquired there is practical virtuosity, where the 'feel for' the task is virtually incommunicable and thus can only be examined in practice itself. The idea of having a 'feel for music' appears to work in a way quite similar to the notion of exercising religious sensibility. Both involve being embedded in a tradition, which makes their beliefs about what note or chord to play next, or how to proceed, something which is rooted in a sense of the appropriateness of responding in just that manner. In neither domain is practice a matter of mimicry, nor is improvisation a case where 'anything goes'. Second, the idea of a 'feel for music' gives 'some content to the notion of immanence in the world by which the world can impose a sense of the things to be done or said, played or sung'.[14] These are both creative responses because our 'feel for' means that we live in that medium, take our prompts from it and can 'play along' with others who do the same. Indeed, this book could not have been written without assuming that we were all 'in tune' with the same transcendental harmony, which presumption both enabled the project to be conceived and supplied its own confirmation in practice.

Not everyone could have joined us, any more than everybody can join a jazz quartet; in both cases it takes an apprenticeship to develop a 'feel for'. It may still be objected that music is a 'respectable practice', because it is ultimately about sense data, as is demonstrated by the phrase 'developing an ear' and the fact that even without one we can all hear something. However, a majority of people do report instances of spiritual awareness in various surveys. Perhaps others have 'turned their heads away', which is not how 'to develop an ear'. Perhaps some have been so busy attending to other things that these occluded what could have been followed up. And perhaps part of it was our fault, because as closet practitioners, we gave no recommendation or encouragement. As was maintained at the start, all human properties and powers, which include the ability to acquire any form of practical knowledge, only exist *in potentia*. If and when religious awareness does develop, then the (above) argument, that it shares many features with other practices, also raises the question as to whether it plays a special and distinctive role in the personal identities of its practitioners. Alternatively, does it simply represent one practice amongst others?

Personal identity and religious concerns

Practice continues to enjoy primacy where the formation of our unique identities as particular persons is concerned. I have argued at length elsewhere[15] that because of the way in which we are constituted, the way the world is, and the necessary interaction between the two, we cannot be other than *concerned* about reality — and the different orders of reality in which we are ineluctably involved. I will first sketch this as a purely secular argument about our ineluctable embedding in the natural, practical and social orders of reality, and then ask what difference relations with transcendental reality make.

All human beings have to confront the natural world, and their embodiment necessarily confers concerns upon them about their physical well-being as they encounter their environments. This concern is embodied in our constitution and, although the imports of nature can be downplayed evalutively, they cannot avoid being viscerally registered or be ignored completely. Second, all people are constrained to live and work in the practical world; necessary labour is the lot of *homo faber*. Performative concerns are unavoidably part of our inevitable engagement with the world. The precise objects of our performative concerns are historically and culturally varied, but the import of our competence in dealing with the practical realm is universal. Third, sociality is also and necessarily the lot of human beings, who would be less than what we understand as human without their social engagements. Participation in the social realm entails concerns about self-worth. We cannot evade becoming a subject among subjects, and with this come 'subject referring properties',[16] such as admirable and shameful. The latter convey the import of society's normative system to our concern about our social standing. These may be very different concerns, since we can choose to stand in very different places, but these are all equally social and thus the impact of some social norms upon our comportment cannot be obviated.

This produces a dilemma for every human being, since most of the time most of us have to live in the three orders of reality simultaneously. Therefore, a task which falls to all is to determine how to deal with imports coming in from the three orders, which take the form of emotional commentaries on our concerns and yet inform us about very different kinds of human concerns: in physical well-being, performative achievement and self-worth. These concerns are real; not to heed the relevant commentaries may be deleterious to us, and yet nothing guarantees their compatibility. On the contrary, to heed, for example, our physical fear could well lead to performative incompetence or to social acts of which we are ashamed. This dilemma can only be overcome if each human being arrives at some *modus vivendi* between their ineluctable concerns.

To do so entails disengaging 'ultimate concerns' from subordinate ones. Such an ultimate affirmation can only be made after evaluating the consequences for self, by taking account of the positive and negative costs to be borne and establishing how much we care. Basically, through an inner dialogue we 'test' our ongoing or potential commitments against our emotional commentaries, which tell us how far we are up to living out the committed life that would be reflective of these ultimate concerns. What we ultimately affirm as being of ultimate concern is both that which we value most highly, and also that which we feel we can live out as a commitment. We are, of course, fallible on both counts; we may make incorrect evaluations about the worthiness of what we have deemed our ultimate concerns to be and we may also be mistaken in judgements about our ability to see these commitments through. In either case, these concerns are revisable.

Our personal identities derive from our ultimate concerns, from what we care about most, together with our other concerns, which cannot be discarded but are accommodated to our prime commitment. As Frankfurt put the matter, our ultimate concerns are definitive of us, in that what our commitments 'keep us from violating are not our duties or our obligations but ourselves',[17] what I am calling our personal identities.

Now, what difference is made if our relations with transcendental reality are introduced? Obviously, those who hold that they have justifiable beliefs in the existence of God also consider that they have good reasons for holding relations between humanity and divinity to be as ineluctable as those pertaining between humankind and the other orders of reality. But what of those who disavow the transcendent and therefore any transcendental concern? I maintain that this denial has the same deleterious consequence for human well-being as ignoring those of our concerns that are vested in natural, practical and social reality. How can this possibly be asserted, since non-believers appear to make out just as well in the world, including often making their way through it with at least as much goodness and generosity as do believers? My proposition is entailed by the belief that God is love, the quintessence of unconditional love. That is what he offers us by his nature. To defend my case, I thus have to adduce some ineluctable human concern that hinges upon our relations with transcendental reality, that is, one which it is universally deleterious for us to ignore and one which is intimately related to our flourishing.

There seems to be every reason to advance love itself as this concern. As an emotional commentary, love also signals the most profound human concern, in that our fulfilment depends upon our need to love and to be loved. Since antiquity it has been debated what makes this particular emotion different from others. The answer seems to lie not in its intentionality, nor in its cognitive and evaluative characteristics, but quite simply in its indispensability. As Robert Brown puts it,

> What makes love unusual among the emotions is the human inability to do without it – whether its bestowal or receipt – and the immense amount of satisfaction that love commonly brings to the people concerned . . . Only love is both completely indispensable to the functioning of human society and a source of the fullest satisfaction known to human beings.[18]

It follows that the unbeliever does not do without love, as she cannot if it is truly indispensable, and may find it in love of nature, of art or of another person – where only in the last case can it be received as well as given. It remains to try to show that someone who settles for anything less than divine love then damages their potential for fulfilment,[19] in a manner roughly analogous to how the ascetic can endanger his physical well-being through an impoverished diet. It goes without saying that the commitment of the hunger striker has this effect.

To care about anything, enough to make it a matter of ultimate concern, entails two elements. First, there is a cognitive judgement about its inherent worth, which is always fallible. Second, there is a deep emotional attachment to it, and must be since it would be strange to say that a person was devoted to X if they felt quite indifferent towards it.[20] The affective element is not fallible; we cannot be mistaken that we love, but nevertheless we can love unwisely by pinning our affections on someone or something of whose worth we cannot give good reason.

Now, if the religious believer's belief is justifiable, he or she cannot be wrong in his or her cognitive judgement that God is, by his nature, inherently worthy of the highest loving concern. This is how they have experienced him to be, and it is these experiences which constitute the justification for their religious belief.[21] Indeed, unbelievers would probably concur that were there a God whose nature is that of pure unconditional love and whose intentions towards humankind were that we should participate in it to the fullest, the judgement about his supreme goodness would not be in doubt. What they doubt is not his putative worth, but his existence. However, were they to become convinced through experience that he does exist, they themselves would admit that previously they had invested their loving in something inherently less worthy which failed fully to satisfy.

We need to go one step further than this to show that complete human fulfilment depends upon perfect love and that only lesser degrees of it derive from imperfect loves. This is possible because, in the long-running Aristotelian debate about whether we love someone or the qualities that they personify, it seems that on either side we settle for the imperfectly worthy. If we love a (human) person 'for themselves', as is often said, the qualities that they do instantiate may well leave out some of those which we value highly, and it is extremely improbable that this would not be the case. Conversely, if we love someone because they (very nearly) embody all the qualities which we value most highly, we will also have to put up with unrelated characteristics to which we are not wholly indifferent: as with the intelligent, handsome and virtuous man who also dominates every conversation. Only a being whose person and nature are identical, and that consists in love itself, is inherently and unreservedly worthy of our highest and unmitigated loving concern. Only God fulfils these desiderata. To be love itself is to love unconditionally, as there is nothing else upon which such a nature can set store without contradicting that very nature. It is also to love unchangeably, since to love less or more would be a contradiction in terms. Of course, consequentiality, conditionality and changeability are the rocks upon which human loving most frequently breaks up. Human love does indeed tend to alter when it alteration finds.

However, to return to the believer, what difference does the love of God make to his personal identity? In his acknowledgement of transcendental relations, he finds an ultimate concern that is cognitively of supreme worth, if he is justified in his beliefs. If so, one new item of information that he will have gained from his religious experience, as opposed to the teaching tradition which contextualises it, is that he is personally loved. Now, it was argued earlier that deeming anything to be one's ultimate concern entailed both cognition and affect. Hence, what is now being asked is *how much we care* about that to which we have cognitively assented, for it is how we respond by loving back (with all our heart, soul, strength and mind . . .) which determines its effect upon our identities.

We humans respond by loving God back with a feeble lack of proportionality. The reason is partly that our transcendental experiences are discontinuous and partly that those other concerns do not go away and we let them get in the way: 'Martha, you worry and fret about so many things and yet few are needed' (Luke 10.41). Mostly, we do not have that kind of trust; our other concerns are indeed ineluctable and generally we act as if only our care for them can ensure our well-being in the other orders of reality. Believers are as familiar with compromise and trade-off as is anyone else about their purely secular concerns. The rich young man from Mark's gospel has often suffered a rough retelling. It was not that he chose a love of Mammon over that of God, because Jesus loved him for the service he already gave, but rather that he would not do that one thing more which would have shown that God was his ultimate concern. Most of us are guilty of wrong ranking rather than rank wrongdoing.

Theosis and being-in-the-world

Nevertheless, those who have experienced anything of the unconditional love of God cannot fail to care about it at all if, as has been maintained, such love is indispensable to human fulfilment. The response may be unworthy, but that does not mean it is non-existent. *Theosis*, or progressive divinisation, is a process that remains incomplete for the vast majority of us believers during our lifetimes. However, given fidelity, it is in process and is increasingly formative of us ourselves. The main *inward* effect of endorsing *any* ultimate concern is that it transvalues our feelings. Such a commitment acts as a new sounding board against which old concerns reverberate: the emotional echo is transformed. Consider something as simple as once having enjoyed a pie and a pint. In the natural order, the newly committed vegetarian may now feel positive revulsion; in the practical order, Olympic competitors may see these as salivating temptation; in the social order, the new executive may consider them as beneath his status. In other words, any serious commitment acts as a prism on the world that refracts our first-order emotions, transmuting them into second-order feelings, for affectivity is always a commentary upon our concerns. In conclusion, what I want to argue is that a religious commitment is constitutive of three new transvalued emotions, which are distinctive of this concern and which differentiate its adherents from those dedicated to any form of secular concern. This affectual transformation is the substantive justification of how transcendental relations are at least as important in forming us, in our concrete singularity, as are our naturalistic experiences and secular commitments.

The first feeling which is discrete to those who have experienced God as unconditional love is sinfulness: of having fundamentally missed the mark, of representing a different order of 'fallen' being, or of our intrinsic unworthiness to raise our eyes. Sinfulness is qualitatively different from the emotions attending dedication to secular ultimate concerns; however high or deep these may be, when we fall short of them the corresponding feelings are self-reproach, remorse, regret or self-contempt. Even the lucky lover, who declares himself unworthy of his beloved, protests something different, namely that he has hit the mark undeservedly. Conversely, disconsolate swains merely feel disconsolate, not sinful. In their turn, these secular feelings are different again from the unemotional state of those without any commitment, whose only attitude is can they get away with whatever they seek to do, which is precisely where cost–benefit analysis rules. Sinfulness is regarded as an emotional commentary which is emergent from relations between humanity and divinity, and is expressive of the quintessential disparity felt between them.

It grows out of those human emotions, such as remorsefulness and unworthiness, but only through their transmutation. This entails a penitential revaluation of our lives, which develops only as the transcendental commitment, and thus the contrast, deepens. Graham Greene's whisky priest in *The Power and the Glory* progressively embraces his loss of social self-worth and endorses service of God as his ultimate concern, which leads to his martyrdom. At the start of this transvaluation, he treasures his old photograph, showing the well-fed and well-respected priest with his immaculate flock, at a time when his vocation had seemed to involve little sacrificial subordination of physical and social well-being. As his ultimate concern becomes ultimately demanding, his emotions towards the photo are transformed, and its eventual loss is simply to be separated from a reproachful irrelevance. The more his divinisation proceeds, the deeper his sense of his sinful nothingness. In Newman's words,

> the truest penitence no more comes at first, than perfect conformity to any other part of God's law. It is gained by long practice – it will come at length. The dying Christian will fulfil the part of the returning prodigal more exactly than he ever did in his former years.[22]

The sense of being a sinner intensifies, whereas the protests of unworthy but lucky lovers fade away as they make good their vows to 'prove themselves'. Growing proofs of divine love may indeed rectify a life, but they simultaneously deepen the feeling of disparity: that whatever we do, we have all fallen short of the glory of God. There seems to be no human equivalent to the affect associated with sinfulness: that the closer we become to our ultimate concern, the further apart and more different in kind we feel ourselves to be.

Second, let us consider the growth of detachment. There are always costs to commitment, simply because promoting one concern is to demote others, yet the concerns in question are ineluctable. Generically, our three secular concerns were not acquired at will; they emerged from the necessary interplay between the way we are constituted and the way the world is. Consequently, it takes a considerable act of will to prioritise an ultimate concern because this means the subordination (not the repudiation) of other concerns, by producing an alignment between them with which the subject believes he or she can live. Struggle is therefore generic to human commitment to *any* ultimate concern, because subordinate concerns do have naturalistic legitimacy. They are about different aspects of our well-being and the emotional commentaries emanating from them signal the costs entailed to the person by the priorities that they have reflexively determined.

However, although such struggle is endemic to the crystallisation and confirmation of what we care about most, and thus to our personal identities themselves, the battlefield is very different for the believer and the unbeliever. Secular struggles are basically about sustaining dedication to an ultimate concern *within* the three naturalistic concerns, and involve not letting these three slip out of the alignment that has been determined between them. Poignant regrets and powerful temptations often recur after an ultimate commitment has been made; costs are recurrent and the bill is frequently re-presented. In a purely mundane sense, religious commitment is even more expensive. This is because the struggle of those who have put their trans-cendental commitment first is that they thereby seek to subordinate *all three* of their naturalistic concerns: physical well-being, performative achievement and social self-worth. Those who try to respond more and more freely to God's unconditional love feel drawn to live in conformity with this supreme good, which explicitly means not being conformed to the world.

Their struggle has always been well understood in the Christian tradition and has been represented as the battle between the two kingdoms, of earth and heaven or, by extension of the military metaphor, as the battle lines between the 'two standards' in St Ignatius's *Spiritual Exercises*. In our own terms, it is the antinomy between transfiguring *theosis* and both the anthro-pocentricism of 'Modernity's Man' and the sociocentricism of 'Society's Being'. This struggle is constitutive of a new transvalued emotion, detach-ment. By definition, such detachment is without secular counterpart, precisely because it constitutes a new view of naturalistic reality and a different way of being-in-the-world with its three concerns. Since it is a transvaluation, its secular precursors are emotions such as resignation towards what has been subordinated, as with the careerist, resigned to the loss of his sporting life, or the mother who reconciles herself to putting her career on hold. However, these secular responses of resignation to the consequences of having made an ultimate commitment are negative emotions, tinged with nostalgia, at best, and bitter regret, at worst. It is the absence of such negativity that distinguishes the growth of religious detachment.

Detachment does not mean that the battle is over, for it never is. Compromise, concession and betrayal are life-long possibilities and assail-ants. Yet, in the lulls, detachment is a new and positive commentary upon being in the world, but not of it. Detachment is a real inner rejoicing in the freedom of unwanting; it is a carefree trusting that all manner of things will be well; it is the ultimate celebration of being over having or not-having. It is the feeling that we are *sub specie aeternitatis* and have been unbound from the wheel; freed from those constraining determinations of body, labour and self-worth, and have glimpsed autonomy in the form of sharing in divine autarky. Under the prompting of this emotional commentary, our orientation towards the world is transformed; since our identity is not primarily vested in it, we are enabled to serve it. In disinterested involvement, true detached concern is possible: for the planet, for the good use of material culture, and for the intrinsic value of every human being and encounter. Thus, comportment towards the three naturalistic orders is itself transfigured. If seeking to be conformed to unconditional love is the ultimate concern, it will be more formative of our way of being-in-the-world than can any other naturalistic commitment.

This is where the argument comes full circle. There are certain ways of being-in-the-world that remain incomprehensible without the admission of transcendence. It has been maintained that there are no good reasons for keeping religious practice out of human being, and that the primacy attached to practice in realism's 'model of man' makes it the only one which can let it in. The relations formed in transcendental 'space' react back upon the world, to which they are not conformed, by sanctifying it. From these relations ripple out concentric circles of unconditional love. Such love is the antithesis of private property; it entails a totalising impulse which reaches out to embrace, and thus to liberate, the world in an upwards redemptive spiral. Thus the *theosis* of our concrete singularity collaborates, combines and coalesces with the universalism of the divine economy. Full human coalescence with the transcendental entails the transformation of the third emotion, mentioned earlier, where gratitude is transmuted into worship as *theosis* and *kenosis* conjoin. This way of being-in-the-world, for the few who ascend to living in love, who give wholehearted priority to God as their ultimate concern, and who are correspondingly generous in the subordination of their secular concerns, is tentatively explored in Chapter 10. Unification with God does come only to the few, but the rest of us need not remain strangers to his purification and illumination.

Notes

1 William Alston, *Perceiving God: The Epistemology of Religious Experience*, Cornell University Press, Ithaca, NY and London, 1991, p. 240 (my italics).
2 'Rational Man' was the term current in Enlightenment thinking. Because it is awkward to impose inclusive language retrospectively and distracting to insert inverted commas, I reluctantly abide with the term 'man', as standing for humanity, when referring to this tradition, its heirs, successors and adversaries.
3 See Kate Soper, *Humanism and Anti-Humanism*, Hutchinson, London, 1986, especially p. 24f.
4 Gary Becker, *The Economic Approach to Human Behavior*, Chicago University Press, Chicago, 1976, p. 8.
5 Gary Becker, *Accounting for Tastes*, Harvard University Press, Cambridge, 1996, especially Chapter 11.
6 See R.S. Warner, 'Work in Progress Toward a New Paradigm for the Sociological Study of Religion', *American Journal of Sociology*, 1993, 98 (5).
7 J-F. Lyotard, *The Postmodern Condition*, University of Minnesota Press, Minneapolis, 1984, p. 15.

8 Richard Rorty, *Contingency, Irony and Solidarity*, Cambridge University Press, Cambridge, 1989, p. 185.

9 Michel Foucault, *The Order of Things*, Random House, New York, 1970, p. 387.

10 The best example of this model is provided by the work of Rom Harré. The leitmotif of his social constructionism is the following statement: 'A person is not a natural object, but a cultural artefact.' *Personal Being*, Basil Blackwell, Oxford, 1983, p. 20.

11 Anthony O'Hear, *Experience, Explanation and Faith*, Routledge & Kegan Paul, London, 1984, p. 45.

12 J.C.A. Gaskin, *The Quest for Eternity*, Penguin, New York, 1984, p. 80 (my italics).

13 Alston, *Perceiving God*, p. 217.

14 Michael Luntley, *Reason, Truth and Self*, Routledge, London, 1995, p. 213. This is Luntley's metaphor for moral judgement; I suspect he will not approve of the uses to which I am putting it.

15 See Margaret S. Archer, *Being Human: The Problem of Agency*, Cambridge University Press, Cambridge, 2000, esp. chapters 6 and 7.

16 Charles Taylor, 'Self-Interpreting Animals', in his *Human Agency and Language*, Cambridge University Press, Cambridge, 1985.

17 Harry G. Frankfurt, *The Importance of What We Care About*, Cambridge University Press, Cambridge, 1988, p. 91.

18 Robert Brown, *Analysing Love*, Cambridge University Press, Cambridge, 1987, pp. 126–7.

19 This is basically St Augustine's argument: 'Fecisti nos ad te et inquietum est cor nostrum donec requiescat in te.'

20 See Justin Oakley, *Morality and the Emotions*, Routledge, London, 1992, p. 65.

21 Note that this is an argument *from* religious experience. Those who come to believe in other ways, such as through tradition alone or from natural theology, will not have personal knowledge of God's nature, in the first case, and may not even ascribe a nature to him, in the second case, where he may simply be accepted as a (mechanistic) 'first cause'.

22 Cited in Owen Chadwick, *The Mind of the Oxford Movement*, A. & C. Black, London, 1960, p. 153.

6 The Masters of Suspicion and secularisation

Andrew Collier

Among the most effective arguments against religion in the past one hundred and fifty years have been those of the three great thinkers who have become known as the Masters of Suspicion: Marx, Nietzsche and Freud. All have given debunking explanations for the prevalence of religion in most human cultures; debunking in the sense that the explanations are in terms not of any evidence for the truth of the religions, but of their power to console people and reconcile them to their unhappy lot: the power of wishful thinking. Thus Marx has famously referred to religion as the opium of the people. This is not in context such an insulting phrase as it might seem: first because, as Graham Greene's Monsignor Quixote points out in the novel of that name, opium was a perfectly respectable drug in Marx's time, a tranquilliser for those who could afford it, so that Marx may be updated as saying that religion is valium for the poor. And second because Marx is not saying that religion is propagated by the rich to keep the poor contented, but that the oppressed themselves produce religion to give themselves the hope and self-respect that oppressive society does not give them.[1] Religion is, so to speak, the identity-politics of the oppressed, which must be given up if they are to be won for the politics of self-liberation. This is very similar to Nietzsche's account, though the class standpoint is opposed. For Nietzsche religion is part of a slave rebellion in morals – a substitute for the unsuccessful slave rebellion in reality. For Marx the aim is to lead the oppressed back from a rebellion in morals to a real rebellion which could overthrow the master class, while for Nietzsche it is to quarantine the slave rebellion in morals so that the master class are kept free from infection with it. But that religion exists because it is consoling to the oppressed is common ground of both.

It would be possible to make out an historical case against Marx and Nietzsche that, at least in certain times and places, religion has been an ideology of liberation rather than consolation for the oppressed, and that this definitely includes the religion of the pre-exilic Hebrew prophets, and arguably that of first-century Christianity. Taoism too has sometimes projected earthly liberation in a 'heavenly kingdom'. But my aim in this chapter is rather to urge that suspicion of this sort could equally be directed against secularism. First, though, there are some philosophical points to clear up.

It should be noticed first what arguments from suspicion do and do not prove. They prove at most that the ideas against which they are directed would have been widely believed whether or not they were true. They do not prove that they are not true. Ideas may be held for very bad reasons, yet may turn out to be true: 'just because you're paranoid, that doesn't mean they're not out to get you.' In this way, arguments for suspicion of religion are not like the explanatory critiques which the Masters of Suspicion also provide (for instance, Marx on the wage-form). Explanatory critiques show both that a belief is false and that it is produced by the social structure.[2] The critiques of religion show at most that it is produced by the social structure, whether true or false. Some people have thought that this fact draws the teeth of arguments from suspicion altogether: if they do not establish whether the ideas of which they treat are true or false, it is said, let us forget about them and attend to the arguments which do give evidence for the truth or false-hood of those ideas. But the Masters of Suspicion are not so easily disposed of. For among the arguments for and against the truth of any idea, testimony (hearsay) will be one of the most important. My knowledge that Australia exists is pure hearsay. It would be paranoid to think that all the testimony of teachers and atlases and television programmes and wine bottle labels about Australia was deception. But if there were really cogent reasons for believing that all the people who produce such things had an interest in deceiving me or were likely themselves to be deceived, the case would be altered. A better, because realistic, example would be scientific testimony. Other things being equal, the rational thing for a lay person to believe about the findings of a science, is what the scientists say. But if their testimony is that a commodity is safe to use, and they are all employees of the company that sells that commodity, the testimony loses all credibility. If it were not for the work of the Masters of Suspicion, the sheer fact that the vast majority of human beings have believed some religion to be true would be over-whelming evidence that religion was on to something real. Whatever the Masters of Suspicion have not done, they have neutralised that evidence.

It is noteworthy that while each of the three Masters of Suspicion debunks (whether successfully or not) many other things apart from religion, all debunk religion. All are secularists, though their secularism is not the same, and it may be necessary to talk about secularisms in the plural, just as we talk about religions in the plural. They debunk religion at greatly different lengths: in Marx it is a matter of a few striking phrases, like the one about opium and the theses on Feuerbach; in Nietzsche the critique of religion pervades his whole work, though perhaps it is clearest in *The Genealogy of Morals* and *The Twilight of the Idols*; in Freud it is the subject of one whole short book, *The Future of an Illusion*. But all more or less take for granted that religion is false, the only question being why a false belief became so widespread. And none considers that secularism could be made the subject of a similar critique. In this they share an assumption common to the modern era,[3] an assumption which prevailed long before secularism became the dominant ideology; the assumption that secular knowledge is obvious, while the onus is on religion to prove its contentions. Is this assumption legitimate?

On the face of it, it would seem (and in the end I think it is so) that if a person has no religious experience it would be rational for them to withhold belief until cogent arguments are presented, while if a person does have religious experience, it would be rational for them to believe unless cogent arguments are presented against religion. The onus of proof is different in the two cases. But are the two cases symmetrical? The secularist may claim that one needs reasons for believing something but that one does not need reasons for not believing something. In reply it could be said that the secularist has, not the absence of belief in religious phenomena, but belief in their absence. The secularist is typically committed to the belief that the religious experiences of those who have them are illusory, that nature is a closed system, and so on. One needs grounds for these beliefs as much as for religious beliefs. Secularity is not a neutral position, and the idea that religion is an extra belief beyond 'ordinary' beliefs is not a neutral description of the case but a partisan, secularist description. The religious description would be rather that humankind is a worshipping animal, and if we do not worship the true God we will worship false gods; the secularist is then seen not as a non-worshipper but as an idolater. Is this a legitimate way of looking at it?

In the first place, this position should be distinguished from the rather facile position which has often rightly annoyed atheists, of saying 'You don't believe in God? Well then, atheism is your religion.'[4] This would be justified only if the atheist worshipped the absence of God. I think that such an atheism is possible, and perhaps Bakunin, Nietzsche and Camus are touched with it. But it is not the usual form of atheism. Most atheists, if they worship anything, worship something which really exists but is not worthy of worship. It might help here to use a phrase of Paul Tillich's[5] and say that the essence of worship is placing ultimate concern in something. The atheist may place ultimate concern in money or their nation-state or their family or human emancipation, just as the Christian or Muslim places ultimate concern in God or the Taoist in the Tao. This also makes it clear why we have to distinguish different secularisms as well as different religions.

It is clear that contemporary European culture is overwhelmingly secular, that is, secularisms have many more adherents than religions. This is less clear of the USA where a large majority claim to believe in God. However, Doug Porpora has shown in his book *Landscapes of the Soul* that there has been what might be called secularisation of the emotions in the USA, leaving assent to the proposition that God exists intact, but without it moving the believers to the feelings and actions that would follow rationally from such belief. An index of this is the idolatrous ceremony of the pledge to the flag which goes on in (secular) American schools. A genuinely religious community would refuse this idolatry, as early Christians refused to burn a taper to the Emperor, and were thrown to the lions for it. Thus it may be said that the economically and politically dominating cultures today are secular, though the Third World is still overwhelmingly religious.

The emergence of this secular culture is unparalleled in human history. If religions and secularisms are simply different placings of ultimate concern, we can ask what is the religious meaning of this unique historical event of secularisation: where has ultimate concern come to be placed? There can be little doubt as to the answer: the history of secularisation and secularity is the history of bourgeois revolutions and capitalism. Religion always poses a problem for capitalism because, by saying that some things are sacred, it insists that not everything is saleable. Of course, there have been corruptions of religion by commerce, whether by the Temple money-changers that Jesus cast out, or in the sale of indulgences in pre-Reformation Europe, or in the gospel-businesses of the modern USA. But authentic religion has always made a whip of short cords to cleanse the Temple of such corruption. In order for capitalism to have a clear path, it needs to profane all that is sacred; there must be no limits to what is saleable. The totalitarian commercialism which is now the established Church throughout the West has come close to achieving this. A party whose constitution still proclaims it socialist (the British Labour Party) can sell time with cabinet ministers to businessmen – a transaction which in any honest society would lead to the dismissal and disgrace of the ministers and the imprisonment of the salespeople; television can arrange blind dates between couples, to be monitored for the amusement of viewers, making commercial pornography look innocent by comparison; and in poorer capitalist countries that ultimate atrocity occurs – the murder of street children to sell their organs on the transplant market.

I have said that for capitalism nothing is sacred, but strictly speaking, like any iconoclasm, it desecrates what it regards as false sanctities for the sake of its god: money. The religious name for capitalism is mammon-worship. The identification of mammon-worship as a religion goes back to Jesus's saying that you cannot serve God and mammon, and to Paul's characterisation of covetousness as idolatry. And like all secularisms, mammon-worship shares surprisingly many of the characteristics of a religion. To name just one: it believes in the 'hidden hand' of the market, making all things work together for good to them that love money.

The grounds for suspicion of secularism are now apparent: it (or the most influential version of it) is *the* ideology of capitalism. There are very good reasons for capitalists to be secularists, and to want their customers to be secularists. But these are not good reasons for believing secularism to be true. Moreover, capitalism is an exploitive system, as Marx has argued so cogently, and as anyone who studies the inequalities within and between the countries of the world today must see. It is therefore *a priori* likely that its ideology conceals realities that if known would make the exploited militant.

However, I foresee two objections to my claim that secularism (or *a* secularism) is the ideology for capitalism. It will be pointed out that early capitalism was associated not with secularism but with Protestantism. And it will be asked how come the communist and (in many countries) socialist movements have also been secularist, often militantly so.

First as to Protestantism: the intrinsic aspect of Protestantism included the idea of salvation by trust in Christ, without need for ritual observances or a legalistic or ascetic morality, the priesthood of all believers, and the protest against the division of this world into sacred and secular parts. These are clearly religious ideas, not secularist ones. But what Protestantism did in the world, its extrinsic aspect, is a different matter. Particularly those forms of Protestantism that were iconoclastic (literally as well as metaphorically) broke down the distinction between sacred and secular by secularising the sacred. For Protestantism in its intrinsic aspect, nothing is particularly holy because everything is holy as the gift of God. Luther taught the ubiquity of the body of Christ. George Fox, the Quaker, objected to the greeting 'good day' because all days were equally sent by God. So sacred particulars – holy places, days, people – are to a greater or lesser extent dispensed with. From outside, this looks like secularisation. The twenty-fifth of December was an ordinary working day in England during the Commonwealth, and soldiers even entered people's houses to check that they weren't cooking Christmas dinner. It was this sort of own-goal that turned people against Puritanism. And this extrinsic aspect of Protestantism was precisely what attracted unscrupulous rulers to it. Henry VIII could plunder the monasteries to replenish the royal coffers after his extravagance had depleted the reserves his father had built up. There was nothing liberating about this for the people: it meant the destruction of the community's main resource for education, health care and hospitality. But it was liberating for capitalists, as it put a whole lot of wealth on the free market which had previously been kept off it. The extrinsic history of Protestantism is the beginning of the history of secularisation. And it is this extrinsic aspect that lasted. By the end of the seventeenth century the intrinsic aspect had burnt itself out. Protestantism was a dead religion,[6] to be revived a couple of generations later by the Pietist and Evangelical movements. The Whig oligarchy was as secular as the Jacobin club (though indeed, one member of the Jacobin Committee of Public Safety was a Protestant minister, Jeanbon Saint André). It is worth saying in passing that the intrinsic aspect of Protestantism survived just as long as the Protestant-led bourgeois revolutions were genuinely movements of liberation (albeit limited liberation which had its down-side as well). Once the bourgeoisie was a secure exploiting class, its consciousness became fully secular. In Marx's phrase, 'Locke replaced Habakkuk'. John Gay's wonderful satire *The Beggar's Opera* indicates to what extent the religion of Whig England was mammon-worship.

Now what about socialist secularism? I shall discuss this mainly with reference to Marx, as the greatest and in many ways a typical secular socialist.

(Though the mature Marx was not as militantly secularist as some socialists, including many of his own followers. He prevented Bakunin from making atheism a condition of membership of the First International, and when his wife and daughter attended secularist meetings he discouraged them, advising them to study the Hebrew prophets instead. Likewise Engels condemned Dühring for aiming to prohibit religion by law in a future society.) It can readily be granted that the secularism of Marx was not the secularism that I have just described as mammon-worship; there are many secularisms as there are many religions. Marx's ultimate concern is not money but human emancipation. But there are three points that need to be made. The first is that whatever may have been the case with Marx, the ultimate concern of many self-styled Marxists in the twentieth century has been not human emancipation but state power. The second point is that there is after all some continuity between bourgeois secularism and Marx's secularism. Marx was brought up in the Rhineland, which had been overrun by the French in the Revolutionary Wars, and governed under Napoleon by the old Jacobin, Jeanbon Saint André. Marx inherited the secularism of the French Enlightenment and the French Revolution, and was a bourgeois secularist before he became a communist. His (and Engels's) bitter tribute to the bourgeoisie in the *Communist Manifesto* shows a sneaking admiration for bourgeois iconoclasm, as well as contempt for bourgeois mammon-worship.[7] Yet these are two sides of the same coin. Moreover, Marx's practical interventions in politics, both in the revolutions of 1848 and in his support for the Eisenachers against the Lassalleans in the German working-class movement, show his total support of bourgeois politics as long as the bourgeois revolution was uncompleted. I am by no means sure that he was right about this. Uncompleted bourgeois revolutions may leave a more favourable ground for working-class politics than completed ones, and certainly allow the survival of non-commercial values which can be retrieved by those who would supplant capitalism. If bourgeois secularism is under suspicion as mammon-worship, I am not at all sure that some aspects of Marx's secularism should not come under suspicion too as influences that he should have cast off when he abandoned bourgeois politics. Perhaps Marx was a secularist because Voltaire was a secularist. But Voltaire was no critic of mammon. And certainly when modern socialists take up militant secularism, they are tilting at windmills which the capitalists would be only too happy to see demolished by the property developers. (For instance, the evacuation of Christian symbols from Christmas festivities by some Labour councils does not leave an ideologically neutral festival – an impossibility – but one dedicated exclusively to capitalist commerce.) After all, the consensus among the religious minority today is definitely to the left of the mainstream secular consensus, as is shown by the Churches' support for the Jubilee 2000 campaign for the remission of Third World debt.

The third point is that there may be aspects of Marx's secularism which are *genuinely liberatory*, but are not really alien to religion, or at least to one religious tradition. For paradoxical as it may sound, there is a project of secularisation within the Judaeo-Christian tradition.[8] It starts with the witness of the pre-exilic Hebrew prophets against Temple worship. In Isaiah and Hosea and later in Deutero-Isaiah there is a scepticism about the value of sacrifices, fasts and trampling the Lord's courts; and a corresponding claim that what God requires is justice and mercy, releasing the oppressed and relieving the poor.[9] This tendency culminates in the prophecy of the author of Revelation that in the heavenly Jerusalem there will be no temple. At its best, Protestant iconoclasm (I refer to inner iconoclasm, not Roundhead vandalism) is in this tradition. Its extreme terminus is in the Ranter sect in Commonwealth England, which rejected all sacred particulars, saw God in everything, and advocated communism as the true fulfilment of Holy Communion. The Ranters are often described as pantheists, but this is incorrect, since they had the idea of God working, and working in different ways at different times.[10] If the extrinsic development of Protestantism was towards bourgeois secularisation and mammon-worship, its intrinsic aspect was towards this liberatory 'secularism', which yet is not secularism in that it postpones secularity to the Kingdom of God. There is something real in common between Marx's view of religion as an alienation-effect, and this religious view which recognises that religion is the result of our alienation from God, but that it is necessary as long as that alienation lasts; religion which projects the supercession of religion along with the supercession of alienation in the Kingdom of God.

What do I hope to have achieved in this chapter? I have certainly not proved secularism false or religion true, any more than the Masters of Suspicion have proved religion false and secularism true. But just as they have removed the force of the consensus of humankind at most places and times as an argument for religion, I hope to have undermined the use of the consensus of modern European humankind as an argument for secularism. And that argument, whatever its intrinsic weakness, has been surprisingly effective. People dismiss religion because 'no one believes that now' or 'modern people cannot believe that'; they take Nietzsche's 'death of God' to be a historical event, datable at some time in the second half of the nineteenth century, which is really only as much as to say that belief in God has become unfashionable since that date. At only a slightly more subtle level, people attribute the 'death of God' to the development of science or some other kind of intellectual progress, though there is nothing in science to contradict any religion but the most extreme fundamentalism, and intellectual progress outside science is largely fictitious. If the secularisation of modern Europe can be explained by a cause (capitalism) which is in no way an argument for secularism, and is suspect on independent grounds, then these arguments have no force, and the prevalent tendency to dismiss religious experience *a priori* is nothing more than a prejudice.

Notes

1 The context of the opium saying is as follows:

> *Religious* suffering is at one and the same time the *expression* of real suffering and a protest against real suffering. Religion is the sigh of the oppressed creature, the heart of a heartless world and the soul of soulless conditions. It is the *opium* of the people.
>
> The abolition of religion as the *illusory* happiness of the people is the demand for their *real* happiness. To call on them to give up their illusions about their condition is to *call on them to give up a condition that requires illusions*.
>
> (Marx, 'A Contribution to the Critique of Hegel's Philosophy of Right', *Early Writings*, p. 244; emphasis in original)

2 See Roy Bhaskar's *Scientific Realism and Human Emancipation*, pp. 169ff. for an account of explanatory critiques; also my *Critical Realism*, ch. 6.

3 By 'modern' I mean roughly the last three and a half to four centuries. I do not use the term 'postmodern', not only because it is an oxymoron but because the present seems in many ways the culmination of the modern period and the intensification of its specific characteristics. If one wants to distinguish the present from the preceding 'modern' centuries, the best distinction to make would be as follows: in the modern period commercial values have been predominant, but not all-pervasive; today they are all-pervasive. The two periods could then be characterised as 'commercialism' and 'totalitarian commercialism'.

4 See Engels, 'Ludwig Feuerbach and the End of Classical German Philosophy', *Selected Works*, p. 612.

5 See Tillich's *Systematic Theology*, Volume 1. Compare Luther: 'A God is simply that whereon the human heart rests with trust, faith, hope and love. If the resting is right, then the God is right; if the resting is wrong, then the God, too, is illusory'. ('Commentary on the Book of Daniel', quoted by Haldane in *The Pathway to Reality*, Volume 2, p. 127)

6 This is a slight exaggeration, as the hymns of Isaac Watts prove. But compared with the passionate and all-pervasive Protestant religiousness of the early and mid-seventeenth century, it is true.

7

> The bourgeoisie, wherever it has got the upper hand, has put an end to all feudal, patriarchal, idyllic relations. It has pitilessly torn asunder the motley feudal ties that bound man to his 'natural superiors', and has left remaining no other nexus between man and man than naked self-interest, than callous 'cash payment'. It has drowned the most heavenly ecstasies of religious fervour, of chivalrous enthusiasm, of philistine sentimentalism, in the icy water of egotistical calculation. It has resolved personal worth into exchange value, and in place of the numberless indefeasible chartered freedoms, has set up that single, unconscionable freedom – Free Trade. In one word, for exploitation, veiled by religious and political illusions, it has substituted naked, shameless, direct, brutal exploitation . . . All that is solid melts into air, all that is holy is profaned, and man is at last compelled to face with sober senses, his real conditions of life, and his relations with his kind.
>
> (Marx and Engels, 'The Communist Manifesto', in *Selected Works*, pp. 37–8)

8 I do not know of any such continuous tradition in other religions, but there are
   some intimations of the attitudes that underlie it. For instance, the Druzes do
   not observe the five daily prayer times of orthodox Muslims because they say it
   would interrupt their continual prayer. There are also sceptical remarks about
   the value of rituals or religious objects in the Taoist and Buddhist traditions.

9 For example:

> What are your endless sacrifices to me?
> says Yahweh.
> I am sick of holocausts of rams
> and the fat of calves.
> The blood of bulls and goats revolts me.
> When you come to present yourselves before me,
> who asked you to trample over my courts?
> Bring me your worthless offerings no more,
> the smoke of them fills me with disgust . . .
> Cease to do evil.
> Learn to do good,
> search for justice,
> help the oppressed,
> be just to the orphan,
> plead for the widow.
> > Isaiah 1.11–13 and 17 (*Jerusalem Bible*)

> Hanging your head like a reed,
> lying down on sackcloth and ashes?
> Is that what you call fasting,
> a day acceptable to Yahweh?

> Is not this the sort of fast that pleases me
> – it is the Lord Yahweh who speaks –
> to break unjust fetters
> and undo the thongs of the yoke,

> to let the oppressed go free,
> and break every yoke,
> to share your bread with the hungry,
> and shelter the homeless poor.
> > Isaiah 58.5–7 (*Jerusalem Bible*)

10 See especially Abiezer Coppe's 'A Flying Fiery Roll' and Joseph Salmon's 'A
   Rout, A Rout, or some part of the Armies Quarters Beaten Up, By the Day of
   the Lord stealing upon them', both in Smith, *Ranter Writings*.

Bibliography

Bhaskar, Roy, *Scientific Realism and Human Emancipation*, Verso, London, 1986.

Collier, Andrew, *Critical Realism*, Verso, London, 1994.

Freud, Sigmund, *The Future of an Illusion*, Pelican Freud Library, Vol. 12,
   Civilization, Pelican Books, Harmondsworth, 1985.

Greene, Graham, *Monsignor Quixote*, Penguin, Harmondsworth, 1983.

Haldane, R.B., *The Pathway to Reality*, John Murray, London, 1903.

Jerusalem Bible, Darton, Longman & Todd, London, 1968.

Marx, Karl, *Early Writings*, Penguin, Harmondsworth, 1975.

Marx, Karl and Engels, Frederick, *Selected Works*, Lawrence & Wishart, London, 1968.

Nietzsche, Friedrich, *Genealogy of Morals*, Vintage, New York, 1969.

Nietzsche, Friedrich, *Twilight of the Idols*, Penguin, Harmondsworth, 1968.

Porpora, Douglas V., *Landscapes of the Soul*, Oxford University Press, Oxford, 2002.

Smith, Nigel, *Ranter Writings*, Junction, London, 1983.

Tillich, Paul, *Systematic Theology, Volume 1*, Nisbet, Welwyn, 1953.

7   Western mysticism and the limits of language

Margaret S. Archer

Realists have frequently recognised the benefits of metaphor in the development of knowledge. Empiricists have not. What is the reason for this? After all, it is a common observation that sense data can be difficult to convey without resorting to tropes. Nevertheless, Hobbes was typical in protesting against the absurdity of the 'use of Metaphors, Tropes and other Rhetoricall figures, in stead of words proper.'[1] His resistance derives from the fear that the metaphor would be taken seriously as pointing to mysterious entities and unobservable processes. Instead, plain facts should be dealt with in plain language. Conversely, in their readiness to acknowledge unobservable generative mechanisms as causal powers, realists like Bhaskar and Harré have drawn attention to the fruitfulness of metaphor in the history of science. For example, familiar metaphors, such as 'waves' and 'springs', enabled the conceptualisation of underlying processes in unfamiliar fields. It is this ability of the familiar to unlock the unfamiliar that recommends the metaphor to realists for (fallibly) fostering scientific development.

   Does this realist encomium extend to the metaphor in relation to all types of knowledge about reality? *Ad hominem* it seems that it should, because basic to realist ontology is the stratified view of reality, which draws upon the geological metaphor. Therefore, it could be expected that realists would at least give a sympathetic hearing to those who employ metaphor in the attempt to disclose more about any domain of reality. That should include the Western mystics, whose aim is to make truth claims through the use of metaphor. Such sympathy might be reinforced because of the antagonism consistently shown towards religious mysticism by the empiricist tradition, from Hume[2] to Ayer.[3]

   Empiricists readily dub the entire corpus of mystical writings as incomprehensible, because it is held to trade in obfuscation, paradox and illogicality. Western mysticism can suffer badly at such hands, for it is quite possible to extract isolated phrases and sentences that fuel the case for incomprehensibility. Here, for example, are three 'candidates', culled from St John of the Cross:

   . . . the soul has to proceed rather by unknowing than by knowing . . .[4]

. . . faith is dark night for the soul, and it is in this way that it gives it light . . .[5]

. . . upon this road, to enter upon the road is to leave the road . . .[6]

However, I had to search seventy pages of text to find these 'examples' and to extract them from a context of systematic exposition, in which their meanings were painstakingly established. Thus, I am not going to delay further with characterisations of the 'mystics' as writers who do not authentically struggle with language to convey something about the divine, but rather revel in linguistic impenetrability.

Instead, let us abandon the words 'mystic' and 'mysticism' altogether, because of these connotations, and use the practitioners' own preferred designation of themselves as 'contemplatives' and of their activities as 'contemplative prayer'. Now, as is well documented for John of the Cross and his close collaborator, Teresa of Avila, such proficients come under considerable pressure to explain their contemplative experiences to others. For both, such pressures came from two sources. Fellow monks and nuns, seeking guidance on this 'way of perfection', pressed each of them to write about it. Equally, antagonistic pressure came from within their own Carmelite Order: John was brutally imprisoned in Toledo, which occasioned some of his most sublime poetry, and Teresa wrote her *Life* and *Confessions* to propitiate suspicious confessors. Both pressures impelled them to try to bridge the gap between their religious experiences and a discursive form that could capture them. The two authors are unanimous upon the difficulties of finding such a language and upon the inadequacies of their writings. Nevertheless, both are seeking to communicate something about the nature of relations between humanity and divinity, as warranted by their own religious experiences. Importantly, the two writers consistently resort to metaphor in order to do so.

The first question is how far did they succeed in communicating their experiences and the beliefs that these grounded for them? It is a fair one to ask a secular readership to consider, because it places no more burdens on the unbeliever than does the anthropological enterprise of attempting to understand 'alien practices and beliefs'. To my knowledge, no anthropologist, whatever his or her personal beliefs, has returned from fieldwork and pronounced the verdict of 'incomprehensible'. At this stage, the point is whether or not we can understand what the contemplatives are saying about divinity through metaphor. Only if that is the case can their truth claims be examined. Therefore, two responses, which prejudge the answer, should be eschewed.

On the one hand, some deem this communicative endeavour to be doomed to failure in advance. Thus, William James lists 'ineffability' as one of the four features characterising mystical experience[7] and W.T. Stace[8] makes 'ineffability' the principal common denominator of his survey of Eastern and Western mystical practices. There are three considerations, which make this conclusion seem over-precipitous. First, the great contemplatives themselves had plenty to say about the practice. The difficulties they had in writing did not amount to impossibility, so their voluminous works appear to count against this point. Second, if contemplation does represent an essentially incommunicable encounter with God, then how is it that we can speak of a Western mystical tradition,[9] where the same themes, images and metaphors are found surfacing and resurfacing? Third, how is it possible that these works still speak to some of us today and that we rejoice in those like John and Teresa, their precursors and successors, whose metaphorical communications we understand – albeit to different degrees?

On the other hand, some consider the success of the metaphorical enterprise to be a foregone conclusion for the contemplatives. This is because the metaphors used cease to be about human/divine relations, which the contemplatives held them to be, but become self or socially referential. For example, David Tracy's treatment of 'Metaphor and Religion'[10] proposes that the real referents of metaphor make no transcendental claims, but are rather about various kinds of purely human experiences. Similarly, Frederick Ferré maintains that 'religious imagery is a kind of symbolism which may function, for those who adopt it, to overcome the threat of the arbitrary on its valuational side.'[11] In both of these authors, the result of collapsing the subject/object distinction is anthropocentrism. What is then at issue is not any attempt at the (partial) disclosure of God, but rather the functions that theistic images have in reinforcing human values. As Janet Soskice concludes, in this way the 'critical issue, that of reality depiction, is pre-scinded'.[12] The metaphor does not strive to bridge earth and heaven, because 'heaven' becomes a piece of human fictionalism, which is functional to a social group. This is incompatible with realism about God and with the contemplatives, whose metaphors should not be decoded as telling us something more about ourselves, or something which is of functional utility to us. Contemplative writing is uncompromisingly intentional; its aim is to tell us something about God. As such it may fail.

Conversely, those who think that the 'otherness' of God precludes real reference to him then endorse a closed system of pan-symbolism. In it, the evasion of divine reality becomes tantamount to a denial of that reality and collapses into idealism, because of the absence of any referential activity. Here,

> the symbol loses its representative function and substitutes itself for reality. Exterior reality becomes a symbol, and the symbol itself becomes the only reality. From an idealist point of view the symbol acquires an autonomous value; from the realist point of view it is bound to the reality it symbolises.[13]

The latter was the case for John and Teresa whose referential intent is indubitable.

In sum, metaphorical religious language can claim (fallibly) to be referring to God and his relations with us, provided that:

1   the subject/object distinction is upheld, i.e. no collapse into anthropocentrism;
2   metaphors are not extended into a seamless web of symbolism, i.e. no collapse into idealism;
3   the nature of divine 'otherness' does not preclude all knowledge of divinity.

The religious metaphor is informative under those conditions, though its claims remain as fallible as all knowledge. This does not pre-empt the question as to how far it does inform.

However, there is agreement between Realists that something more is required of the metaphor than its coinage *tout court*. It needs further explication if it is to be genuinely informative, because in *some* respect anything can be likened to anything else. Thus, in science it would be uninformative to talk about the 'sea of light', without singling out the 'wave' as that which captures something about the properties and powers of light. Yet disagreement surfaces between Realists, working in the religious domain, over what form of further exposition is required. This is the issue of 'irreducible metaphors', and accord only goes so far as agreement that if a metaphor is intransigent, amenable to no elaboration, explanation or exposition, it lacks informative significance. Indeed, one doubts that such instances are metaphors at all. Beyond that, there is a parting of the ways. On the one hand, those following Soskice[14] will accept 'irreducible religious metaphors', providing that the metaphor can be elucidated by extension, *even* if this further exposition is by means of further tropes. On the other hand, William Alston[15] has made a strong case for the necessity of '*partial* reducibility', namely that part of any metaphorical utterance about God must be susceptible of construal *in part* by literal terms. This does not demand exhaustive literal paraphrase, but it does require that some literal predicate terms be disengaged which can be attributed to God propositionally.

These two arguments occupy the rest of this chapter. In it, I will be using the works of St John of the Cross, partly because his four books, *Ascent of Mount Carmel, Dark Night of the Soul, The Spiritual Canticle* and *Living Flame of Love*, represent the sequence of the spiritual journey, though not of composition. John is also an ideal choice because of his own preoccupation with the mode of communication. He is distinctive in beginning each work with an entirely metaphoric poem, upon which he then supplies a commentary, first stanza by stanza and then phrase by phrase.[16] His commentaries switch to elucidation, often by means of illustrative similes, and an overview was condensed into a drawing of the route up the 'Mount of Perfection'. However, there comes a point when John finds the 'words proper' running out and then he does indeed resort to 'irreducible religious metaphors', meaning that these cannot be elucidated literally. Soskice's distinctions provide a good fix upon *where* this point occurs in his description of the spiritual journey. It is also when his explication of metaphor resorts only to further tropes that John becomes manifestly dissatisfied and uncomfortable with his exposition. However, by following Alston's procedure of 'partial reduction' through to its conclusion, we can arrive at an understanding of *why* literal exposition necessarily fails in talk about God.

Where religious metaphors become irreducible

Let us begin by following Soskice's approach through the sequence of John's four books. Here I want to show how her criterion of metaphorical corrigibility, namely that metaphors are susceptible of further elaboration *and* explanation, holds for John's first stages of the journey (for the *Ascent* and for most of *Dark Night*, the two being one thematic work). However, John himself voices his increasing dissatisfaction with religious language when he treats of the ultimate stage of 'unification', especially in the peon that is the *Living Flame*. The question for us is why does he accept the irreducibility of religious metaphors at precisely this stage, and concede that any further extension of his meaning can only (and reluctantly) be by further resort to the metaphorical?[17]

The architectonic image, uniting John's works, is darkness and light. The spiritual journey begins in the endarkened spirit, which enters into the experience of 'night'; proceeds towards that which we can only see 'through a glass darkly',[18] until a very few attain to unification with light itself. The *Ascent*, which deals with setting out upon this journey, is a long systematic and scholastic treatise, which John himself called 'solid and substantial instruction'.[19] In form, however, it is taken up with explicating the following two verses from the prefatory poem:

> *En una noche oscura*
> So dark the night! At rest
> and hushed my house. I went out with no-one knowing
> upon a lover's quest
> – Ah the sheer grace – so blest,
> my eager heart with love aflame and glowing.

> In darkness, hid from sight
> I went by secret ladder safe and sure
> – Ah grace of sheer delight! –
> so softly veiled by night,
> hushed now my house, in darkness and secure.[20]

There is no doubt that extension and elaboration follow here: forty pages are devoted to elucidating the first line, 'On a dark night'. Here he explains how sensual attachments occlude the soul and that only by embracing the dark void of detachment (that is, 'hushing one's inner house') can we begin to climb ('by secret ladder') towards the light. John maintains a distinction between metaphor, largely confined to the poem itself, and illustrative similes, which are extensively used throughout the commentary for metaphorical clarification. The metaphor discloses reality; the simile is used for redescription by comparison with similars. Thus, in the following passage, which expounds upon detachment, we find that the metaphorical disclosure is repeated in the first sentence and is then redescribed by a cascade of illustrations or likenings. The hope is that the reader will catch on to one of them and thus allow the architectonic, which enfolds this brief exposition, to be unfolded further.

> The evil that the desires cause in the soul is that they blind and darken it. Even as vapours darken the air and allow not the bright sun to shine; or as a mirror that is clouded over cannot receive within itself a clear image; or as water defiled by mud reflects not the visage of one that looks therein; even so the soul that is clouded by the desires is darkened in the understanding and allows neither the sun of natural reason nor that of the Supernatural Wisdom of God to shine upon it and illuminate it clearly.[21]

John uses this device repeatedly and, having brought his readers to an understanding of the dark occlusion caused by sensual attachment, can then allow one famous simile to bear the weight of explaining how the slightest flaw in detachment can prevent soaring ascent.

> For it comes to the same thing whether a bird is held by a slender cord or by a stout one; since, even if it be slender, the bird will be as well held as if it were stout, for as long as it breaks it not and flies not away.[22]

John's exposition of detachment from desire is one that any reader can find intelligible. It successfully models the process of being stripped down which awaits and attends those who are drawn to making the ascent, which is far from everybody. The text is not meant to convert anyone to undertake the journey, but to 'give instruction and counsel'[23] to those who have already committed themselves to it. *Ascent* is not an argumentative text, seeking to win over the agnostic, but a manual giving encouragement and guidance for tyro practitioners. Nevertheless, the metaphorical elucidation succeeds in conveying to any agnostic reader, who is interested enough to finish it, what kind of life-shaping enterprise these beginners are undertaking. They must move from sensory occlusion to darkening their desires willingly. John states that he could have expounded upon detachment at greater length, but also records his satisfaction at having written enough, and well enough, to disclose what embracing it will be like in practice. 'That which has been said suffices; for we believe we have made it clear in what way the mortification of these desires is called night, and how it behoves us to enter this night in order to journey to God.'[24]

Matters are very different with *Living Flame* which deals with the arrival of the 'very few' who come to union with God. The first hint of difference is the brevity of this work on the 'spiritual marriage'; a mere sixty pages, not much more than was devoted to the first phrase of the *Ascent*. The second presage is the reluctance that John recounts about producing it, because the words have been stretched and strained and he himself doubts that they can carry the burden of expressing his meaning.[25] In the opening sentence of the Prologue he is quite overt about this. 'I have felt some unwillingness . . . to expound these four stanzas . . . for they relate to things so interior and spiritual that words commonly fail to describe them, since spirit transcends sense and it is with difficulty that anything can be said of the substance thereof.'[26] The third indicator is that the use of illustrative similes almost disappears, which signals the sheer paucity of commonly shared referents to which this state of union may be likened.

The opening stanza of the poem goes as follows:

> *! Oh llama de amor viva . . . !*
> Flame, alive, compelling,
> yet tender past all telling,
> reaching the secret centre of my soul!
> Since now evasion's over,
> finish your work, my Lover,
> break the last thread, wound me and make me whole!

Significantly, John's first comment, in his attempted exposition, deals with the initial word; he draws our attention to the fact that each stanza opens with 'oh' or 'how', expressing exultation about what follows. 'Each time they are used they show that something is passing within the soul beyond that which can be expressed by the tongue.'[27] The commentary itself holds this note, for the attempt to convey ecstasy is light years removed from communicating 'solid and substantial instruction'. Instead, the *Living Flame* is his own Magnificat, not a manual of guidance for others.

His ecstatic experience is extruded, but not explained, by dense reliance upon a traditional metaphorical corpus. He reaches back to the *Song of Songs*, works through Scriptural marriage imagery about the relationship between Christ and his Church, and battens on to secular love poetry, given the organic continuity that he ascribes to human and divine love. What the text basically tells us about the ecstasy of this transformative union is that it belongs to the same family of experiences as the above, only is vastly 'more so'. Can these love metaphors successfully model the 'spiritual marriage'? I think they do work but only one-sidedly, that is, in successfully conveying John's own joyous fulfilment. They can be pressed into service for witness, testimony and praise, but then the 'words are flexed and eventually left behind',[28] as John himself avows. 'There are no words to expound such sublime things of God as come to pass in these souls; whereof the proper way to speak is for one who knows them to understand them inwardly and enjoy them and be silent concerning them.'[29]

As Iain Matthew aptly comments, the *'Flame* ends in this kind of willing defeatism'.[30] By the last paragraph of the manuscript, John simply breaks off his attempt to explicate the breath of God's spirit, felt within, and signs off. 'I should not wish to speak, neither do I desire now to speak; for I see clearly that I cannot say aught concerning it, and that, were I to speak of it, it would seem less than it is . . . And for that reason I leave speaking of it here.'[31] The end.

In the course of describing this spiritual journey, I have tried to show how metaphor can disclose much at its start and little at its finish. However, can one be more precise about where the use of irreducible metaphors sets in, particularly since the two 'middle' texts have not been touched upon here? Matthew, I believe, gives us a clue as to 'precisely where' when he notes of *Living Flame* that there is 'one feature which pervades the poem, so obvious that it could be missed. It is this; in the verses all the initiative belongs to the other.'[32] The fulcrum between where metaphorical referentiality works literally, but then tips over into irreducibility, coincides exactly with the transition from active to passive contemplation. These terms relate to when grace-aided, but still human, exertions give way to the infusion of a pure divine gift, which requires only the stillness of receptivity. Textually, this 'where' occurs in stanza 22, when the Lover and the Beloved finally embrace in silence.

If I am correct about the 'where', we can press John a little further about 'what is going on here'. His answer is clear and extremely radical: nothing less than human transformation into the divine.[33] Usually, we qualify *theosis* as 'progressive', thus accentuating the process rather than accepting the full implications of it as an end-state. Yet it is to this culmination that the last lines of the stanza refer – 'Finish your work my Lover/break the last thread, wound me and make me whole!' The threads which have already been broken are those of *temporality*, i.e. the soul now participates in God's timelessness; of *intentionality*, i.e. the soul's inclinations are now purged, purified and Godlike; so that the last web to be broken is human *corporeality*, i.e. the soul now wishes to shed its embodiment through death, to effect permanent union.[34] In sum, divine unification is meant to be taken very seriously: God 'absorbs the soul, above all being, in the Being of God'.[35]

If we are prepared to entertain the reality of this state (certainly for others!), then it is *not* one in which the subject/object distinction fails to be maintained, but where this distinction no longer *does* maintain. The differentiation of subject and object, which is necessary if metaphor is to bridge it, has itself been transcended. The divinized subject now shares 'God's eye view', and thus has moved over the human divide into that mode of divine being where 'the heavens are as high above the earth as my ways are above your ways, my thoughts above your thoughts' (Isaiah 55.9). Our generic human limitations, which include the limits of language, preclude divine nature from being conveyed by other than 'irreducible metaphors'. Literal elucidation works well only when the focus is upon humanity in relation to God. Conversely, God's own actions, towards us and within us, can only be extended by tropes, amplified by further tropes.

Why metaphorical reduction necessarily fails

If the above argument is correct, it should follow that the limits to metaphorical reduction are confronted when religious language attempts to treat of God himself. Conversely, William Alston has sought to maintain that we humans may capture something of divinity, if our human meta-phors can be partially but literally rendered in relation to God.[36] I believe that this 'partial reduction' does not work, but also that we can learn something extremely valuable about *why* this is the case by following through his enterprise.

Alston's aim, in seeking to bring about the 'partial reduction' of religious metaphors, is that we should be able to assign predicates to God literally. If that were the case, at least some of the terms in which we regularly discuss creatures and their doings would be the same ones in which we could talk about God and his doings. As Alston puts it,

> theists have long felt a tension between the radical 'otherness' of God and the fact that we talk of God in terms of talk drawn from our talk of creatures. If God is radically other than creatures, how can we properly speak of him acting, loving, knowing, and purposing? Wouldn't that imply that God shares features with creatures and hence is not 'wholly other'?[37]

In maintaining that God is not 'wholly other', Alston is clearly not saying that God is so 'wholly like' us that every creaturely predicate can be trans-ferred from us to him; he is only making a claim about the *partial* reducibility of our metaphorical talk. So are scientists, who are not claiming that radio waves are like sea waves in every, or even most, respect(s).

However, Alston does try to convince us that we can properly speak of God being an agent, in terms modelled upon human agency, *despite* his 'otherness'. The latter does not preclude a divine–human sharing of funda-mental agential properties. God, qua agent, is not so 'other' that we cannot properly speak, in the same terms, of his doing those things which are generic to agency *making a difference in the world* – by 'intending', 'acting' and 'producing' outcomes. In opposition to this, I will follow through the arguments about these three predicates, and maintain that God's ontological 'otherness' does preclude literal talk in these terms.

If my counter-argument is successful, three consequences will follow from it. First, it will have established that there is no real communality between God's agency and ours. Instead, in so far as we can grasp God as an agent, this can only be by reference to his own distinctive properties. Second, it will also follow that in exercising his properties and powers God abrogates the categorial structures through which alone human agency can be exercised – namely, time, space and causality. Therefore, if we wish to impute agency to God, and I agree with Alston that we do, we will have to regard his nature as a generative mechanism, *sui generis*. Third, it is because this generative mechanism is at work, yet constitutes a different kind of agency, that we creatures who are bound by time, space and causality will not be able to conceptualise it by a literal explication of the metaphors we use about divinity. This is the reason *why* our human religious language about God *necessarily remains metaphorical*. That it does so is not a matter of human epistemological limitations, but is because of God's ontological difference, i.e. he is related to reality in an entirely different way from us.

To proceed, it is necessary to ask the non-theistic reader to entertain a being, God, who is eternal, non-corporeal and omniscient.[38] This is no different from what we do in science, when, for example, the early physicist was asked to countenance the implications of 'invisible waves'. The logic of the argument does not depend upon faith, and so it should enable the non-theist to understand why the theist has real difficulties in talking about God in 'words proper'. The three divine properties they are being invited to entertain are among the classical Thomist divine attributes. They are properties that St John of the Cross endorsed, and ones which Alston accepts, despite his neo-classicism,[39] which need not concern us here. Now let us consider these three divine properties and powers in relation to God's agency, and how it differs from ours, in order to evaluate Alston's claim that these attributes do not make God so 'wholly other' that predicates applicable to human agents cannot be literally attributed to him.

As far as human beings are concerned, any exercise of their agency involves **temporality**. Time is required for goal formation, processes take place in real time, and the outcome produced entails temporal succession. If we first concentrate upon the human process of determining a goal, Alston is clear that there are many respects in which this differs from 'goal setting' by God, as a timeless being. For example, (i) God does not temporise as we do, whilst sorting out desires, interests, disinclinations and moral commitments; (ii) God does not have to work inferentially, which takes time with us, for he knows all logical consequences and the falsity of all their contradictories; (iii) our intended actions may be suspended by the temporal intervention of contingencies (such as our own internal 'second thoughts' or intrusions from the world as an open system, as in 'between cup and lip . . .'). This is not so with God, because there is no time gap between divine intention and action. Alston agrees that such differences are sufficient to preclude the application to God of those human psychological terms that are involved in our temporal goal formation. Instead, he is seeking 'only to show that the terms for psychological *functions* can be devised that apply in just the same sense to God and creature'.[40]

In relation to goal formation, Alston accepts that the causal connections, which involve temporal succession in humans, cannot fit his functionalist bill. Instead, he invites us to consider that 'laws of coexistence' can be applied literally to God and to us. Temporality is not involved in the following formulation of intentionality. 'If S wants X more than anything else and realises that doing A is necessary for getting X, and believes that doing A is possible, then S will intend to do A.' Such a law of coexistence deals with nothing but the temporal now: S has intention A, if S's current desires and beliefs are now related as specified.

However, Alston accepts that this *formulation* cannot be right, because it assumes that the divine psyche is subject to laws, which entails God being law-governed. Theists will rightly object that since God freely decides which laws are operative, the operations of his own psyche cannot be made to depend upon laws. However, Alston thinks that the remedy is simple, and consists in replacing God's law-governedness with God's nature. 'That is, the stable dependence (of intentions on conative and cognitive factors) will be rooted in His nature rather than in laws to which He is subject.'[41] Yet this cannot be correct either, and nor does it provide us with a model of intentionality that applies in the same way to God and to human subjects.

First, it entails thinking of 'God's nature such that He will, for example, have a certain intention whenever His conative and cognitive factors are such-and-such'.[42] Yet, if his willing and his knowing are variable, divine intention formation becomes a process, for a determinate relationship has to be *established* between these factors. But how can there be a process without temporality? Second, since the model of coexistence has now been rewritten to refer to God's own nature, it cannot perform the functionalist task it was meant to do. This is because no human analogue can be found where our intentions depend solely upon our 'human nature'. Our autonomous reactions (such as withdrawing a hand from fire) are exclusively dependent upon our physiology, but cannot count because they do not involve intentionality. Conversely, satisfaction of our biological needs, such as eating, requires an intentional specification (what we want to eat, what is available, and so forth), which means that our intentions do not spring directly from human nature.

The first criticism relates to a temporalising of divine nature; the second concerns a misrepresentation of human nature. Therefore, Alston has not shown that we can talk about human and divine intentionality or goal-setting in the same terms. If we cannot, then, in this respect, God's nature and will must remain mysterious, that is, resistant to literal modelling on the human agent.

Turning to the processes by which agency acts to bring about changes in the world, the second stumbling block to conceiving of these in the same terms for humanity and divinity concerns spatiality. Every basic action of a human being entails their embodiment, for even the enunciation of reasons, considered as causes, involves use of the vocal cords to articulate them – or neuronal activity to express them internally. The problem here is that God, as a spaceless and incorporeal being, is quite different. So, Alston asks, what is crucial to our bodily movements *as actions*, rather than autonomic jerks? This is the classical Wittgensteinian question about what is left over if I subtract the fact that my arm goes up from the fact that I raise my arm? The answer generally given is 'my intention', thus making intentionality the core concept in human action, rather than bodily movement.

The problem that now faces Alston is, 'can an intention cause whatever substitutes for bodily movement in incorporeal basic action?' – that is, God's actions. In other words, bodily movements are just what human beings depend upon for their basic actions, but Alston argues that it 'is conceptually possible for any change whatsoever to be the core of a basic action'.[43] Therefore, we would have to allow that, for God, intentions give rise directly to changes in the world. This is something which Alston admits is indeed outside our 'ordinary experience'. However, he immediately goes on to state, 'I can see nothing in our present understanding of the psyche and of causality that would show it to be impossible in principle.'[44] Thus the consideration of spatiality has now led to a revision of the notion of causality, in relation to divine agency. Causally, it is 'just that we will have to think of God as bringing about changes in the "external" world directly by an act of will – not indirectly through moving His body, as in our case'.[45]

The difficulty with Alston's exercise is that we can engage in extreme 'concept stretching', such that in an abstract and functionalist philosophical sense, the term 'agency' can arguably be applied both to humanity and to divinity. However, that in fact results in *accentuating* the difference between God as agent and us as agents, when it was meant to do precisely the opposite. This is because we are confronted by a being whose actions *depend* upon abrogations of the fundamental categorial structures of space, time and causality upon which human agency is totally *dependent*. (These are not categories that our minds impose upon nature; they are the naturalistic categories through which the natural world works.) In terms of causality, this means accepting that in divine intentionality, actions and outcomes are compacted into a single '*fiat*'. It is not merely that this is beyond our 'ordinary experience', it is that we cannot get our human heads round it at all. '*Partial reduction*' has not yielded a God whom we now understand better in common literal terms, but has simply plunged us more deeply into the intransigent mystery of God's nature and the *modus operandi* of his will. We are forced to conclude that divinity and humanity are not just very different kinds of agents, but perhaps even more different than we thought at the beginning of this exercise. This is because we are now fully aware that God transcends time, space and causality – the only categories through which we humans can act in the world. Because God's ontological difference means that every one of his actions overrides those categorial structures that are intrinsic to human agency, we also lack common terms in which to refer to his doings. Metaphorical reduction *necessarily* breaks down because of the ontological break between the nature of God and the nature of human agency.

Moreover, we have still not exhausted the matter by accentuating the difficulties that a finite being confronts when trying to conceptualise the doings of an infinite being in the same terms. The root problem is as much about *subjectivity*[46] as it is about the objective differences just examined – and it is the former that preoccupies St John in *Living Flame*. There he was not trying to conceptualise God's agency; he was trying to convey the *experience* of his indwelling. To take John at his word, namely that through 'unification' the human soul is absorbed into 'the Being of God' (see page 99), means that he also experiences God in *something of the same way that God experiences himself*. Subjectively, the rest of us are necessarily confined to that incomprehension which Thomas Nagel highlighted in his argument that we cannot understand 'what it is like to be a bat'.[47]

Nagel's point is that, however much we know about bats-as-agents, which negotiate the world by sonar or echo location, there is no reason to suppose that we can imagine the bat's subjective experiences. Because my imagination is experientially restricted by my human status, it can only tell me what it would be like for *me* to pretend to be a bat; it cannot give me knowledge of what it is like for a *bat* to be a bat. Bat-experience necessarily has a specific subjective character, which lies beyond our human capacity to conceive of it or to describe it. As Nagel concludes,

> (r)eflection on what it is like to be a bat seems to lead us, therefore, to the conclusion that there are facts that do not consist in the truth of propositions expressible in human language. We can be compelled to recognise the existence of such facts without being able to state or comprehend them.[48]

This is the second reason why our metaphors are irreducible and our 'words proper' run out – when they apply to God himself.

Both the believer and the unbeliever can agree that were God to exist, and bear the classical properties discussed, his subjective character would be even further removed from our own and thus from our powers of literal human description. Now St John sincerely claims to have attained unification with God, and logically it is indeed only if he has crossed the human–divine divide that he can know (something of) 'what it is like to be God'. Equally he knows that human language cannot convey it directly – but only obliquely by metaphor pointing to further metaphor. Correspondingly, we who are far removed from unification could not understand John, whatever language he used, since we lack the experiential basis for such understanding. Now, unbelieving readers may think that they have *empirical* reasons for doubting John's claims, but they have no more *logical* reason for rejecting this explanation of metaphorical irreducibility than were this the result of someone hypothesised to be in St John's position. If philosophers of mind can ask us hypothetically to entertain both human fission and fusion, or Twin Earth, then 'unification' can similarly be entertained for the same kind of purposes.

In sum, God is not an agent like us and we experience this most profoundly when we become aware (to whatever degree) of his 'indwelling', which is an action entirely without human parallel. We recognise this indwelling as pure, unconditional and unmerited love, the internal expression of the divine nature within us, but we cannot model its conference by the literal use of human concepts. In the end, Alston admits that if we want to go beyond philosophical 'concept-stretching', then 'we will be thrown back on the familiar array of alternatives that are open, with respect to the total meaning of theological predicates, to those who deny that any terms (concepts) we can form can be literally applied to God: the alternative of analogy, metaphor and symbolism etc.'[49] In other words, we have come full circle back to Soskice's position, but at least we can now understand why religious metaphors become irreducible at a certain point. They do so when we directly (if only partially) experience divinity in our lives; when God is most active towards us, then we are, perforce, most tongue-tied about him.

Thus, Aquinas talks of the 'life of grace' as a 'participation in the divine nature'.[50] This is what Teresa takes up in her bridal theme of the seventh mansion. It is what St John of the Cross called divinisation: becoming caught up in 'the being of God'. It is also that to which Alston himself assents, when he takes 'the goal of sanctification to be . . . a full communion with God, the fullest possible sharing in the divine nature'.[51] To encounter God, as pure unbounded love, is the summit of religious practice, whose experience defies literal discursive formulation. After such an encounter, St Thomas Aquinas concluded that 'all he had written in comparison to what he had then seen is so much straw.'[52] He did not finish the *Summa Theologiae*, because 'words proper' were inadequate.

Conclusion

If the foregoing arguments are correct, what are their implications for Realism and particularly for the secular realist? I have been exclusively concerned with questions surrounding 'epistemic relativism' in relation to St John of the Cross, because were his writings impenetrable, it would be impossible to exercise 'judgemental rationality' towards them. However, to understand the contemplatives' difficulties with language and dependence upon 'irreducible metaphors', it is essential to recognise that contemplation is a practice, a 'doing', which in this case means praying. The knowledge derived from it takes the form of a practical skill, a 'knowing how'. Thus it belongs to that family of activities where proficiency is a matter of the subject acquiring a 'feel for' the activity, as in developing a 'palate' for wine', a 'grasp' of how to back a trailer, 'appreciation' of how to produce effects in art. Because practical knowledge involves the active process of 'doing', it is procedural rather than declarative in kind. The former never translates readily or fully into 'words proper'. Thus, practical knowledge is tacit and takes the form of developing skills rather than enunciating propositions.

Nevertheless, to admit that there are great difficulties in rendering tacit, procedural knowledge discursively is not to say that the enterprise fails entirely. 'Irreducible metaphors' can succeed if (some) readers catch on to (some of) the further tropes that are used to extend them. If they do so, the subsequent exercise of their 'judgemental rationality' will *also* need to be practical in form. It will involve participation, just as becoming able to evaluate how best to address a golf ball entails holding a club and practising many swings. No one can acquire this skill if they protest 'I wouldn't play golf' – and the same goes for contemplation. Ultimately, the achievement of the great contemplative writers does not lie in overcoming the limits of language, but rather in conveying enough of their experience of divine love to recommend the practice of contemplation.

Notes

1 Thomas Hobbes, *Leviathan*, Dent & Sons, London, 1914, p. 20–1.
2 David Hume, *Dialogues Concerning Natural Religion* (ed. Henry D. Aiken), Part IV, Hafner, New York, 1948.
3 A.J. Ayer, *The Central Questions of Philosophy*, Penguin, Harmondsworth, 1976.
4 St John of the Cross, *Ascent of Mount Carmel* (ed. E. Allison Peers), Burns & Oates, Tunbridge Wells, 1983, p. 26.
5 St John of the Cross, *Ascent*, p. 69.
6 St John of the Cross, *Ascent*, p. 72.
7 William James, *The Varieties of Religious Experience*, Modern Library, New York, 1902, pp. 371–2.
8 W.T. Stace, *Mysticism and Religion*, Macmillan, London, 1961.
9 See Bernard McGinn, *The Presence of God: A History of Western Christian Mysticism*, 4 volumes, SCM Press, London, 1992.
10 David Tracy, 'Metaphor and Religion' in S. Sacks (ed.), *On Metaphor*, University of Chicago Press, Chicago, 1979, pp. 89–94.
11 F. Ferré, *Basic Modern Philosophy of Religion*, Allen & Unwin, London, 1968, pp. 395f.
12 Janet Martin Soskice, *Metaphor and Religious Language*, Clarendon Press, Oxford, 1985, p. 105.
13 A. Léonard, 'Studies on the Phenomenon of Mystical Experience', in *Mystery and Mysticism: A Symposium*, Blackfriars, London, 1956, p. 108.
14 Soskice, *Metaphor*.
15 William P. Alston, 'Irreducible Metaphors in Theology', in his *Divine Nature and Human Language*, Cornell University Press, Ithaca, NY, 1989.
16 This is the format announced and repeated in most volumes, but it is followed more strictly in some than others. For example, *Ascent* and *Dark Night* only

fully explicate the first two stanzas of their common poem, and begin on stanza three.

17 Soskice distinguishes that stage, which John reaches, from one of radical inexplicability, where a metaphorical 'text resists all attempts to elucidate its meaning, if we can expand upon it or clarify it in no way at all, we would be justified in saying that it lacked significance', *Metaphor*, p. 94.

18 St John of the Cross, *Ascent*, pp. 19–20.

19 St John of the Cross, *Ascent*, Prologue, p. 15.

20 Trans. Marjorie Flower, *The Poems of St John of the Cross*, The Carmelite Nuns, Varroville, Cabra Printing Service, New South Wales.

21 St John of the Cross, *Ascent*, p. 39.

22 St John of the Cross, *Ascent*, p. 50.

23 St John of the Cross, *Ascent*, Prologue, p. 12.

24 St John of the Cross, *Ascent*, p. 53–4.

25 Exactly the same is true of St Teresa's discussion of the 'seventh mansion' which treats of the same 'arrival'; 'These chapters lack the verve characteristic of her writing. The reason why is simply *that there is nothing that can be said about the seventh mansion.* Entering into it we are in a world where human words are meaningless.' Ruth Burrows, *Interior Castle Explored*, Sheed & Ward, London, 1981, p. 110; italics in original.

26 St John of the Cross, *Living Flame of Love* (ed. E. Allison Peers), Burns & Oates, Tunbridge Wells, 1987, p. 13.

27 St John of the Cross, *Living Flame*, p. 20.

28 St John of the Cross, *Living Flame*, p.22.

29 St John of the Cross, *Living Flame*, second redaction, pp. 150–1.

30 Iain Matthew, *The Impact of God*, Hodder & Stoughton, London, 1995, p. 22.

31 St John of the Cross, *Living Flame*, p. 113.

32 Matthew, *The Impact of God*, p. 24.

33 This is also what Roy Bhaskar dares to assert in *From East to West: Odyssey of a Soul*, Routledge, London, 2000.

34 St John of the Cross, *Living Flame*, pp. 34f.

35 St John of the Cross, *Living Flame*, p. 38.

36 Alston, 'Irreducible Metaphors'.

37 Alston, 'Functionalism and Theological Language', in *Divine Nature and Human Language*, p. 64.

38 St Thomas Aquinas, *Summa Theologiae*, Volume 2 (ia. 2–11), *Existence and Nature of God* (ed. Timothy McDermott), Eyre and Spottiswoode/Blackfriars, London, 1964.

39 See Alston, 'Hartshorne and Aquinas: A Via Media', in *Divine Nature and Human Language*.

40 Alston, 'Functionalism and Theological Language', p. 73; italics in original.

41 Alston, 'Functionalism and Theological Language', p. 80.

42 Alston, 'Functionalism and Theological Language', p. 80.

43 Alston, 'Can We Speak Literally of God', in *Divine Nature and Human Language*, p. 61.

44 Alston, 'Can We Speak Literally of God', p. 62.

45 Alston, 'Functionalism and Theological Language', p. 72.

46 Subjectivity is also an ontological difference. For a discussion of 'first person

ontology', see John R. Searle, *Mind, Language and Society*, Weidenfeld & Nicolson Ltd, London, 1999, pp. 42f.

47 Thomas Nagel, 'What Is It Like to Be a Bat?', in David M. Rosenthal, *The Nature of Mind*, Oxford University Press, Oxford, 1991.

48 Nagel, 'What Is It Like', p. 424.

49 Nagel, 'What Is It Like', p. 102.

50 Aquinas, *Summa Theologiae*, Iae 2a, Q 100, art. 4.

51 Alston, 'The Indwelling of the Holy Spirit', in *Divine Nature and Human Language*, p. 252.

52 David Farmer, *Oxford Dictionary of Saints*, Oxford University Press, Oxford, 1997, p. 472.

8 A propaedeutic to a propaedeutic on inter-religious dialogue

Douglas V. Porpora

The title of this chapter may be one of the strangest I have ever affixed to anything I have written. Although in part, the title is facetious, it is also meant to be serious. In part, what follows is a propaedeutic for myself because I am admittedly a newcomer to the literature on inter-religious dialogue. In part, however, the title also describes what the newcomer to this literature actually finds. What the newcomer to this now vast literature largely finds is Christian theologians writing about the need for inter-religious dialogue, how it should be done, and what its implications are for Christianity. As the interlocutors in this exchange seem to be other Christian theologians, it can hardly be described as a dialogue that is itself inter-religious.[1] It itself seems more of a propaedeutic to inter-religious dialogue, although I will argue that it is also something more than that.

That the literature on inter-religious dialogue seems not itself to be inter-religious raises an important question for a critical realist approach to religion: Can believers in different religions sit down together and argue over their rival truth claims in a manner that has any prospect of persuading anyone of anything? I am convinced that, from a philosophical perspective, this can be done in principle but that politically, perhaps, it cannot or should not be done now.

I describe myself as a newcomer to the literature on inter-religious dialogue, but I am hardly a newcomer to inter-religious dialogue per se. Inter-religious dialogue occurs whenever two or more from different faith perspectives sit down to talk about religion – or about the bearing of their religious perspectives on matters that are not themselves, strictly speaking, religious. I have been involved in such discussions many times as in inter-faith responses to peace and justice issues. I have also been involved in inter-religious dialogue closer to home. Although I am a Catholic, I was raised by a Presbyterian mother and was myself baptised as a Presbyterian at birth. I was married in a synagogue, and even now every Passover, my wife removes all leavened products from our kitchen – not just bread, but also rice and beans and all else 'chametz,' anything that can conceivably cause food to rise. Most Christians think that Judaism is just Christianity without Christ. That may have been true in the first century, where popular Christian understanding of Judaism ends, but rabbinic Judaism has been developing for two thousand years since then. What Judaism actually is today is something I learned from the twenty-year ethnographic experience that is my marriage.

Among theologians addressing inter-religious dialogue, John Cobb has become one of my favourites. At one point, Cobb speaks of inter-religious dialogue as holding the promise of an eventually Buddhised Christianity and a Christianised Buddhism.[2] I like to think that Cobb would be pleased with me. Like many Catholics today, my Catholicism is very Protestantised, but it is also Buddhised, Hinduised, Stoicised, and certainly very Judaised and Marxified. Even before September 11, I had been working on Islamifying it.

When we three authors began, none of us was well versed in the literature on inter-religious dialogue. Of us three, I was the one who most pressed the need for a chapter on the subject. My felt need for such a chapter in this book had little to do with an ecumenical agenda, which all three of us share, but was motivated instead by strictly philosophical concerns relating to critical realism. This book argues that it is both possible and fruitful to adopt a critical realist approach to religion. That approach entails the possibility of adjudicating among the rival truth claims lodged by the different religions. Adjudication hardly means that we must inevitably judge each of these truth claims to be either totally wrong or totally right – although a good many may well turn out to be one or the other. It is also possible, however, for many rival claims each to turn out partially right, either because each reflects a limited perspective on a single, larger truth or because, as Cobb suggests, the different religions may actually be pointing to different ultimate truths.[3]

Of course, it could also turn out that no truth claim made by any religion is even partially correct. As some atheists might expect, all religious truth claims could turn out to be so much bunk. For that reason, despite the apparent oddity, atheism in all its forms must likewise be an interlocutor invited to what is called inter-religious dialogue.

The oddity of including atheism is more apparent than real. Cobb and other theologians express misgivings about religion as a designation for different approaches to life.[4] One problem with that designation is that it seems illegitimately essentialist. A possible implication is that, despite the plurality of religious forms, there is something that religion essentially is, which all hold in common. It is unclear what that something is. It cannot be a belief in God or gods because, in at least some of their forms, religions like Buddhism and even Judaism do not necessarily believe in any such thing. Cobb suggests 'ways' of life as a more felicitous designation than religion. Such a designation would include non-theistic and non-ritualistic philosophies of life, such as Marxism and secular humanism.

I am less troubled by the term religion. As Wittgenstein has taught us, many kinds of things – like games – lack necessary and sufficient criteria and share only family resemblances. Thus, although I agree that dialogue should proceed among all philosophies of life in so far as they address what is ultimate, I will continue to speak of them and of the dialogue as religious.

The fact remains that if we cannot adjudicate among the rival truth claims of different religions and philosophies of life, we must entertain serious doubts about a critical realist approach to religion. For a critical realist approach to religion, different religions are akin to different paradigms in science. Just as critical realism argues that rival claims can be adjudicated across scientific paradigms, so too would a critical realist approach to religion maintain that rival claims can be adjudicated across religions.

Some who accept a critical realist approach to science might demur over its applicability to religion. Such reticence may in part reflect the belief that whereas scientific paradigms at least refer to empirical realities, religious concepts have meaning only in relation to the other concepts of the religion to which they belong and no meaning outside of that socio-linguistic system. This is a position popularised by Clifford Geertz in anthropology, by R.B. Braithwaite in philosophy, and by George Lindbeck in theology.[5] The implication is that religious concepts do not refer to anything at all outside the 'prison house of language'.

We have termed this position 'fictionalism', and Chapter 3 is expressly directed against it. In its Geertzian form, fictionalism assumes that because words and concepts acquire their meaning in relation to each other, they therefore do not refer to realities outside of language. The logic here fails to follow. If it did follow, it would apply to science as well as to religion. The reason is that scientific concepts like mass, energy, force and acceleration all, likewise, acquire their meaning in relation to one another. For a linguistic ideology to ask us to conclude from this that such scientific concepts do not refer to anything real is to demand a faith far more strenuous, I think, than a homely belief in God.

To the extent that academic linguistic ideology itself assumes the qualities of a religious faith, then, as Cobb suggests, it too should take its place in inter-religious dialogue – not as privileged broker but as humble co-participant.[6] In that forum, it must respond to the counter-evidence Cobb presents. 'Buddha-nature', Cobb points out, is a concept that derives its meaning in relation to Buddhist concepts and Buddhist practices, much as the socio-linguistic position maintains. Yet in the course of inter-religious dialogue and inter-religious meditational practice, Christians too have managed not only to learn what Buddha-nature means but also to incorporate it within their own Christian concepts and practices. How is this possible, Cobb asks, unless Buddha-nature refers to something understandable and even experienceable apart from the socio-linguistic system that first picked it out?[7]

For all the faults of fictionalism in the abstract, inter-religious dialogue is a site where the pressure towards some kind of fictionalism remains philosophically strong. The pressure is strong for political reasons. Fictionalism is an even-handed way of leaving everyone unmolested. If religions are all non-referential, but instead are alternative ways of affording community and shared identity, they no longer oppose each other as do rival accounts of truth.

Since no one who is open-minded – and I include myself – wants to molest other faith traditions or their faithful, fictionalism commends itself as a tolerant philosophy and sociology of religion. Fictionalism undeniably is tolerant, but, as we have said elsewhere in this book, it extracts too high a price from all the religions. If fictionalism promotes tolerance, it is because fictionalism withdraws from all religions any claim of saying anything true or consequential.

At this price, fictionalism's tolerance actually amounts to a form of disrespect. I tolerate you because you cease to make any claims on me, particularly the kind of claim that truth makes. In that case, I need not even heed what you are saying. At most, I can regard you with the unengaged eye of a tourist.[8] It accords vastly more respect to the 'Other' to regard the Other as claiming something that on grounds of intellectual honesty might compel me to alter my own beliefs. In his book, *On Christian Belief*, Andrew Collier points out that to believe something is to regard it as true.[9] If we are serious about our religious beliefs, we should be serious about their truth, and if we are serious about their truth, we should be prepared to question their truth. Being prepared to question the truth of our religious beliefs is not, however, the same as actually doing so. We will only question if we are given reason to question. That others believe something different from us is in itself a reason to question our own beliefs, but the reason only becomes truly compelling when we find that those others have better warrant for their beliefs than we have for ours. That discovery only comes out of argument. Thus, inter-religious debate on truth claims would seem as important in religion as in science to their respective quests for truth. In this sense, inter-religious dialogue is not just something in which we engage to sponsor amity – however important that may be – but also to keep ourselves intellectually honest about our own religious convictions.

Thus, it is initially surprising to find in the literature on inter-religious dialogue a strong reluctance to debate the rival truth claims of different religions. In the lists of dos and don'ts about inter-religious dialogue, it frequently appears that a dialogue is not a debate.[10] The function of inter-religious dialogue, we are told, is to listen, to understand, and to build community. Even Cobb is dismissive of the utility of debating rival truth claims.[11]

Among the different religions, Buddhism appears to have the tradition most strongly opposed to inter-religious debate. There is a story ascribed to Gautama Buddha in the *Lotus Sutra* that tells of a traveller who wished to get across a river. In the absence of either a bridge or a ferry, the man proceeds to build a raft. The question the Buddha raises is what the man should do with the raft once he has crossed the river. Should he continue to carry the raft on his back?

The obvious answer is that the traveller should abandon the raft once he has traversed the river. The point of the story, as traditionally accepted, is that it is the same with religious doctrines. They, too, should be abandoned once enlightenment is reached. From the Buddhist perspective, the value of a religious doctrine inheres in the assistance that it lends a person's spiritual transformation. A religion, even if not entirely satisfactory, is true to the extent that it embodies the eight-fold path and encourages selfless charity, compassion and understanding.

There is thus a strong strain within Buddhism to evaluate other religions not in terms of their truth but in terms of their effects. The Dalai Lama expresses precisely this point of view.

> Philosophical teachings are not the end, not the aim, not what you serve. The aim is to help and benefit others, and philosophical teachings to support those ideas are valuable. If we go into the differences in philosophy and argue with and criticise each other, it is useless. It is better to look at the purpose of the philosophies and to see what is shared – an emphasis on love, compassion, and respect for a higher force.[12]

Asked by a questioner whether Christian theism conflicts with Buddhism, the Dalai Lama is careful to say that 'the different religions teach different doctrines which help to transform the person.' Yes, he further admits, from a philosophical point of view, the idea of a creator God conflicts with Buddhism, according to which 'the universe has no first cause and hence no creator.'[13] Still, despite these doctrinal conflicts, the Dalai Lama affirms an identity of purpose in the two religions. Just as different people like different dishes, the Dalai Lama says, so different people like different doctrines.

Pressed further on whether Christians and Hindus can attain liberation, the Dalai Lama responds that not even Buddhists attain liberation in a single lifetime. Thus, he says, 'when I meet the followers of different religions, I always praise them, for it is enough, it is sufficient, that they are following the moral teachings that are emphasised in every religion.'[14]

Still not satisfied, the questioner asks whether it is only Buddhism that grants ultimate salvation. Finally, the Dalai Lama reluctantly concedes that 'liberation in which "a mind that understands the sphere of reality annihilates all defilements in the sphere of reality" is a state that only Buddhists can accomplish.'[15]

I have mixed feelings about this exchange. On the one hand, I totally concur that it is enough for a person to develop love and compassion – I do not even care about acknowledgement of a higher force – and needless to believe this or that. I am further moved by the compassion behind the Dalai Lama's refusal to engage in argument with proponents of other religions. What most worries the Dalai Lama is that in challenging another's religion, the challenger may not succeed in converting the other to Buddhism but only leave the other with a weakened faith in his or her own religious path.

To the extent that the other's religious path serves love and compassion, I agree that this consequence is to be avoided.

On the other hand, the critical realist in me empathises with the frustration of the questioner and cheers his or her success in finally pulling the Dalai Lama on to ontologically solid ground. It is only when ontological ground has been touched that philosophical debate can begin.

Not all Buddhists are as reluctant as the Dalai Lama to espouse ontological commitments. Even for the Dalai Lama, it is important to see that, however much certain strains of Buddhism attempt to distance themselves from ontological commitments, they ultimately must hold them.[16]

Ontological commitments are important, important even to the furtherance of love and compassion. Many of us Christians who pursue the development of love and compassion do so because, for us, these virtues have an ontological status that is bound up with the ontological status we accord Jesus. Thus, just as the Dalai Lama seems to fear, we are troubled to hear that, were we at a further stage of enlightenment, we would regard Jesus more truly as just a raft. To the extent that Jesus is the *raison d'être* of our own love and compassion, those of us who think about truth must wonder whether or not the hold Jesus has over us can be replaced emotionally by something truer or deeper or if it is the Buddhists who are mistaken. And, yes, just as the Dalai Lama fears, for those of us who think about truth, the discrepancy between our two religions must also raise the question of whether or not either Christianity or Buddhism is true and if love and compassion are as ontologically fundamental as both Christianity and Buddhism maintain.

Such reflections are why those of us who think about truth seek inter-religious debate. We seek it because it is our own, admittedly dangerous, path to growth. We seek debate less to convince others of anything than to convince ourselves. Ultimately, what we may want to be convinced of is that love and compassion are truly ontologically fundamental. For us Christians, our stake is in Jesus, but if it is the truth we are seeking, then, should the weight of argument demand it, we are prepared, as Cobb puts it, in faithfulness to Jesus even to give up Jesus for the sake of truth. It follows that inter-religious debate cannot be confessional, a debate where Christians in particular hold back some ultimate faith in Jesus that can never be relinquished.[17] When one enters such debate, all cards must be placed on the table.

True, each of us will still enter the debate from his or her own faith perspective. My assumption in such a case is that what will and should operate is a kind of personal standpoint approach, where the burden of proof is asymmetric. In other words, whatever faith perspective we come from, the burden will always be on the other to convince us that our own faith perspective is in error. For Hindus, then, the burden of proof will be on non-Hindus to show that Hinduism is in error – and the same for subscribers to every other religion. I say this is as it should be because no one should be expected to give up both what is important and in accord with one's own experience without sufficient warrant, a sufficiency that will vary depending on one's personal religious experience. Still, while each accords one's own religious doctrine a *prima facie* privilege, as a *prima facie* privilege only, our religious beliefs remain susceptible to eventual rejection should the weight of argument demand it.

One reason why many proponents of inter-religious dialogue are reluctant to approve debate is that they are worried that inter-religious dialogue will serve as a pretext for conversion. Attempted conversion strikes me as not philosophically illegitimate if it is allowed to go both ways. To the extent that conversion means persuasion, conversion is what all parties to a debate are out to achieve. Yet, I have spent more than enough time arguing with Christian fundamentalists to know that when one party expects the persuasion to go only one way, what is supposed to be a dialogue ceases to be one. Then, we are talked at rather than talked with.

To the extent that most people cannot handle challenges to their own religion, perhaps inter-religious debate should not be encouraged for everyone. On the other hand, it should be something that can be handled by theologians and their counterparts in other religions.

Still, there is a broader reason for resisting inter-religious debate, which keeps inter-religious dialogue where it now is. Although there is a great deal of inter-religious dialogue going on at different levels, much of it is of the 'getting to know you' variety: people of different religions praying together, inviting each other to their respective religious observances, and sharing their different points of view. The goal is to broaden inter-religious understanding and appreciation and, specifically, to break down stereotypes.

Describing these dialogues as 'getting to know you' sessions sounds dismissive. I confess that as I came to write this piece I was more than a little impatient that this is mostly what there is and mostly what is being called for. Yes, I wanted to say, of course we should listen and understand and appreciate, but what then? When do we get to the good stuff? What about the debate that is the inter-religious search for truth?

I now reflect that as important as an inter-religious search for truth may be, the world is not ready for it. My empiricist American colleagues sometimes accuse me of being more of a philosopher than a sociologist. In the case of my impatience for religious debate, I so charge myself. Thus, I am chagrined to admit, it has taken a theologian, Leonard Swidler, to remind me that inter-religious dialogue is not something practised by isolated individuals but by communities.[18]

As a practice of communities rather than individuals alone, inter-religious dialogue is a more complex undertaking. In the first place, we need to consider the larger socio-historical context in which inter-religious dialogue takes place. At a communal level, interest in inter-religious dialogue is a virtue. In the case of Christianity, however, it is a virtue that comes as a gift of hegemony and imperialist oppression. If, as seems the case, Christianity is more prepared for inter-religious dialogue than other religious communities, that preparedness partly results from Christianity's longer history of contact with other faith communities.[19] This longer history in turn involves a connection with imperialism in which Christianity itself aggressively sought to win over members of other faiths and in which it did not refrain from persecution to do so.

This historical context does not inspire trust in any ostensibly dispassionate call from the Christian side for an inter-religious debate on truth. Judaism today in particular has been greatly shaped by its history of negative treatment at the hands of Christianity. When I was about to marry, I was prepared to become Jewish as well as Christian. For a Christian, there is no doctrinal difficulty in being both. To my surprise, however, I was quickly told by the rabbi who would perform the service that this option was impossible.

One can be Jewish without believing in God. As far as I can tell, one can even be a kind of Buddhist Jew. In contrast, one cannot be Jewish and accept Jesus in anything like the Christian way. Cobb is tendentious when he speaks of some Jews who believe in Jesus as the Messiah.[20] From the standpoint of the larger Jewish community, such Messianic Jews are no longer Jews. They are instead despised as a Christian fifth column.

Philosophically, I continue to have difficulty with this Jewish position. Jews say that whenever you get two of them together, you will invariably get three opinions. Never, however, is one of those opinions allowed to be Christianity. What bothers me philosophically is the *a priori* closure of one possibility in a religion otherwise so doctrinally open. If it is allowable for Jews even to disbelieve in God, why should it not be allowed to have an admittedly peculiar belief for a Jew about how God once chose to manifest himself to us?

For all my philosophical difficulty with the Jewish position on Jesus, it is fully understandable sociologically. Unlike Christianity, Judaism is not just a religion but a culture, and culturally Judaism has survived in opposition to Christian intolerance, so much so that not being Christian is now part of what it means culturally to be Jewish. Thus, to accept Christian beliefs is culturally to cease being Jewish. To that extent, accepting Jesus is tantamount to threatening Jewish survival and to betraying the victims of the Holocaust.

History is not the only issue here. There is also Christianity's continued dominance in the world. At Christmas, I sometimes complain to my wife about how the world treats this sacred Christian holiday. My wife in turn asks me to consider what it is like to be Jewish when the entire world seems to be honouring Jesus. Although, despite the odds, Jews have endured for thousands of years, they remain a tiny fraction of the world's population. They, more than Christianity, are hurt by inter-faith marriages such as my own.

I, too, think it important to the world that Jewish culture endures. If that means placing certain philosophical possibilities off-limits, it is perhaps a trade-off that, from a sociological perspective, must be. This tension between sociology and philosophy is one way in which inter-community dialogue is more complicated than a dialogue among isolated individuals.

There is yet another complication with inter-community dialogue and so another reason why I repent of my earlier dismissiveness of what I called the 'getting to know you' level of much inter-religious dialogue. Communities are composed of people, people who are at many different levels of knowledge about other religions. Within each community, few are at the level of theologians. A great many remain parochial, uninformed and even positively ethnocentric. The director of our campus Hillel chapter recently told me that when she was in Texas, many people had never even met a Jewish person. On learning that she herself was Jewish, one Texan expressed genuine surprise that she lacked horns. I remember doing a double-take. True, Texas is the home state of George W. Bush and the execution capital of the world. Still, even in Texas, such ignorance is almost too preposterous to be believed.

In the face of such ignorance, an inter-religious search for truth is very far from being placeable on the agenda. I concede: by all means, we must do everything we can for different religious communities to get to know one another.

Now, after September 11, it is particularly important that Westerners get to know Islam better. In America, Christians and Jews both persistently associate Islam with extremism and terrorism. Extremism and terrorism are admittedly there, just as they are in Christianity and Judaism. Here, it is important to heed the second of Swidler's desiderata of inter-religious dialogue: avoid comparing our faith's ideals with another faith's practice.[21]

Clearly, comparing our faith's ideals with another faith's practice is a recipe for making ourselves look good. As we hardly live up to our own ideals, we should not expect those from another faith tradition necessarily to live up to theirs. Since people's ideals generally exceed their practice, in comparing our ideals to another's practice, we appear loftier. But it is an unfair comparison. If we want to focus on another faith community's practice, then it is our own practice we should examine. If we want to focus on our ideals, then it is their ideals that we should compare with ours.

When it comes to ideals, Islam's are much in line with those of Christianity and Judaism. Many Westerners may be surprised at how much of Judaism and Christianity is contained in the Koran. The Koran mentions Noah, Abraham, Lot and Moses. It teaches that God made a covenant with Israel. It ranks Jesus as a great prophet of God, who was born of a virgin and worked miracles. Although, like the New Testament, the Koran reports that Jesus was sentenced to crucifixion, it reveals that God actually preserved Jesus from death by lifting him up beforehand to the divine presence. The Koran denies, of course, that Jesus is in any special sense the son of God – who is affirmed as quite beyond having offspring – but even so, Jesus appears as no poor second to Muhammad, who was not virgin-born, did not perform miracles, and who was not lifted bodily into heaven.

Not only does Islam share much with both Judaism and Christianity, there is even in Islam a certain reverence for the specific ideals expressed by Jesus. Within some Muslim quarters, Jesus is in fact criticised for exclusively teaching an ethical standard too high for all but saints; he should rather have also taught an acceptable lower standard to be followed by lesser mortals. Consider, for example, the comments of Seyyed Hossein Nasr.

> Christian ethics is seen by Muslims as being too sublime for ordinary human beings to follow, the injunction to turn the other cheek being meant only for saints. That is why Sufis call Christ the prophet of inwardness and the spiritual life. But since all human beings are not saints, this Christian morality is seen by Muslims as neglecting the reality of human nature, and of substituting an unattainable ideal.[22]

This criticism reflects among Muslims a shared valuation of the ethical ideals taught and embodied by Jesus. For many of us Christians, it is the very sublimeness of Jesus's teaching and practice that evokes in us the numinous awe associated with the 'wholly other', which prompts us ultimately to see in Jesus the incarnation of the divine. Even if Muslims do not draw the same conclusion, it is welcome to see Muslims, too, moved by the ethical ideals that Jesus represents. To the extent, furthermore, that Islam incorporates this Christian ethical ideal, Muslim and Christian ideals coincide.

From the opposite direction, the Muslim criticism (also) coincides in a way with a criticism I myself have levelled at Christendom. In my book, *Landscapes of the Soul*, I interviewed people of different religious backgrounds.[23] When I spoke with Christians, I invariably asked what ethical standard they thought Jesus taught. Invariably, the Christian answer was the golden rule: do unto others what you would have them do unto you.[24] Against this interpretation, I went on to argue that the golden rule was not Jesus's ethical standard but a watered down version of it, an undemanding ethic for everyday souls. What Jesus actually preached, I said, was a demanding, supererogatory ethic, better called the 'platinum rule': do unto others as God does unto you. Jesus called us in other words not to a human standard of goodness but to God's. By watering down Jesus's ethic from the platinum to the golden rule, Christians, I argued, were letting themselves off lightly.

The implication of the Muslim criticism is that my argument is as unrealistic as Jesus's original teaching. The platinum rule may be an ideal, but ordinary people need a lesser standard towards which to strive. Although I am not sure I accept the implicit, essentialist distinction between saints and ordinary people, the evidence seems against me. In a world where we have enough difficulty conforming to the golden rule, perhaps the platinum rule is an unrealistic standard. In any case, on their own, Christians clearly have innovated the 'more realistic' ethical standard that Muslims find missing from Jesus's original message. In the end, as both popular ideal and as practice, Muslim and Christian ethics converge.

As an activity conducted by communities rather than isolated individuals, inter-religious dialogue has other important objectives that lie in between getting to know each other and jointly searching for truth. Among the important objectives that lie in between is joint action for a better world.

Among the most successful of these initiatives is the inter-faith formulation of a global ethic. Hans Kung, a Catholic theologian long devoted to inter-religious dialogue, had been pressing for such a formulation since his book, *Global Responsibility: In Search of a New World Ethic.*[25] Kung's interest coincided with that of the Council for a Parliament of the World's Religions, which was formed in 1988 in order to plan a centennial celebration of the first such parliament, held in 1893. Kung was accordingly approached to submit a first draft of a world ethic for consideration at the second parliament in 1993.

Kung did so, and with some revision a global, inter-faith ethic was approved at the 1993 parliament. Since some two hundred authoritative representatives of the world's religions were among the signatories, the formulation carries no little weight.[26]

Although in the approved global ethic the world religions do not converge on the platinum rule, they do at least agree on the golden rule, expressly endorsing non-violence and human rights. It is remarkable that any ethical consensus at all could be achieved. It is an achievement that is not just socially but also philosophically important. Such convergence indicates that, at some level at least, the world's religions, despite their diversity, all point in the same ethical direction.

The philosophical question raised is what explains this convergence. The ability of widely different religions to reach basic consensus on ethics suggests that religious languages are hardly as incommensurable as post-modernists would allege, and that ethical sensibilities are not as wildly subjective as ethical relativists would maintain. It is almost as if there are some objective ethical considerations to which the world's great faiths are all simultaneously attending.

It is true, as Cobb would warn, that agreement on a common ethical statement does not ensure that the statement will be read in the same way by all signatories.[27] Cobb, nevertheless, still expresses amazement at what has been accomplished. What is particularly significant is that the parliamentary statement affirms the universality of human rights as something neither relative nor subject to cultural variation. Instead, for the Parliament of Religions, the humane treatment of both men and women is an ontological bottom line.[28] With the world's major faiths all united in their acceptance of the concept of human rights, the burden of proof would seem to shift decisively to those secular philosophies that would characterise human rights as just a social construction.

I said at the beginning of this chapter that most of the literature on inter-religious dialogue seems more like a Christian propaedeutic to such a dialogue than the actual dialogue itself. I went on to say, however, that the literature is actually more than just that. True, as far as I can tell, most of the dialogue is intra-religiously Christian rather than inter-religious. Still, rather than a propaedeutic, the literature represents one half of the dual dialogue that must occur when it is communities that are the interlocutors. Let us hear one last time from Swidler: 'Inter-religious, inter-ideological dialogue must be a two-sided project within each religious or ideological community and between religious and ideological communities.'[29]

Because inter-religious dialogue is corporate, Swidler points out, the results of the conversation between communities must be shared and digested through dialogue within each community. What is required, then, is both a forward dialogue across communities and a series of backward dialogues within each. It is the requisite backward dialogue of this project that the Christian literature on inter-religious dialogue actually represents. The peculiarity is that this backward dialogue is taking place without much of the forward dialogue across communities that would make the whole genuinely inter-religious.

In a sense, the Christian community is carrying on an inter-religious dialogue with interlocutors from other religions who are largely – although not completely – *in absentia*. More forward dialogue with other communities would certainly be better. Its relative absence, however, does not prevent the Christian community's backward dialogue from being either a dialogue or inter-religious. The Christian community's backward dialogue is definitely a dialogue, and it is just as definitely inter-religious to the extent that it is resolutely addressed to the reality of religious pluralism. In this sense, Christianity's dialogue with other religions is akin to science's non-verbal dialogue with the world.

The question central to any backward dialogue in any religious community is what to make of the other religions. Their very existence constitutes a challenge to received doctrine, which is typically totalistic. The question then is which totalistic elements need to be softened and which, if any, need to be affirmed and defended. Alternatively, an entirely new metatheory may be needed in which the truths of all religions are partially relativised. In particular, in so far as many of the major religions have historically been framed in terms of personal salvation or liberation from something, an immediate question for each is whether salvation can be attained and by whom outside the faith community.

Within the backward dialogue of the Christian community four major reactions to religious plurality can be identified: exclusivism; inclusivism; pluralism; liberationism.

Strong Christian exclusivism maintains that Christianity is the one correct religion whereas all the others are in error. A natural although not strictly necessary corollary is that only Christians can be saved – whatever salvation may mean. Although today Christian exclusivism appears almost a caricature, it was the received view throughout most of Christian history. Until Vatican II, it found expression in the Catholic position, 'Outside the Church, no salvation'. Similarly, according to the Protestant neo-orthodoxy of at least the early Karl Barth, religion is a form of unbelief in which humanity tries on its own to make its way to God. Only by abandoning religious hubris and accepting the true revelation of God's own initiative in Christ can one be saved.

After Vatican II, the Catholic Church adopted a more inclusive line, carried forward most forcibly first by Karl Rahner and, subsequently, by Hans Kung. Rahner introduced the notion of 'anonymous Christians', believers in other faiths who, through their devotion and goodness, submit to Christ without knowing it.[30] Rahner further granted other religions even their own share of truth. Kung and others have since gone even further in abandoning Christianity's claim to total and exclusive truth.[31] Today, it is inclusivism of some sort that most Catholic and Protestant theologians both affirm.

The theoretical problem for inclusivism is the essential tension between openness to the truths of other religions and the distinctive value placed on the life, death and teaching of the one, historical man, Jesus of Nazareth. To the extent that only Christianity – by its own lights – fully appreciates the significance of Jesus, Christianity, against the other religions, seems to possess a distinctly crucial piece of ultimate truth.

Kung attempts to negotiate this tension by distinguishing between ordinary and extraordinary revelation.[32] All religions – and even secular philosophies, Kung says – may be in receipt of ordinary revelation or knowledge of ultimate reality; in contrast Christianity is also distinctly in possession of extraordinary revelation. Other theologians, such as Dupuis, distinguish between the Christ incarnated in Jesus and the transcendental Logos of history who is otherwise at work in different ways in other religions.[33] Still other theologians assign a similar task to the otherwise under-worked Holy Spirit.

Pluralism is the view championed by the Protestant philosopher and theologian, John Hick. What most impresses Hick is that, despite a diversity of experience and interpretation, all religions affirm the reality of the transcendent. This transcendental reality is the common truth that Hick discerns behind the diversity of religion. Hick speaks of it as occupying a fifth, spiritual dimension.[34]

Much else in the doctrines of individual religions – including Christianity – Hick is content to consider as culturally specific speculation that we need not worry about and that need not keep the religions apart, especially as there is no way to decide who is right. The Buddhist Pali Canon, Hick observes, lists ten unprovable propositions, among them that the universe is infinite or eternal or, conversely, that the universe is finite and not eternal; similarly, that there is a soul that lives on after death or that there is no soul or at least not one that survives death. Following the Buddhist prescription that religious doctrines are primarily a means for human transformation, Hick maintains that we should not be overly concerned about doctrinal differences regarding such matters. 'What we need to know', says Hick, 'is how to behave here and now', and 'it is the basic teaching of all the world religions that we should behave towards others as we would wish others to behave towards us.'[35] In the end, Hick's pluralism adopts an explicitly critical realist view that out of their epistemically relative cultural contexts, the different religions equally apprehend in part a larger spiritual reality that is truly there.

Much philosophical and theological criticism has been levelled against Hick's version of pluralism. It does seem peculiar for an avowed critical realist to dismiss so cavalierly so many religious reality claims as undecidable and not worth thinking about. What is or is not decidable would rather seem to be a conclusion that can only be drawn after a case-by-case debate. In particular, it seems that science might be able to establish whether or not the universe is infinite or eternal. Similarly, there are fairly good – although perhaps inconclusive – grounds on offer in the philosophy of mind for doubting the existence of anything like a soul. It may be that these questions are not yet decided, but it appears premature as an opening gambit to declare them all undecidable in principle.

To dismiss so much of individual religious doctrines as undecidable superfluity comes close, without argument, to vindicating secular humanism or at most Unitarianism. Again, I would agree that our moral posture is more important than the specific doctrinal beliefs that get us there. Yet, to the extent that we only do get there through one or another set of doctrinal beliefs, their truthfulness ought to remain of consequence to each of us on the journey. Whether the Buddhists are actually right that religious doctrines are just ethical instruments is something that itself should be the subject of debate, and, as we have seen, Buddhism itself ultimately holds out for the truth of its own ontology.

More fundamentally, Hick has been much criticised for simply presuming that the ultimate spiritual reality to which the religions point is all the same. Yet, at least for some important strands of Hinduism and Buddhism, ultimate reality is impersonal whereas for the Western religions 'of the book', ultimate reality – God – is deeply personal. Are these two ultimate realities truly the same? If not, is one right and the other wrong or one actually more fundamental than the other?

Hick does address these questions. He answers by appeal to the Kabbalistic distinction between the personal God we encounter in relation to us and the Godhead or infinite or God *Ein Sof*. The latter, God without relation to us, is more ultimate than the God of Western religious experience, conforming more to the infinite, ineffable, category-transcendent reality of Eastern religious experience. Yet, in so far as the Kabbalah and even Christian mystics have also spoken of the ineffable Godhead, there is an underlying convergence, Hick believes, between East and West.

Liberationism is the fourth major Christian approach to religious pluralism. Its proponents include Catholic theologians Paul Knitter and Aloysius Pieris.[36] According to liberationists, theological discussion has often been too preoccupied with personal salvation. What is more important than the question of personal salvation, the liberationists say, is the convergence of major strands within each of the world's religions on the need for collective salvation from oppression, social injustice and environmental degradation.

I personally commend the change in theological emphasis that the liberationists want to effect. Although a preoccupation with personal salvation arguably goes back to the first Christians, it is a preoccupation that I have always considered a diversion from the higher Christian calling. The question, it seems to me, is not whether it is works or faith that gets us into heaven. Rather we should not be thinking over much about heaven at all. For me, to be a Christian is to feel called to emulate the divine love exemplified by Jesus, not for what it will get us now or later but simply because, in this loving kindness, we conform to God's image. Jesus said that those who would save their lives will lose them. I think the same applies even to our souls.

At the heart of the Christian message is a call to forget ourselves. It is the same self-forgetfulness that is prescribed by Buddhism, which is why many find it easy to incorporate Buddhist practice into Christianity. Where Christians must part company with Buddhism is in the idea that all attachment is to be relinquished. To the extent that even a selfless love for others is an attachment, it is one attachment that, from a Christian perspective, should not be renounced but fostered. Buddhism itself seems inconsistent in this regard for it frequently speaks of compassion as the positive result of abandoning all attachment. If this is not an inconsistency, there is something about Buddhism I at least still do not understand. In any case, a Buddhised Christianity would recommend itself less as a better means to personal salvation than as endorsing the abandonment of personal salvation as an ultimate goal. Instead, to the extent that love and compassion presuppose justice and harmony, the goal becomes, as liberationists and bodhisattvas both would have it, the deliverance of the world.

Whatever its merits, the liberationist perspective does not solve all the theological problems that Christianity confronts in a religiously plural world. Even if personal salvation fades as an issue, there remains the unique status Christianity alone assigns to Jesus. If that status is to be upheld, some form of Christian inclusivism seems required. To go as far as Hick, for example, is to abandon Christianity in favour of a pluralistic meta religion. That is not to say that Hick is wrong, that his theology could not be the one at which we arrive at argument's end, but only that Hick's theology is one that no longer is specifically Christian.

This chapter is not the place to debate Christianity's four major theological responses to religious diversity. What is important to keep in mind is that they all represent part of the backward dialogue that the Christian community is having with itself in response to religious plurality and inter-religious dialogue. The four responses are not primarily contributions to Christianity's forward dialogue with other religions. While specifically Christian dialogue with other religions should always begin with and reflect a Christian perspective, forward dialogue ought to be more exploratory and less committed to any specific theological conclusion.

One sociological problem is that, in the absence of much actual forward dialogue, Christianity's backward dialogue with itself can be misunderstood as itself being forward dialogue. It is this mistake the Hindu, Bibhuti Yadav, seems to make when he lambastes Hans Kung's inclusivist theology as covertly imperialistic. 'Hans Kung', Yadav says, 'is authorised to say that Krishna's birth was not a case of Logos becoming flesh, that Vaishnavism is based on a popular superstition and is unhistorical and mythical.'[37] Yadav goes on:

> His [Kung's] redemptive theology is too fat to be confined to diplomatic niceties, however; it makes God look naively ridiculous. God [being a] Christian and committed to [the] equality of man has revealed himself to all, but not as absolutely and conclusively as to those who happened to be in Jerusalem. Not that the world religions do not have truth concerning the true God; they indeed do. They are only in error, and proclaim the truth of the true God in spite of the fact that they are in error.
>
> It is not that Hans Kung does not love his Buddhist and Hindu brothers. On the contrary, he finds 'no foundation for any theory or practice that leads to discrimination between man and man or people and people'. He only insists that the 'just Father' loves him in a 'special' way, an 'extraordinary' way and his brothers in a 'general' way, an 'ordinary' way.[38]

If Kung were offering his inclusivist theology to Hindus as an opening to further, forward dialogue with them, Hindus would have every reason for offence. Why should Hindus continue a dialogue that presumes at the outset that they possess only partial or ordinary truth, whereas Christianity alone possesses the full truth that comes from both ordinary revelation and its own extraordinary revelation?

Kung's theology, however, is not forward dialogue at all. It is a contribution to Christianity's backward dialogue with itself, an attempt by the Christian community to accommodate its own truth claims to what Griffiths calls the 'alien truth claims' of other religions.[39]

The implication is not that a faith community's backward dialogue is immune to criticism from other faith communities. The implication is rather that forward and backward dialogues cannot be judged on the same grounds. Whereas forward dialogue must proceed without assigning public privilege to any community's truth claims but rather with all truth claims being equally up for inspection and debate, backward dialogue must proceed from what each community currently regards as truth.

It may well be that certain strains of Hinduism interpret alien truth claims more generously than does Christianity. Generous and tolerant inclusivity is an important quality, but does not in itself decide the truth. If inclusiveness were the sole criterion, we could declare Hick's religious pluralism the victor at the outset. On the contrary, however, it could turn out that some version of Christianity or some other equally rigid religion is actually correct and others are simply wrong. I am not saying that matters will turn out this way but only that they could. How they will turn out can only be decided by an actual debate over rival truth claims that employs all the normal criteria for deciding truth. In this regard, against Yadav, it certainly does seem pertinent – although how decisively is another matter – that Jesus was an historical person while Krishna is not. In any case, it follows from the principle of epistemic relativism that each religious community must struggle towards truth from wherever it currently is.

In closing, I return to the question with which I began this chapter and which originally motivated it: is it possible for believers in different religions to adjudicate their rival truth claims through dialogue? After introducing myself to the literature on inter-religious dialogue, I am no longer certain that such dialogue can or should be done now. The reason, however, is political or social rather than philosophical. Our different religious communities do not seem ready to conduct such a dialogue dispassionately or harmoniously. That being the case, we probably should not engage in it.

This conclusion, however, hardly means that in principle no such dialogue can be conducted. On the contrary, philosophically speaking, such dialogue seems entirely possible. Biblical criticism has raised strong doubts about the historicity of much that is in the Bible. If people named Noah, Lot and even Moses ever existed, their histories in the Bible are clearly far from historical. Similarly mythical rather than historical are the infancy narratives of Jesus, including his virgin birth. To the extent that the Koran seems to accept uncritically the historicity of all this Jewish and Christian material, there is reason to adopt the same doubts about the Koran's unmediated transmission from God as we have learned to entertain about the Bible's.

Similarly, there is much that Jews and Christians can say to one another about the historical person of Jesus. This conversation has already begun, and the trend in Christian Biblical criticism today is to paint a much more Jewish picture of Jesus. Perhaps when this picture has been fully painted, Judaism may one day be able to reappropriate Jesus as one of its own.

Even between East and West, there is much that can and already has been said. Is reincarnation to be taken literally or, as Herbert Fingarette has proposed, is it better understood as a mythical expression of an existential truth about this one life we live?[40] If reincarnation is to be taken literally, is some mind–body dualism implied? If so, there are all sorts of conceptual problems that will need to be confronted. On the other hand, we must all remain open to surprise. For a non-reductive materialist like me, for example, it has been pleasantly disconcerting to come across Ian Stevenson's documentation of what do seem like cases of literal reincarnation.[41]

In terms of the applicability of critical realism to religion, it does not matter that politically inter-religious adjudication of truth claims is something we cannot or should not do now. What matters philosophically is that it be something we could do. There is no principled reason for supposing otherwise. True, we lack an Archimedean standpoint from which to adjudicate rival religious claims, but we are in the same position with regard to rival scientific claims. Critical realism holds that rival scientific claims can still be adjudicated even without such an Archimedean standpoint. If one disputes that premiss, one has problems with critical realism itself rather than with the particular application of critical realism to religion. Conversely, if such adjudication can be accomplished in science, there is no reason in principle why it cannot also be accomplished in religion.

The truth is, it must be accomplished in religion – at least by each of us individually. Today, each of us believers lives in a pluralist context where we regularly confront those who believe differently. This context presents us with what Peter Berger calls the 'heretical imperative'.[42] The heretical imperative is the imperative for thinking people to choose rather than simply imbibe their religion. As long as we see people who believe differently, it must occur to any of us who are thinking persons that someone believes wrongly. The thinking person must certainly wonder whether that someone is him or her. To address that doubt in a self-critical, fair-minded way, the thinking person must – at least for himself or herself – adjudicate among rival religious truth claims. Perhaps the time will come when this can be done not just by us internally and individually but as members of the religious communities to which we belong.

Notes

1   The only book I found that contained a truly inter-religious dialogue was Paul Griffiths', *Christianity Through Non-Christian Eyes*, (Orbis, Maryknoll, 2001). Now in its seventh printing, it was first published in 1990. It contains a good but sparse response to Christianity from other religious perspectives. Griffiths (p. 247) notes that the only other such collection appeared a quarter of a century before his.

Mohamed Talbi, an Islamic author of one piece in Griffiths' collection wrote in 1986 that 'as far as I know we cannot mention one real Muslim Christologist to set besides the numerous Christian lay people and clerics who are Islamologists' (p. 86). See Talbi, 'Islam and Dialogue – Some Reflections on a Current Topic'. The situation may have changed since 1986. Yet a perusal of the bibliographies of different books on inter-religious dialogue reveals interlocutors who are almost exclusively Christian authors.

2 See John B. Cobb, Jr., *Transforming Christianity and the World: A Way Beyond Absolutism and Relativism*, edited and introduced by Paul Knitter, (Orbis, Maryknoll, 1999), which is an edited collection of Cobb's essays, each introduced by Knitter. See particularly pp. 46–7 in the essay 'The Meaning of Pluralism for Christian Self-Understanding'.

3 See Cobb, *Transforming Christianity*, p. 44, 'The Meaning of Pluralism for Christian Self-Understanding'.

4 See Cobb, *Transforming Christianity*, pp. 62–75, 'Beyond Pluralism'.

5 See Clifford Geertz, 'Religion as a Cultural System' in M. Banton (ed.), *Anthropological Approaches to the Study of Religion*, Routledge, London, 1990; R.B. Braithwaite, 'The Nature of Religious Belief', in Basil Mitchell, *The Philosophy of Religion*, Oxford University Press, Oxford, 1971; and George Lindbeck, *The Nature of Doctrine: Religion and Theology in a Postliberal Age*, Westminster John Knox Press, Philadelphia, 1984.

6 Cobb, *Transforming Christianity*, p. 148, 'Proclaiming Christ in a Pluralistic World'.

7 Cobb, *Transforming Christianity*, pp. 161–2, 'Can Comparative Religious Ethics Help?'.

8 Douglas Porpora, *Landscapes of the Soul: The Loss of Moral Meaning in American Life*, Oxford and New York, Oxford University Press, 2001.

9 Andrew Collier, *On Christian Belief*, Routledge, London, 2003.

10 See, for example, Jason Barker's electronic piece 'Christians and Inter-religious Dialogue', http://www.watchman.org/reltop/christiandialogue.htm

11 Cobb, *Transforming Christianity*, p. 73, 'Beyond Pluralism'.

12 See H.H. The XIVth Dalai Lama, 'Religious Harmony' and 'Extracts from the Bodhgaya Interviews', pp. 162–70 in Griffiths, *Christianity*, p. 164.

13 Griffiths, *Christianity*, p. 167.

14 Griffiths, *Christianity*, p. 169.

15 Griffiths, *Christianity*, p. 169.

16 Griffiths makes this point in his editor's section-introduction *Christianity*, pp. 162–3.

17 Cobb, *Transforming Christianity*, pp. 45–6, 'The Meaning of Pluralism for Christian Self-Understanding' and pp. 183–4, 'Concluding Reflections'.

18 Leonard Swidler, 'The Dialogue Decalogue', an electronic article, http://www.silcom.com/-origin/sbcr/sbcr265.

19 Talbi, in Griffiths, *Christianity*, concedes that Christianity does seem more prepared for inter-religious dialogue.

20 Cobb, *Transforming Christianity*, p. 154, 'Proclaiming Christ in a Pluralistic World'.

21 Swidler, 'The Dialogue Decalogue'.

22 Seyyed Hossein Nasr, 'The Islamic View of Christianity' in Griffiths, *Christianity*, pp. 126–34, 130.

23 Porpora, *Landscapes*.

24 Following my analysis, Anna Wierzbicka coined the term 'platinum rule' for what I identified as Jesus's ethic. See Wierzbicka, *What Did Jesus Mean?: Explaining the Sermon on the Mount and the Parables in Simple and Universal Human Concepts*. Oxford University Press, Oxford, 2001.

25 Hans Kung, *Global Responsibility: In Search of a New World Ethic*, Crossroad/Herder & Herder, New York, 1991.

26 See Daniel Gomez-Ibanez, former Executive Director of the Parliament of the World's Religions, 'Moving Towards a Global Ethic', an electronic piece, http://wwwsilcom.com/-origin/sbcr/sbcr231

27 Cobb, *Transforming Christianity*, pp. 167–78, 'Can Comparative Religious Ethics Help?'.

28 Cobb, *Transforming Christianity*, pp. 167–78. See also the ethic itself on the website for the Parliament of the World's Religions, http://www.conjure.com/CTS/ethic.html

29 Swidler, 'The Dialogue Decalogue'.

30 Karl Rahner, 'Christianity and the Non-Christian Religions', pp. 19–38 in John Hick and Brian Hebblethwaite (eds), *Christianity and Other Religions: Selected Readings*, Oneworld, Oxford, 2001.

31 Hans Kung, 'Is There One True Religion? An Essay in Establishing Ecumenical Criteria', pp. 118–45 in Hick and Hebblethwaite, *Christianity and Other Religions*.

32 Kung, 'Is There One True Religion?'.

33 Jacques Dupuis, *Toward a Christian Theology of Religious Pluralism*, Orbis, Maryknoll, 1997.

34 John Hick, *The Fifth Dimension: An Exploration of the Spiritual Realm*, Oneworld, Oxford, 1999.

35 Hick, *The Fifth Dimension*, p. 227.

36 See Paul Knitter, 'Christian Theology of Liberation and Interfaith Dialogue' (pp. 146–55) and Aloysius Pieris, 'The Place of Non-Christian Religions and Cultures in the Evolution of Third World Theology' (pp. 59–87), both in Hick and Hebblethwaite, *Christianity and Other Religions*.

37 Bibhuti S. Yadav, 'Vaishnavism on Hans Kung: A Hindu Theology of Religious Pluralism', pp. 234–46 in Griffiths, *Christianity*, p. 242.

38 Yadav, 'Vaishnavism', p. 243.

39 Griffiths, *Christianity*, pp. 7–9 in volume introduction.

40 Herbert Fingarette, *The Self in Transformation: Psychoanalysis, Philosophy and the Life of the Spirit*, Doubleday, New York, 1977.

41 Thomas Shroder, *Old Souls: Compelling Evidence From Children Who Remember Past Lives*, Fireside, New York, 2001.

42 Peter Berger, *The Heretical Imperative*, Doubleday, New York, 1980.

9 Natural theology, revealed theology and religious experience

Andrew Collier

Most modern Protestant theology, in the wake of Karl Barth, rejects the idea of natural theology and insists that all theology is revealed theology. Often, though not always, this theology is suspicious of appeals to religious experience, and tends to assimilate experience-based religious epistemology to natural theology. The argument of this chapter is that while the motives behind the rejection of natural theology are worthy of respect, what is needed is a certain kind of caution with regard to natural theology rather than outright rejection of it; and that so far from the epistemology of religious experience being compromised by the dangers of natural theology, it is essential to any account of revealed theology.

Natural and revealed theology

The distinction between natural and revealed theology goes back to the Middle Ages. It was held, for instance, by Thomas Aquinas, that parts of theology – for example, the existence of God – could be proved with certainty by pure reason, while other parts – for example, the Trinity – could not, and depended on revelation vouchsafed by the authority of the Church. Belief in these was equally certain, but was 'faith' not 'knowledge'. This did not mean, though, that it was groundless: it was held that belief in the authority of the Church was rational, just as we (by and large) regard the authority of the scientific community as rational today.

There are, I think, several things wrong with this view. First, no area of substantive knowledge (i.e. of knowledge outside logic and mathematics) is demonstrable with certainty by pure reason. It is all based also on experience, and is fallible. So if natural theology is conceived in the rationalistic way that it was in the Middle Ages, there really is no natural theology. Second, even the most rationally well-founded authority – the scientific community, for instance – is also fallible, and must justify its (fallible) authority at the bar of reason and experience in any instance. Just as science can point to its experiments and the power of its hypotheses to explain natural phenomena, so the Church, if it is to be believed, must be able to give an account of the reasons for its beliefs; it cannot simply say: believe this because we say so.

However, there might still be both natural and revealed theologies consisting, in the words of the Quaker Swarthmore Lecture of 1982, not in unreasonable certainties, but in reasonable uncertainties.[1]

Is there any natural theology of this kind? Let us look at the teleological argument. As stated by Thomas Aquinas, I think this can be paraphrased as consisting of three steps:

1   there is teleology in nature (that is, at least some natural things are directed towards goals);
2   teleology always requires an explanation;
3   the only explanation available for teleology in nature is design by a non-human intelligence. (In point of fact Aquinas coalesces points 2 and 3, but it is useful to distinguish them.)

Note that step 1 does not say that there is design in nature. It says that natural processes work towards an end, or that natural objects are explained by their function. When modern biologists deny that there is teleology in nature, they usually mean either that we do not need to postulate an intelligence to explain natural phenomena, or that teleological phenomena in nature have a non-teleological (Darwinian) explanation. They are denying step 3 or affirming step 2, not denying step 1. Once this is recognised, I think it becomes highly implausible to deny step 1. When we have discovered what the function of an animal's organ is, we have discovered why it has got it. When we have discovered that the dance of various species leads to mating, we have discovered why it occurs. That is teleology. Step 1 does not have the indubitability of logic or mathematics, but it comes as near certain as anything else does. Step 2 is slightly more dubitable: one might believe that teleological phenomena are the result of extraordinary coincidences. But it is pretty plausible. By itself, a teleological explanation looks like backwards-running causality: the mating which will happen in half an hour's time explains the dance that is happening now. But this mystery is removed when the teleology itself is explained: the kettle is boiling now because I am going to have a cup of tea in five minutes. This is not mysterious since my desire for the tea precedes the boiling of the kettle. So teleology becomes non-mysterious when there is an intelligence behind it. *One* way of making teleology in nature non-mysterious is by postulating a non-human intelligence behind it. And there needs to be *some* way of making teleology non-mysterious: it requires explanation.

But step 3 states that a non-human intelligence is the *only* way of explaining teleology in nature. That must have seemed true in Thomas Aquinas's time, but not today. For we are familiar with another explanation of teleology in nature, namely natural selection. Since Darwin, the functionality of animal organs, the goal of animal dances, can be explained in evolutionary terms, without recourse to a designing intelligence. So for the teleological argument to work, one would need to show that there were some teleological phenomena in nature that cannot be accounted for by natural selection. And it seems that there are, namely the so-called 'anthropic coincidences' in cosmology and the 'Gaia phenomena' in ecology. Of course, a third explanation for teleological phenomena, apart from natural selection and intelligence, may yet be discovered. But at the present state of knowledge, the idea of an intelligence behind nature looks like an odds-on bet. 'An intelligence', of course, is consistent with, but does not imply, 'the God of Biblical religion', or any other theistic concept. But more of that later.

Now let us look at the Protestant objections to natural theology. While this is most trenchant in Barth, it has its roots in the Reformation, so let us look first at two theses presented by Martin Luther for disputation at Heidelberg in 1518.

> 19. The one who beholds what is invisible of God, through the perception of what is made [cf. Romans 1.20], is not rightly called a theologian.
> 20. But rather the one who perceives what is visible of God, God's 'backside' [Exodus 33.23], by beholding the sufferings and the cross.[2]

What is the motive for this preference for the theology of the cross over creation theology? We must remember that Luther, prior to his experience connected with the verse 'the just shall live by faith', experienced God as a frightening, hostile being. The theology of the cross counteracts this by setting forth God's self-sacrifice for humankind. The hostile god was for Luther primarily the god of law and retribution, but God as creator could be seen in the same way, as the source of famine, disease and death. Of course, Luther does not deny that God is creator: he goes on to say that the problem is that 'without a theology of the cross, man misuses the best things in the worst way' (Dillenberger, *Martin Luther*, p. 503). In other words, once we know from the cross that God is in essence unconditional love, we can worship God as creator (and indeed as law-giver) without danger. But if we *start* from creation theology, we will end with a hideous idol whose nature is to destroy as much as to create. In so far as the theology of the cross is revealed theology and natural theology is necessarily creation theology, we can say that Luther's position does not rule out natural theology, but insists that revealed theology must always be the judge of it.

The case of Barth is rather different. The political stimuli of many of his theological breakthroughs are becoming increasingly well known.[3] Paradoxically, what political events stimulated him to do was to draw as sharp a line as possible between politics (and indeed human culture generally) and theology. It started with the outbreak of the war in 1914, and the shocking discovery that many of the liberal Protestant theologians on whom Barth had been brought up – many of his own teachers – had signed the statement of support for the Kaiser's war aims. One of them, Adolf von Harnack, had helped to draw it up. What was wrong with their theology that made this possible? For Barth, their identification of the Kingdom of God with a purely human phenomenon, namely bourgeois civilisation. Although Barth was a lifelong democratic socialist, and active at different times in the Swiss and German Social Democratic Parties, his objection was not that the theologians had misidentified the work of God on earth – had opted for bourgeoisie not proletariat – but that they had identified the divine work with a human work. He came to have a rooted objection to any conjunction of a sacred adjective with a secular noun: Christian civilisation, a Christian state, a Christian party, the Christian family, and so on. Hence his advice that a Christian might by all means join the socialist party, or the army, but should not become a 'religious socialist', or an army chaplain.

When Hitler came to power, this line of Barth's became the theological backbone of resistance to Nazism within the Protestant Churches. Nazism was idolatry: it identified a purely human movement with the will of God. So far so good. But Barth also took exception to natural theology as the supposed epistemological basis of Bismarckism and Nazism. The roots of this are in the words of one of his teachers, Wilhelm Hermann: 'a proved God is world, and a God of the world is an idol.'[4] During his struggle with Nazism, he insisted that the founding heresy that led inevitably to Nazism was natural theology.

Yet this is very odd. In the first place, the nineteenth-century liberal Protestantism in which, according to Barth, the rot set in, was not given to natural theology in the true sense. It either followed Schleiermacher in basing its epistemology on religious experience, or it followed Ritschl in locating religion on the moral side of the Kantian gulf between epistemological and moral reason. So Barth's hostility to natural theology inherits rather than breaks with the tradition of nineteenth-century liberal Protestantism. Barth seems to think that the openness of that tradition to the secular philosophies of its day was itself a concession to natural theology; but in the first place this is not so: for a theology to engage with and use a secular philosophy is not to deduce its theological conclusions from natural premises, and may even (if that philosophy is Kantian, for example) preclude doing so. And in the second place, the permeation of Nazi ideas into the Churches did certainly not come about on philosophical grounds. It is curious that Barth was surprised when Bultmann joined the (anti-Nazi) Confessing Church; he had expected him to join the 'German Christians'; this because, despite Bultmann's closeness to Barth over natural theology, Bultmann was openly influenced by a secular philosophy, existentialism. Furthermore, the main advocates of natural theology in the twentieth century have been neither liberals nor Nazis, but Catholics and Protestant fundamentalists.

Barth's linking of natural theology to Nazism is just one instance of that activity which few twentieth-century thinkers – particularly left-wing ones – have been able to resist: tarring their intellectual opponents with the brush of political perniciousness. But any intellectual position can lead to any number of political tendencies depending on which other beliefs it is combined with. Natural theology – more specifically the teleological argument – can in fact quite easily lead to pernicious politics, but only when combined with a particular philosophical fallacy, namely the epistemic fallacy.

To make this clear, let us start with one of Hume's objections to the teleological argument – the only one that holds any water. From a watch, one can infer a watchmaker, but not a watchmaker who is also a faithful husband and a fine operatic tenor. He may be, for all we know, but we have no reason to believe so. From teleology in nature we can (for the sake of argument) infer an intelligence, but not an infinitely wise and loving intelligence. So far Hume is absolutely right. But one cannot rule out the possibility that he[5] is infinitely wise and loving either, and one may have independent grounds for believing so. If, however, one commits the epistemic fallacy – the reduction of questions of what is to questions of what we can know – one will reduce the being of the intelligence proved by the argument to the qualities proved by the argument itself; one would then be led to postulate a finite and imperfect, partly creative but partly destructive intelligence to account for those qualities in the nature from which he is proved. If our pagan ancestors had been philosophers of religion, they might have argued for Woden, Frey, and so on along just such lines. Nordic paganism is not an option for most people today, though it was for some Nazis. But there really are those who, while they heap all the superlatives of traditional Judaeo-Christian religion on the Deity, derive his nature from that of nature in just this way. Look at the world, they say: it clearly isn't designed for human happiness. Therefore, God doesn't intend human happiness, so we shouldn't either. This view can take an explicitly neo-pagan form: immanent will, manifest in nature as destructive as well as creative power, legitimating destructiveness in human life; sanctified social Darwinism. Again, some of the Nazis believed this. But it can also take Christian forms, for instance, in the theodicy of John Hick. Either way it is an abuse of natural theology. But as long as the epistemic fallacy is avoided, natural theology need not be abused in this way. But for it not to be, Luther has to be followed: the nature of God as unconditional love as revealed in the Cross has to judge the data of natural theology, and the judgement poses the question: why then is nature destructive as well as creative? Biblical religion, of course, answers with a doctrine of the fallenness of creation.

So much for natural theology, which has a legitimate but limited place: philosophically limited, because it at most proves that an intelligence behind nature is likely; and theologically limited, because it at most proves an intelligence, not an infinitely wise and loving one.

Revealed theology and religious experience

Now we come to the question of revealed theology and its relation to religious experience.

The first thing to say about this is that every case of revelation is also a case of religious experience: revelation implies someone to whom God has revealed something, and for that person the revelation is experienced. If God wrote the ten commandments on stone and placed the stone in a cave on Mount Sinai for the gerbils to play on, no revelation would have taken place. If God revealed the ten commandments to Moses who read them to the people, it has. Furthermore, any revelation is known only by virtue of the experience that someone has of it. There is no revealed knowledge aside from religious experience.

The relation in religious contexts between the two verbs 'to reveal' and 'to experience' is this: revelation is always revelation by someone of something to someone; in the present context, revelation by God, of some aspect of himself, to human beings. Experience is always someone experiencing something: in this context, a person experiencing aspects of God. Where genuine revelation has taken place, the two verbs denote the same process from two sides. But it is possible to experience some quality as belonging to God when it does not. In this case, no revelation has taken place, and the experience is illusory.

A word is perhaps necessary about my statement that revelation and (veridical) religious experience are the same process seen from two sides. For I have described the two verbs in an asymmetrical way: revelation as a three-place relation (God reveals something to someone) and experience as a two-place relation (someone experiences something).

I have said that what God is revealing and what the recipient of the revelation is experiencing is some aspect of God's nature. One might then say that experience is only a two-place relation because it is always only *some* aspect of God's nature that he reveals, never himself in his fullness. But someone might object: no, what God is revealing is *the truth about* some aspect of his nature. We do not experience that nature directly, we merely hear the word about it. This objection obviously stems from the idea that revelation is always by means of the word, and ignores the testimony of the great mystics that what is revealed in their special sort of experience is never fully expressible in words. However, since I agree that it is normal for revelation to be mediated by words, and that any revelations that are not are preceded by ones that are, I need to reply: if after hearing the word we have more information at our disposal about God but no experience of him, a revelation has not taken place. A genuinely revelatory hearing of the word of God carries with it an experience of God himself.

However, from the fact that all revelation is known through religious experience, it does not follow that what is known is simply the experience and not revelation at all. To focus on the experience rather than the revelation (except for special, limited purposes) is to falsify the experience, for the experience is focused not upon itself but on the revelation. A theology that takes as its subject matter religious experience rather than revelation goes astray in the same way that Berkeley led empiricism astray about human knowledge in general. However, theology cannot bypass religious experience in its rightful focus on revelation, because there is no access to revelation aside from religious experience. We need to hold to two truths here, in order to avoid the epistemic fallacy: (1) our only access to revelation is through religious experience, and (2) religious experience can be false, can present as revealed what God has never revealed and what contradicts what God has revealed. Hence, two errors are possible which arguably Schleiermacher and Barth respectively are at least prone to, if not always guilty of: one can take all religious experience at face value and obliterate the distinction between that which is true and that which is false; or one can take for granted what the content of revelation is (a particular book or creed or the confessions of a particular Church) and refuse to answer the legitimate questions 'How do we know? Why this putative revelation and not that one?'

The position which defends revealed theology but ignores religious experience may concede that each case of revelation is a case of religious experience, but play down the importance of this concession by saying: since religious experience itself is focused on revelation and is of value even in its own terms only in so far as it is a reception of revelation, theology can pass over it and concentrate directly on revelation. The answer to this has three points, corresponding to the threefold analysis of knowledge in critical realism: within ontological realism there is epistemic relativity, and within this, judgemental rationality. First, ontological realism: revelation, if it is what it claims to be, reveals God's nature (or on some accounts, his will) as it is. If a putative revelation does not do this, it is false and hence no revelation at all. Only because there is some truth about God's nature can there be such a thing as a revelation of it. And that truth is independent of our knowledge of it. Hence, any particular putative revelation (that is, any religious experience) is fallible. Second, because there is no access to revelation independent of experience, we are thrown back in our attempt to establish what is really revealed on the relativity of our fallible experience. But, third, this does not mean that we are not able to judge in a rational and well-founded (though still fallible) way between different religious experiences yielding conflicting information about God, because we can argue rationally about religious experiences – for instance, about whether a given religious experience is internally coherent, agrees or conflicts with other religious experiences and with information known from other sources, meets the criterion 'by their fruits you shall know them', and so on. It is because of the realist assumption that it is rational to argue in this way, despite the relativity and fallibility of experience. Religious experience itself demands that we do so, because it presents itself as experience *of* something, of God or his word.

Let us not be misled by the fact that, grammatically, 'experience' is a noun. We do not understand what experience is unless we understand that 'to experience something' is a transitive verb.

These considerations give us the basis for a religious epistemology based on religious experience, and oriented towards revealed theology.

It may be possible here to throw some light on a long-standing dispute within theology. Great store has often been placed on which is prior out of the Word, the Church (or equivalent institution in other religions), or religious experience. Traditionally Catholics give priority to the Church, mainstream Protestants to the Word, and Quakers and charismatics to religious experience. But the argument about primacy collapses as soon as one asks: primacy in what respect? One of the first lessons of clear thinking is that when any A is related to any B, one rarely has primacy over the other in all respects, so proof of primacy in one respect does not prove primacy in any other. In the case of the Word, the Church and experience, the relation is rather like the game of scissors–paper–stone. Experience is almost always the result of an encounter with the Word: 'faith comes by hearing and hearing by the spoken word (*rhema*) of God.' The Word exists only when preached by the Church. But the Church is believed only because after it has preached the Word, what it has preached is experienced by the hearers themselves, so that its authority is derivative of the authority of experience. There is no second-hand faith, even though second-hand hearing always precedes faith.

At least this is the *normal* relation between the three things. Of course, in a literate community an individual may encounter the Word without encountering the Church, but religious literature exists only because religious institutions have preserved, printed and disseminated it. And Margaret Archer has convinced me that there are experiences which owe nothing to language or society, and it is conceivable, though exceptional, that a religious experience might fall into this category. But normally the three are circularly dependent.

I hope that I have given some grounds for (1) treating natural theology with respect as providing arguments for the existence of an intelligence behind nature; (2) relying not on natural but on revealed theology for the knowledge of the nature of that intelligence; (3) looking for the evidence of revealed theology in religious experience; and (4) treating that experience as fallible and testable by reason in the same way as other experience.

Postscript

On re-reading this chapter, I feel that it could lead to a false impression on one issue: the impression that revelation occurs as a series of discrete revelations by God to individuals in their private experiences. This is not my point at all. The revelations of God could not come about except by religious experience, and are verified to each individual by religious experience; but they are preserved in and communicated through religious traditions as a reservoir of potential revelation, which can be tapped by individual experiences. This potential revelation is communicated in propositions and makes possible the individual experiences in which the revelation occurs, and which confirm the propositions. Just as scientific theory makes possible the experiments which confirm it. This relation of mutual dependence between theory and experiment in science, or between tradition and experience in religion, is not circular, since each side is dependent on the other in different ways.

Notes

1 Gerald Priestland, *Reasonable Uncertainty*, Quaker Home Service, London, 1982.
2 John Dillenberger, *Martin Luther: Selections from his Writings*, Anchor Books, New York, 1961, p. 502.
3 See, for example, T. Gorringe, *Karl Barth: Against Hegemony*, Oxford University Press, Oxford, 1999.
4 Quoted by Karl Barth in 'The Principles of Dogmatics according to Wilhelm Hermann', *Theology and Church*, SCM, London, 1962, p. 243.
5 I follow tradition in using the male pronoun for God, with the proviso that if one rejects anthropomorphism, as all mainstream Churches have, one cannot believe that God is sexed. Hence, there is no objection to the feminine pronoun, but by the same token no need for it. There is an objection to the neuter pronoun 'it' since it suggests impersonality; and there is an objection to 'he or she' since it suggests unsureness as to sex, rather than the view that God created both sexes in his own image. I suspect that my difference from both those who object to the feminine pronoun for God, like C.S. Lewis, and those who insist on it, like some feminists, is anthropological rather than theological. They believe that there are deep metaphysical differences between the sexes. I believe that the differences all concern predicates which can't apply to God anyway.

10 On understanding religious experience: St Teresa as a challenge to social theory[1]

Margaret S. Archer

Throughout this book we emphasise religious experiences as legitimate, though fallible, warrants for religious beliefs. The problem is that many modern thinkers find religious experience incomprehensible in its own terms and respond by explaining it away in secular terms. First, they believe that their own lack of belief explains the unintelligibility of putative religious experiences. Second, since they assume that it is unnecessary to justify their own disbelief, they consider themselves justified in substituting their secular accounts for the account given by the believing subject. I will argue that they are wrong on both counts and do so with reference to St Teresa, whose own testimony about her experience has always encountered resistance.

On the first count, the distinction between the believer and the unbeliever does not coincide with those who find her religious experiences explicable and inexplicable. We can see this in Bernini's sculpture of the 'Ecstasy of St Teresa', because the central figures representing Teresa and Love were problematic to both the secular and religious powers of her day. The complete sculpture, in Santa Maria della Vittoria, is flanked by two opera boxes of these *notables*, engaged in altercation with one another or dissociating themselves from the scene. It seems from this that explaining Teresa's ecstatic love was no easier to the faithful than to the faithless four hundred years ago. What became her large book of *Confessions* was an attempt at self-explanation, imposed upon her by incredulous clergy – especially watchful for heresy in the mid-sixteenth century. The challenge here is whether or not for most people *verstehen* can extend to Teresa's experiences. I will be arguing that on the basis of our common humanity and common (Western) tradition, her account of them is understandable to people in general.

If that is the case, then on the second count, nobody is justified in 'explaining her experiences away'. However, whilst the two main post-war explanatory programmes in social science both embrace 'religious behaviour' as part of their brief in explaining the social world, they simultaneously expunge the divine from the explanations offered. On the one hand, methodological individualism's central principle states that 'the ultimate constituents of the social world are individual people who act more or less appropriately in the light of their dispositions and understanding of their situation.'[2] First, this principle is entirely anthropocentric, for, as its doyen states, 'Methodological individualism means that human beings are supposed to be the only moving agents in history'[3] – which gives no house-room to any form of divine agency. Second, individual dispositions are the 'terminus of an explanation'.[4] Although methodological individualism does not prohibit attempts to explain the formation of such dispositional characteristics, it does prescribe that these dispositions are 'to be explained only in terms of other human factors and not in terms of something *in*human'.[5] On the other hand, the socio-centricism of collectivism is even more inhospitable to the transcendental, because it is even more dismissive of individuals' accounts of what they consider motivates them. Instead, Teresa is an epiphenomenon of her times and circumstances. These shaping social forces are more important than she is – the malleable individual who is moulded by them.

This means that when confronted with events involving someone like Teresa, who gives her own account of her actions and of the religious experi-ences in which they are grounded, these are systematically expunged from both types of explanatory account. Such accounts are not *supplementary* explanations, legitimately introducing factors of which Teresa may have been unaware. They are *substitute* explanations (guilty on count two above), advanced in purely secular terms. Any reference to the terms of Teresa's own account are expurgated; in the place of transcendence, individualists substitute the influence of 'other people', and collectivists substitute the effects of 'social forces'. It will be maintained that whilst the two types of substitution evade the need to examine her experiences, they both leave behind them huge problems of adequately accounting for her actions.

Let me illustrate the difficulties of both individualist or collectivist explanations, by telling a story – one whose point is to demonstrate the deficiencies of both, but whose greater significance lies in pointing beyond this dichotomy to the need for incorporating the experiences that moved Teresa to act as she did. If this is indispensable, as I maintain, then it is neces-sary to question the assumption (count one) that religious experience is radically incomprehensible to the unbelieving social theorist – or any other unbeliever. This will take up the latter half of the chapter.

1 Anthropocentric and sociocentric accounts

The date is 1560–63, the place Avila, and this is the first instalment of the story,[6] for I will tell it in two parts. The central character in Part 1 is a professed Carmelite, aged 45, born Teresa Sáchchez de Cepeda y Ahumada, with a supporting caste of a very extended family, a variety of sisters (of both kinds), numerous confessors, sundry nobles, a grand inquisitor and two nuncios. It can be told as 'The Storming of the City' – a sixteenth-century *el alma/el alamo*, which begins outside the city walls in the Carmelite Convent of the Incarnation – a place which according to Teresa's autobiography rather resembled a salon.

(a) The story begins one evening in September 1560 with Teresa and a small group of nuns talking over the origins of the Carmelites (who had no founder – other than the hermits of Mount Carmel, listening alone like Elijah after a whisper in the breeze). Their talk was of a desire to return to the austerities of the desert fathers – brushed aside by the 1432 Bill of Mitigation, which allowed the previously 'discalced' Carmelites to put their shoes back on.

(b) The vision grew in clarity, of a strict contemplative enclosure, a 'discalced' house for a handful of committed religious and lay women. In origin it was *not* born out of discontent, for Teresa wrote in her Journal: 'I was very happy in the house where I was. The place was much to my taste, and so was my cell which suited me excellently'.[7] *Nor* was it envisaged as an evangelistic assault on the city (on society), for it was to be enclosed behind walls, without the city walls.

(c) The growing support depended on personal persuasion, largely by Teresa of her confessors, Francis Borja (SJ), Pedro de Alcántara (Franciscan) and Pedro Ibañez (Dominican), often after initial doubts and resistance. Sanctity and stratagem went hand in hand, for the cunningness of serpents equalled the gentleness of these doves. The house was to be purchased by Teresa's sister and brother-in-law, Juan de Ovalle, in the names of two lay widows. We even have the wandering made-good brother Lorenzo, sending in his needed 200 ducats from the New World for conversion of the property into St Joseph's Convent.

(d) The growth of opposition is classic conflict theory in its individualism. Resistance comes from the city where Teresa finds herself discomfited from the pulpit of St Thomas's, when the priest inveighed against 'nuns who left their convents to go and found new orders'. Her sister Juana was refused absolution unless she gave up the idea and asked Teresa to do so. She wrote, 'I was now very unpopular throughout my convent for wanting to found a convent more strictly enclosed. The nuns said that I was insulting them; that there were others who were better than myself, and so I could serve God quite well where I was.'[8] The city fathers, not wanting another convent, prevailed on the Carmelite Provincial, Angel de Salazar who opposed the project in view of public hostility.

(e) At this point, Teresa was summoned to a royal house in Toledo to a depressive widow, Donna Luisa de la Cerada, early in 1562. The project appeared stillborn. Yet it was gestating more clearly, more austerely and more uncompromisingly after Teresa learned that the ancient rule enjoined such poverty as precluded communal possessions – endowments. Henceforth, she thought of St Joseph's as living on alms or *sin renta*, in genuine detachment from the world and dependence on God.

(f) Much opposition to this new 'extremism' now came from her supporters. These, she wrote, 'put before me so many contrary arguments that I did not know what to do; for, now that I had learned the nature of the Rule and realised that its way was that of greater perfection, I could not persuade myself to allow the house to have any revenue. True, they sometimes convinced me; but, when I betook myself to prayer again and looked at Christ hanging so poor and naked upon the cross, I felt I could not bear to be rich. So I besought Him with tears to bring it about that I might become as poor as He.'[9] She now has to try to win over her supporters to this more radical vision.

(g) Arriving back in Avila, the key players were assembled; permission was received from Rome authorising the foundation of St Joseph's in the name of two widows, thus outflanking the hostile Carmelite Provincial, Salazar, and placing the convent of St Joseph under the Bishop of Avila, Don Alvaro de Mendoza. The city walls were breached when he was reluctantly persuaded by Teresa to accept a foundation *sin renta*, in the knowledge of the public outcry that would ensue at the idea of supporting a new foundation. On 24 August 1562, the first convent of the reformed or discalced Carmelites opened and the first mass was said for its seven sisters.

The story does not end here. So far it has been told in the standard terms of methodological individualism; the 'ultimate constituents' have been individuals, the explanatory variables, their dispositions, and the outcome, the result of the conflictual interplay between named 'other people'. Thus, the explanatory account has been in reductionist form, presenting a non-reified social context described through the strategy of 'personalisation', involving only inter-personal factors such as persuasion, influence, strategy and resistance. At this point the realist would advance the standard critique and question if this is a truly individualist account. For the players have played from roles (Provincial, confessor, nuncio, noble women, Bishop) and many of the constraints and enablements they wielded rested in the role not the incumbent; in the institutions not the individuals; in vested collective interests not individualistic dispositions; in structured locations of power not personal powers. Without these social forms the players would not have held the cards they did, nor been able to play in this drama at all. However, it is not the 'structure and agency' debate that concerns us here.

Much more important for the present argument is the fact that the 'terminus of an explanation' for the methodological individualist is 'individual dispositions'. As Gellner puts it, 'by 'dispositions' . . . is meant something 'intelligible', a conceivable reaction of human beings to circumstances; not necessarily one we share'.[10] This is the problem. Teresa's 'dispositions' are not shared but are also incomprehensible to secular individualists, who have outlawed the participation of 'something *in*human' in the formation of such dispositions. What are supposed to constitute the bedrock of their explanatory accounts are not, to them, intelligible dispositions on her part. Thus, in all the inter-personal cut and thrust that would preoccupy an individualist account, what motivates Teresa would be left blank. A void of incomprehension is a very unsatisfactory 'terminus of an explanation'. All that can plug it is a bland assertion that Teresa is so disposed as to wish to found a convent. This is what 'dispositions, which are open and law-like'[11] reduce to, namely overt and stable preferences – registered rather than understood by the investigator.

Let me continue the story, but transform the telling to the collectivist mode. This entails being able to account for the fact that the opposition of the city intensified. How can we explain it and answer the puzzlement that Teresa expresses in her autobiography?

> How everyone thought that twelve women and a prioress (for I must remind those who opposed the plan that there were to be no more) could do such harm to the place when they were living so strictly. If there had been any error in their project it would have concerned themselves alone; harm to the city there could not possibly be, yet our opponents found so much.[12]

Well, the collectivist would respond, taking up the story:

(a) Late sixteenth-century Spain had a total population of something less than 8 million; by the end of the century the number of monks alone is estimated at 400,000. Although female religious were less numerous, it was probable that one in twelve fell outside the active population by reason of vocation, withdrew family capital in the form of dowries when professed, or required municipal support as members of charitable foundations. The charge on the society increased with the falling value of money, after the influx of American gold. This meant the devaluation of their endowments whose inadequacy then threw them back on the city – to be supplemented by alms or subsidies. And the number of convents continued to grow: at the beginning of the sixteenth century, Avila had four convents, but fifty years later there were at least six more and talk of this new one. The same battle raged all over Spain, as economic devaluation and the expansion of religious foundations coincided. For example, the same struggle over a new discalced Carmelite House was played out in Madrid several years after Teresa's death (1582). In other words, this is just a pattern produced by the play of socio-economic forces.

(b) The Bishop of Avila bowed to the papal bull, which instructed that no authorities, either ecclesiastical or lay, should attempt to hinder the foundation of St Joseph's. Opponents in the Church may have been silenced by the power of Rome, but the city was not – society repudiated it. Penniless nuns begging beneath the city walls, from a surreptitiously planned and then coercively imposed convent, were a slight to the authority of the Corregidor and City Fathers. Tradesmen closed their shops to demonstrate and the Inspectorate of Fountains declared that the convent buildings would interfere with the city's water supply. The City Council met in emergency session and some hammered at the doors of St Joseph's, behind which the nuns barricaded themselves.

(c) The Bishop sent a representative who read the townsmen the papal bull, insisting on the ecclesiastical and civil authority conferred upon him. The militants on the City Council renewed their pressure. Unable to dissolve the convent directly, they referred their case to the Royal Council. Delegates were nominated and funds raised for a protracted lawsuit. Teresa's friends began to pool money (Teresa had none) and to prepare counter-representations. When the Royal Council official arrived in November to take statements from the contending parties, a compromise was mooted between the City and the foundation. If the convent was adequately endowed, and thus less likely to be a burden on local resources, the City Fathers would tolerate it.

(d) Teresa bowed to these powers, accepting that she must yield on the question of endowment. A compromise was worked out for signature, when Teresa suddenly asserted her unwillingness. At prayer she had reflected that, once endowed, they would be for ever constrained to forgo poverty. To silence her opponents a petition was dispatched to Rome asking specifically for the convent to be allowed to continue *sin renta*. The unusually swift December papal ruling granted the nuns of St Joseph's the privilege 'to possess no goods, either individually or collectively, but to maintain themselves freely from the alms and charitable assistance which pious Christians may offer and bestow'.

(e) The lawsuit before the Royal Council remained unsettled and rumblings continued to drift over the ramparts of the City of Knights; in June 1563, records mention the case still dragging on. Passions cooled slowly as litigation costs outweighed charitable donations. Avila had finally accepted the small convent.

Why? On this *collectivist* account, because of the two collective entities involved, the Church had overpowered the city and the crown had insufficient interest to act as other than umpire. Here we have collective agents alone, whose *positions prises* are determined by their vested interests, and the outcomes of their confrontations are determined by the relative distributions of power and resources. Issues begin when vested interests are invoked and end when continued confrontation literally costs too much. The figure of Teresa is a pretext; the same struggles between city and Church were being played out all over Spain. The reasons for this lay outside Spanish social structure altogether: in the new world's economic devaluation of the old world and in the Eternal City's ecclesiastical hegemony over the cities of western Christendom. In all these contending social forces, Teresa becomes a tiny spot of local Avilian colour.

Will such an account do – with Teresa and the rest of the caste reduced to *träger*, where they are the marionettes playing out events, never the makers of history (under times and circumstances not of their choosing)? Of the many difficulties of this position, the prime one that this story highlights is the unworkable nature of the 'passive agent' which collectivism presents. This explanatory account also expunges Teresa's own account from it. Personal experiences, including her claim to be motivated by her religious experience, are simply 'white noise' where *träger* are concerned.

Yet, Teresa was not an agent of some reified, homogeneous church, not a sleeping agent, not an unconsciously prescient pawn of it – she was as much of a nuisance within it as outside it. Her ideas (using Weber's 'switchmen' simile) nudged parts of the Church on to a different line, accentuating the Church's ideal interests over its material ones and actualising the contradiction between Church and society in the country where the possibility of their collaboration had seemed more convincing than anywhere – one which had been welded into a nation by *los reyes catolicos*. Again, a complete explanation has to let Teresa back in. There is no need to doubt that social factors played a role (of which Teresa may have lacked full discursive penetration), but so did she. And if she did, social theorising cannot evade hermeneutics – the need to understand what prompts an active agent to act.

Thus, if we grant that Teresa had some influence over the course of events because of her religious experiences, we must take her and them seriously, just as seriously as the times and the circumstances which were not of her choosing. And if we take *both* seriously, we have to reject reductionism of any kind – that is, the individualistic version which would make Teresa the mistress of her circumstances, and the collectivist version, which reduces her to an expression of her times.

If we do take her own account seriously, we have to confront the task of trying to understand her *religious* experience. Neither form of explanation can evade it, though both would try to do so. Individualism excludes transcendental reality by reducing it to human terms, to 'Teresa's account' – whose referents she held were properly to transcendence. Thus, in individualism, beliefs become merely what believers believe. Teresa's claim to have experienced a contemplative relationship with divinity (which is an ontological claim) is *automatically* reduced to 'Teresa's own dispositions' (to her epistemology). In parallel, collectivism has to find societal reasons for the appearance of motives like Teresa's. It does so in typical Durkheimian[13] fashion by dismissing the content and referent of Teresa's beliefs and pointing instead to their social functions – such that she becomes the mouthpiece of religious institutions in relation to secular powers.

Hence, in individualism, listening to Teresa's account becomes reduced to 'learning more about Teresa's epistemology'. In collectivism, listening to Teresa becomes reduced to 'learning more about her society'. What they would rule out, in their respective anthropocentrism and sociocentrism, is that her experiences *could* be taken seriously. What I hope to have shown is that they must be incorporated, and therefore understood, if adequate explanations are to be advanced. We can now turn to the question of whether or not this is possible for secular social theorists, rather than assenting to their pre-judgement about the incomprehensibility of religious experience.

2 The light the Enlightenment tried to extinguish

The difficulty with taking her religious experience seriously is that this has generally been interpreted as a matter of taking her *beliefs* seriously, of assessing what evidence is there to support them. But evidential talk is grounded in the explanatory model of Enlightenment science – a model of matter-in-motion. To Michael Buckley[14] this entailed the disastrous move of substituting impersonal scientific evidence in place of a personal God. Instead of being the result of religious experience, religious belief became the product of a process of inference, the result of a series of arguments about evidence from the physical world. Natural theology's star rose and revealed theology's declined – the climacteric of this process being publications like William Paley's *Evidences of Christianity* (1794). Religious experience, which depends upon a non-observable generative mechanism (divine action towards us), and its equally non-observable sensing (by human subjects), was thus doubly disqualified by the Enlightenment project. This was paralleled in social theory by the erection of an iron curtain between *erklaren* (explanation) and *verstehen* (understanding), which *détente* has not yet fully dismantled.

So let us try a different tack based upon revising the modernist view of both humanity (like Teresa) and of God. First, this consists in accentuating that we humans are unlike matter. We have sensibilities which matter does not; our *human experience* is not that of objects, responding automatically to stimuli, for which external evidence is forthcoming. Rather, it turns on the fact that what we do depends on an internal, reflexive and 'largely inarticulate sense of what is of decisive importance' to us as human beings.[15] Second, revisionism involves reclaiming a non-scientific view of God, who is not merely a mover of matter, a physicalist 'first cause' (to which mechanics relegates him). He is not conceptualised as a depersonalised object, but as the (partially) immanent subject (see Chapter 2) of the Judaeo-Christian tradition. By working through these two revisions, religious experience can be conceptualised in a manner that makes it understandable to non-believers – at least, this is the claim I will try to uphold.

Restoring the human subject (Teresa)

To begin with us; the Enlightenment gave a *logocentric* view of human beings. Since truth was defined in terms of formal logical deductions performed on symbolic systems, this model was incompatible with explaining religious experience, which is not fully propositional. On Teresa's understanding, contemplation depends on our capacity to have experiences that are not enjoyed by all life forms, let alone by machines like digital computers, designed to work inferentially. In the religious domain these are capacities for spiritual sensibility, which proficients have cultivated but no computer can ever simulate – namely the 'purification', 'illumination' and 'unification' regularly described as the experiential stages of contemplation.

The formal model of Enlightenment rationality enforced a distinction between 'logos' and 'pathos', between our rationality and our sensibility. As the two became pushed apart, the 'head' and 'heart' dualism ensued. On the logocentric model we have emotions and desires, with reason acting as the slave of these passions by telling us instrumentally how best to maximise their fulfilment. But reason cannot evaluate the ends sought themselves. Therefore, we have no moral careers. Actions and their desired ends are a function of taste (aka 'preferences') alone – and *de gustibus non est disputandum* – serviced by instrumental rationality. Exit the *vertrationalität*, including religious commitment, as no end is pursued for its own sake, rather than because it can leave us 'better off', in terms of some notion of 'utility'.

So, on this model Teresa has a 'preference schedule', whose priority is to found a convent. All we can do is to look at *how* she went about it, whilst others, with different preferences, tried to stop her. (This is the *metaphysical* individualism of modernity that lay behind the *methodological* individualistic account I gave in Part 1.) But we can neither ask nor evaluate *why* she desired it. So the response to Bernini is banal – she is just that way inclined. Yet, unlike an object, she wants to tell us – she wants to justify herself by giving reasons to her confessors which is why she wrote her *Life*. On Hume's model it could have gone on a postcard; 'I desired it, my desires are unquestionable, and I applied my reason to achieve my desired end.'

Teresa becomes no more understandable by substituting Kant's stern Voice of Duty for her Humean religious 'passions'. Kant's is a 'head' versus 'heart' model and depends on 'free will' informing us of our duty, which we then must seek to universalise. Kantianism is often reproached for failing to explain the 'Will's' choice, and why it can move us against our inclinations. But this does not help with Teresa, who is not moved by duty and is in the awkward position of knowing how she thinks she ought to act, but not whether it is her duty to act in this way.

Do we fare any better in understanding Teresa's religious experience if we cut through this distinction between reason and the emotions? Now, unless we were affective beings, no amount of knowledge could move us to anything. (St Augustine makes this assumption when talking about the incompatibility between apathy and morality: 'if *apatheia* is the name of the state in which the mind cannot be touched by any emotion whatsoever, who would not judge this insensitivity to be the worst of moral defects.')[16] If it is granted that emotions are the basis of moving us, it also needs to be recognised that the 'passions' are not blind and mysterious urges. Contra Hume, they involve information and cognition. Reason is implicit in *all* emotions: it has the cognitive task of informing us (fallibly) about how things are in themselves (not how we subjectively take them to be). For example, everyday promptings towards 'generosity' take a lot of cognitive skill, for it is not enough that a gift be the one we would like to receive!

This means that feelings are not just felt, they relate to the nature of their object. What makes an emotion appropriate or inappropriate is nothing self-referential but the nature of the emotion's object. Fear of open spaces is inappropriate and most agoraphobes seek therapy for it. Conversely, the appropriate response to goodness is love, but love of the object itself and not because of its value to us – which makes the moral glory of humanity the fact that we need not be anthropocentric. Love certainly moves one to action and it does so in the sense that the loved object is a moral end in itself. (This cuts through the modernist idea that beings cannot be moral ends because ends must be abstract entities like propositions, desirable states of affairs, facts or events.) It means that the quality in question, here goodness, must inhere in the object, but, and this is the cognitive element, we may of course be wrong.[17] We are fallible and could behave *as if* the object had intrinsic value. This is the problem. Many unbelievers would say that Teresa was loving and acting appropriately *if* God existed, but she was wrong and I cannot prove her right by advancing a proof of the existence of God! Are we stuck at this point? I want to argue 'no', though it will take several more stages to do so.

On the human side, the argument depends upon our redrawn human agents who are not modernist rational calculators. With her head now reunited with her heart, the reconceptualised Teresa seeks to communicate four things, *inter alia*, about her religious experience:

1   she is in love (the *personal* statement);
2   she loves that most worthy to be loved (the *worth loving* statement);
3   she maintains that the greatest love is due to supreme goodness (the *ultimate worth* statement);
4   she enjoys a personal relationship with God, the supreme good (the *relational* statement).

We will need all of this but let us begin work on the last item, her claim to have a personal relationship with God.

Reinstating the God of revelation

This is the point where we have to take God out of the grip of the Enlightenment because you cannot love a 'first cause' or relate to an impersonal causal mechanism. We also have to move beyond natural theology, which may create a space for the notion of a creator, but at most it is an empty space containing a being who may be quite indifferent to human beings. If we ask instead how a (non-mechanistic) God could bridge the gap between the infinite (his ontological transcendence) and the finite (limited human beings), we confront the notion of divine self-revelation and the conditions of its possibility. Now, ontological transcendence need not imply his unknowability (see Chapter 2), if God makes himself known in ways that can be grasped by us. Were he to be granted this power, his revelation is a fact about him and not a matter of our judgement, which is a fact about us. This will be accepted logically by unbelievers, who reserve their doubts about his existence in the first place.

I want to work on the notion of self-revelation through a suggestion of Feuerbach's which he never took seriously because he concluded that God was an alienated projection of human wants (in yet another anthropocentric theory). The insight is that God is constrained by the nature of his creation because, to Feuerbach, 'in the scheme of his revelation God must have reference not to himself but to man's power of comprehension'.[18] He is constrained if he wishes to communicate himself. This does entail accepting limitations to omnipotence, which we are willing to concede, though many theologians would not be. Now I want to borrow left-handedly from one of our more anthropocentric philosophers, David Wiggins, who regards the idea of non-human persons or communication with them as impossible – here he has in mind Martians and automata, but God 'fits' his category too. To Wiggins, we cannot 'make sense of non-human creatures, become attuned to them, or be in a position to treat their feelings as if they were our own'.[19] He goes on to argue that faced with an automaton or Martian we cannot have the expectations which enable us to interpret them, given their inscrutable sources of satisfaction, *unless*, and this is crucial, these creatures were synthesised by carbon-copying the contingencies of our human frame and constitution. That is, we could not understand them and they could not communicate with us, unless by accident or design they conformed to human form and human consciousness.

If we now consider a non-human God, desirous of communicating with us, we come to the notion of God-in-struggle. As the Fourth Eucharistic Prayer of the Roman Catholic Church expresses it: 'again and again you offered a covenant to man, and through the prophets taught him to hope for salvation. Father, you so loved the world that in the fullness of time you sent your only Son . . .' The incarnation satisfies Wiggins's condition – a divine conformation to human form and consciousness. By 'laying his godhead by', we could understand what divinity was like if it came to us in human shape. Hence the essential role of Athanasian teaching that Christ was simultaneously fully divine and fully human – the joint conditions for the possibility of a revelation of divinity which was fully communicable to humanity. On those conditions, Wiggins is right to wonder 'how far the process (of communication) can go'. Teresa is trying to tell her contemporaries and us that it goes much further than has been imagined. Now our unbelieving modernists will presumably respond that my case and

Teresa's is now twice as bad. If they cannot accept a 'first cause' they certainly will not swallow the notion of incarnate God.

3 'Anyone who lives in love lives in God' (1 John 4.16)

Here they have a problem themselves; they will not accept the incarnate Christ, but they cannot deny the historical Jesus. Indeed people today readily make this dichotomy when they say, 'Well, I'm not religious but I do subscribe to Jesus's moral code', or 'Jesus was an example of a very good man'. This is household Arianism. Of course, such was not Teresa's response; her imitation was of incarnate Love. But this is the difficulty for the unbeliever. She is in love, and they cannot hold her mistaken about her own feelings, but with the *same person* whose moral qualities they have just deemed worthy of love because of his goodness. They *can* understand her for they (a) understand loving supreme or at least very great goodness, and (b) often themselves love persons they have never met (celebrities or heroes and heroines), even to the point (c) of fantasising meetings and conversations with them. Teresa is not an enigma to them, but is she simply a fantasist like them? For we admitted that the cognitive basis of our emotions was humanly fallible and therefore corrigible. Here is the big difficulty for the faithful: it seems we have got as far as we are going to get in gaining assent that she is genuinely in love with a supremely good, but dead, man, Jesus. We are not going to persuade any of the faithless that she is in loving communion with God, as she asserts.

Having conceded this much, how is it possible still to maintain that unbelievers can understand her contemplative experiences? The key comes from the fundamental notion that 'to live in love is to live in God'. We cannot make anyone assent to her 'living with God', but they can accept the assertion that someone is experiencing a life of love – indeed nobody can dissent from 'the *personal* statement', because when we love we cannot be mistaken about that.

The next stage is to build upon the notion of 'loving' itself, by making use of the reconceptualisation of human beings as creatures of sensibility. We are not logocentric jugglers of symbolic strings, for our ultimate concerns are what we care about most, and caring is not derived inferentially. Ultimate concerns are not a matter of pure reason adopting a series of moral propositions – a detachable moral code of 'do's' and 'don'ts' which define moral living as *acts* (of commission or omission). Moreover, those sensibilities which give us our orientation to the good are not optional extras because our judgements of value (the things we care deeply about) are central to *who* we are and to *how* we see our place in the world. In other words, to care is to love. Like Teresa, we love that which we consider most worthy to be loved (we assent to 'the *worth loving* statement'). Since this defines who we are, most of us are not strangers to 'living in love'. Therefore, it is understandable by all and provides the bridgehead to understanding Teresa's *religious* experience of it.

To Teresa, the life of incarnate love supplies the role model for 'living in love', since she maintained that the greatest love is due to supreme goodness. Not only do unbelievers assent to the latter, but they also find that the life of the historic Jesus is intelligible and often acceptable as a standard, even though they do not see this as imitating the Son of God. Thus, we are not necessarily forced to accept one definition of supreme goodness for the unbeliever and another for the believer, because the two will frequently refer to the same source themselves, under different descriptions – but this is the only way in which we can know anything at all. That means that there is a substantial group of unbelievers who join believers in endorsing 'the *ultimate worth* statement' as applying to Jesus, and therefore find its acknowledgement understandable. For those who do not, this is not a question of their lack of faith or of understanding, but of the diversity of morals.

What differentiates Teresa now is not the subject of what she cares about, compared with most unbelievers, but *how much* she cares. Teresa cares totally about incarnate love and seeks to personify it, whereas others dilute the same standard into less demanding codes of behaviour. Thus, Porpora[20] tells us that the majority of Americans believe that the 'golden rule' epitomises Jesus's ethical teaching, namely 'do unto others as you would have them do unto you'. Now this is morally active because it involves seeking the good of others. Nevertheless, it is hardly the highest standard in ethics since: (i) our desires themselves may not be morally commendable; (ii) it is quite compatible with self-fulfilment on our own terms; or (iii) it can become merely an ethic of conventional reciprocity designed, like Utilitarianism, to bring about the smooth running of everyday life. It does not call us to any kind of extraordinary goodness. All the same it is more demanding than the earlier 'silver rule', which can be formulated as 'that which you would not want others to do to you, do not do unto them'. This is more morally passive for it largely places negative constraints on our behaviour, but this very refraining from harming others could be based on purely prudential grounds of self-interest. Although there is no positive admonition to virtue here, the silver standard is still higher than the 'tinsel rule', 'treat others as they deserve', which requires that they have to earn moral treatment, they have to gain respect, and even win their place in the 'kingdom of ends'.

The three rules are a hierarchical structure of increasingly demanding injunctions, but simultaneously they disclose the limitations of that which can be expressed sententially. What they miss is the 'platinum standard', the radical demand of one life on others, summed up in Jesus's new commandment to 'love one another as I have loved you'. This is a call beyond convention into supererogation; a call to perfection in a love that includes enemies as well as friends. As such it is a call to model ourselves on love in a manner that is too all-embracing to be interpreted in terms of procedural ethics, as with the other three rules. What has to be emulated is a life in its fullness and the urge to do so engages all our personal sensibilities in a moral vision of 'discipleship', something defying codification into rules because it has outdistanced banal procedural horizons and has resisted routinisation into the rule-governed.

What does the moral praxis of 'living in love' look like? This notion of 'discipleship' treats moral knowledge as practical wisdom and falls between Ryle's 'knowing now' (as in swimming) and 'knowing that' (which is propositional). 'Living in love' is much more akin to playing music by ear, involving an immersion in the whole musical enterprise, an engagement with its traditions, repertoires and maestros, much of which is not mediated by ratiocination – hence little of which can be distilled into propositions. All lovers of music, as of wine, communicate at best by metaphor, and talk of 'attacking notes' or of a 'flinty taste', which are metaphors that cannot be cashed in. 'Discipleship' is in part imitation, in part swimming in the stream of its traditions and exemplars, but it is also developing a reflexive self-adjustment, the capacity to make one's own judgements about the appropriateness of actions in new unscripted contexts. This 'living in love' has nothing to do with juggling sentences, but much more to do with acquiring a 'feel' because it is feelings themselves that are moved.[21]

The core skills are nothing mysterious since the historical knowledge on which they are based is found in the Scriptural canon, whose own constitution Frances Young has interestingly compared with musical composition.[22] Acquiring the basic repertoire entails personal immersion in this thick tradition comprising the core canon and subsequent commentaries, including the lives of proficients themselves. The saints are the master musicians in this training and (ideally) canonisation can be seen as convergent judgements that such lives were indeed conformed to the 'platinum standard'. This living tradition represents the golden nugget within the collectivist account. We are indeed inducted into a corpus of knowledge, techniques and practices which is never of our making, since it predates us, has autonomy from us, and yet can causally affect us. Nobody invents the entire Christian cultural conspectus *de nova*; their Christian lives begin as apprenticeship. Probably in this delicate task of religious education the reason why so many do not develop a career of discipleship is their frail acquaintance with the collective tradition and a lack of contact with sufficient of its living journeymen.

Simultaneously, the core skills themselves evolve, for there is nothing purely mimetic in discipleship. Proficient lovers increasingly develop their faculty of judgement, including a critical appraisal of their own discipleship, out of which they elaborate novel strategies for living in love in new times and circumstances, where no code of established practice is available. Like musicians with a good 'feel', they improvise creatively on the theme laid down and collaborate together in this evolving improvisation. They acknowledge personal responsibility for creating something novel out of their inheritance in response to new exigencies in the present. They respond to what went before and themselves lay down some of the parameters of what will come next, for tradition itself is elaborative over time, as is revelation.

Thus Teresa produced her *Way of Perfection*, the *Interior Castle* and poetry, besides her autobiographical and confessional works. These innovative texts of discipleship represent the kernel truth of individualism: we are active agents not passive marionettes and the opposition incited from others is correctly seen by individualists as the tension through which tradition evolves. However, what is being elaborated are not additions to a sentential code, but new words for describing the essentially practical experience of 'living in love', which represents an educated capacity to improvise on life and not merely to mimic the past, for discipleship is also creative.

Conclusion

A serious appreciation of 'discipleship' probably represents the limits to an understanding of Teresa's *'relational* statement'. But the same hermeneutic limits to intelligibility also attach to the dispositions that emerge from any relationship. These limitations attend our understanding of other people's loving in general – whether of a person, a cause or an abstract principle. Such restrictions are inescapable, for they consist in the ineradicable difference between third-person and first-person accounts. As third persons, believers and unbelievers are in the same position *vis à vis* Teresa's experiences. We can all understand their grounding in the Christian tradition and we can all understand their public outworkings, but none of us can share her own inscapes.

All the same, the faithless may still express resistance because they hold there to be a crucial difference between two statements. On the one hand, there is the statement that they would readily make about a happily married man, 'I don't understand what he sees in her', and, on the other, the statement they would make about Teresa, 'I don't understand her deep love of God'. This difference rests on empiricism; the wife can be seen, but not believed (to possess lovable qualities), whereas God could be believed (to possess these qualities), but cannot be seen to exist. However, empiricism does not cover the whole spectrum of loving, and the above distinction fails when someone loves a cause or an ideal. In fact, I suggest, most of us would find good and intelligible reasons for Teresa's absorption in unconditional love, whilst we could not do so for someone's commitment to fascism or pursuit of sadism. We do make such judgements on 'kinds of loving', but we make them within hermeneutic limits, for we can no more *have* Teresa's ecstatic experiences than we can share a Nazi's exultancy at a Nuremberg rally or enter into the exquisite agony of the Marquis de Sade.

As Weber rightly insisted, *verstehen* or understanding is not the same thing as empathy. Our individual empathetic registers have different ranges, and many believers find themselves in the same position as unbelievers –

personally they cannot imagine themselves having experiences like Teresa's. As was maintained at the beginning, believers and unbelievers stand in no clear-cut relationship to finding her experience intelligible or not. Conversely, and within its necessary limitations, every (normal) human being has the same hermeneutic handle to her experiences, because all understand loving, since it is indispensable to humankind (see Chapter 5). For the figures on Bernini's balconies and for social theorists alike, it is not Teresa's *religious* experiences that they cannot enter into, but her *personal* experiences – which cannot be shared.

Max Weber declared that he was himself 'religiously unmusical', but he did not therefore conclude that there was no music to be heard, although all he could see were dancers moving to a silent orchestra. He did follow those moving harmoniously through the world's ballrooms and he had much to say about the pattern of the dance as a way of being-in-the-world. In this he acknowledged the limitations of secular social theory and its inability fully to grasp or legitimately to explain the music away. Thus he also endorsed the need to incorporate that which social theory could not explain and should not reinterpret in secular terms – the love of transcendence on the part of many of its subjects.

Notes

1 This chapter is based upon an earlier one which appeared in Kieran Flanagan and Peter Jupp (eds), *Virtue Ethics and Sociology: Issues of Modernity and Religion*, Palgrave, Basingstoke, 2001, and appears with the editors' permission.
2 J.W.N. Watkins, 'Methodological Individualism and Social Tendencies', in May Brodbeck (ed.), *Readings in the Philosophy of the Social Sciences*, Collier-Macmillan, London, 1971, p. 270.
3 Watkins, 'Methodological Individualism', p. 271.
4 Watkins, 'Methodological Individualism', p. 274.
5 Watkins, 'Methodological Individualism', p. 275; italics in original.
6 Biographies, bibliographical commentaries and historical background on St Teresa include: E. Allison Peers, *Handbook to the Life and Times of St Teresa and St John of the Cross*, London, 1954; Efrén de la Madre de Dios and Otgar Steggink, *Tiempo y vida de Santa Teresa*, Madrid, 1968; Alberto Barrientos (ed.), *Introducción a la lectura de Santa Teresa*, Madrid, 1978; Stephen Clissold, *St Teresa of Avila*, Sheldon Press, London, 1979; Rowan Williams, *Teresa of Avila*, Geoffrey Chapman, London, 1991.
7 All quotations from St Teresa's *Life* are taken from *The Complete Works of Saint Teresa of Jesus*, Volume 1 (ed. E. Allison Peers), Sheed & Ward, London, 1982.
8 Peers, *Life*, op. cit., p. 224.
9 Peers, *Life*, op.cit., p. 243.
10 Ernest Gellner, 'Holism versus Individualism', in May Brodbeck (ed.), *Readings in the Philosophy of the Social Sciences*, Collier-Macmillan, London, 1971, p. 257.
11 Watkins, 'Methodological Individualism', p. 280.
12 Peers, *Life*, p. 256.

13 Emile Durkheim, *The Elementary Forms of the Religious Life*, Allen & Unwin, London, 1964.

14 Michael Buckley, *At the Origins of Modern Atheism*, Yale University Press, New Haven, 1987.

15 Charles Taylor, *Human Agency and Language, Philosophical Papers 1*, Cambridge University Press, Cambridge, 1985, p. 38.

16 St Augustine, *City of God*, (trans. H. Bettenson), Penguin, Harmondsworth, 1984, pp. 564–5.

17 I owe this bold statement of realist ethics to Andrew Collier, *Being and Worth*, Routledge, London, 1999.

18 Ludwig Feuerbach, *The Essence of Christianity*, Prometheus Books, Buffalo, 1989, p. 207.

19 David Wiggins, 'The Person as Object of Science, as Subject of Experience and as Locus of Value', in A. Peacocke and G. Gillett, *Persona and Personality*, Blackwell, Oxford, 1987, p. 71.

20 Douglas V. Porpora, *Landscapes of the Soul*, Oxford University Press, Oxford, 2001. The paragraph that follows is drawn from his argument and evidence.

21 Again a debt must be acknowledged, despite our disagreements, to Michael Luntley, *Reason, Truth and Self*, Routledge, London, 1995.

22 Frances Young, *The Art of Performance*, Darton, Longman & Todd, London, 1990.

11 The human project

Douglas V. Porpora

Scale is the theme of the Frederick Phineas and Sandra Priest Rose Center that houses the new Hayden Planetarium in New York. Tom Hanks, narrator of the sky show, tells us that to be good citizens of the cosmos, we must appreciate our own place in the whole.

The Planetarium wants us to understand how physically minute that place is. Thus, as we begin our simulated voyage through the universe, we quickly traverse the five billion miles to the edge of our own solar system. Earth itself is now all but lost from sight. Yet we have not even left our block, let alone our neighbourhood. From a still more panoramic view, even our sun becomes a speck, indistinguishable from all the other specks that constitute the some 200 billion stars of our Milky Way galaxy. Visually depicted in three dimensions, those stars fall toward us like endless snowflakes. Within our own galaxy, our sun is not even at the centre, where the action is, but on the periphery alongside one of the spiral arms.

With still another zoom-out, we find that the Milky Way is only one of a thousand comparably sized galaxies circling the Virgo Cluster. In the final vista, the entire dome above becomes an intricate honeycomb of such supergalactic clusters. All this represents just the visible universe, 13 billion light years across. Beyond is an unknown expanse perhaps infinite in size. And this universe of ours, it is now considered, may be only one of possibly an infinite number of others.

Temporally, too, our place is late and inconsiderable. The Heibrunn Cosmic Pathway wraps around the Rose Center one and-a-half times. With each step, we traverse 75 million years. When we arrive at the end, 360 feet later, we find the whole of human history encompassed by a width no greater than a single human hair.

Considering how infinitesimal humanity is in time and space, can anyone imagine that individually or even collectively we are of any cosmic significance? And if we are of no cosmic significance, what then is the meaning of our lives? Is it as the existentialists suggested, that the only meaning of our lives is the meanings we ourselves give them? Perhaps herein we see the force behind the postmodern retreat from grand meaning to smaller meanings that are only local.

Yet meaninglessness and a sense of human insignificance need not be our only reaction to the scale of the universe. In the first place, size is not the only measure of importance. As infinitesimal as we are in comparison with supergalactic structures or even a solitary star, we represent a singular development in the history of the universe. With us, the universe becomes conscious of itself. It awakens from slumber. Our brains may be small, but our minds can encompass the whole. In a sense, we are the universe's soul. Surely, an important vocation is attached to this station.

Today, we are ever wary of hubris, of arrogating to ourselves more status than befits the inhabitants of a minor planet circling a minor sun on the periphery of a wholly unremarkable galaxy. Surely, we suppose, even if we are the universe conscious of itself, this is a post we share with numerous others. The Planetarium's sky show reinforces this view. As we plunge through billions and billions of stars, it is hard to resist Carl Sagan's suggestion that the universe is 'brimming over with life'.[1] Should even only a small percentage of stars harbour life, there are still so many of them as to make life – and even intelligent life – quite prevalent.

It comes as a surprise, therefore, that Sagan is very likely mistaken. Instead, intelligent life is probably so rare as to require a universe of such gigantic proportions just to produce it even once. In *Contact*, the movie based on Sagan's book, Jodie Foster pores into the vastness of space and asks, 'Is anyone out there?' As worthwhile as the Search for Extraterrestrial Life (SETI) project definitely is, we should prepare ourselves to be met only by silence.

How can it be that with all the stars out there, none but our own contains intelligent life? Is that not the height of arrogance? No. Consider first that for a planet to yield any kind of life beyond microbes, it must be of just the right size and circle its star within what is called the 'continuously habitable zone' (CHZ). Around a star like our own sun, the CHZ is very narrow. If the earth were just 5 per cent closer to the sun than it actually is, it would be subject to a runaway greenhouse effect that would leave it as uninhabitable as Venus. Just 15 per cent farther away and it would be subject to a runaway glaciation, making it equally uninhabitable. In neither case could more complex life have evolved.[2]

For a planet to orbit a star in the CHZ, the star must first have a CHZ. Stars less than 83 per cent of the mass of our sun are not sufficiently luminous to have a stable CHZ. On the other hand, stars that are more massive than our sun by even 20 per cent burn out their fuel much too quickly for life to have time to evolve.[3] All told, only about 4 per cent of all stars fall within the right range. By stellar standards, our sun may be quite ordinary, but in terms of its life-yielding potential, its specifications are highly select.

Still, with some 200 billion galaxies, each with billions of stars, even 4 per cent can present us with perhaps a trillion stars of the requisite type. Yet, we have only begun to enumerate the specifications required for the emergence of complex life. In our own neighbourhood, about two-thirds of solar-type stars occur in binary or multi-star systems. These are generally inhospitable to complex life because they induce highly elliptical planetary orbits that pass in and out of the CHZ.[4] Presumably, then, we next have to trim our initial trillion candidates by as much as two-thirds.

Galactic location is also important. As Peter Ward and Donald Brownlee observe, many places in space are just 'dead zones'.[5] Our own sun's position in an outer rim of the Milky Way may seem to place it in the cosmic boondocks, but it is only in the boondocks that more complex life has any chance of evolving. Closer in towards the galaxy's celestial metropolis, stars are too densely packed for safety. With greater gravitational pulls from neighbouring stars, planetary orbits are once again erratic. With intense radiation from nearby novas or supernovae, all evolutionary progress is suddenly wiped clean.

Clearly, the conditions required for life are more complex than just the number of stars in the sky. With each additional constraint – and there are many more – the odds in favour of complex, extraterrestrial life become bleaker and bleaker. And even complex life is not yet human-level consciousness.[6]

We finally need to ask how likely it is for human-level intelligence to emerge, should an evolutionary process even get started. Stephen J. Gould for one considers it almost astronomically unlikely. Replay the course of our own evolution again and again, Gould observes, and in all likelihood we would never reappear.[7] In the end, if earth is not the only place where the universe has become conscious of itself, it may be one of only a precious few.

From this perspective, the scale of the universe takes on a different significance. If the entire immensity of the universe was required for intelligent life to emerge even just once, then that vastness is perhaps not a measure of our insignificance but a marker of our almost exorbitant importance. The question asserts itself: Were we or something like us meant to be here? If so, what are we here to do? If this entire, immense universe went through all the trouble of coming into existence to yield something like us, what pursuit befits our arrival?

It is not so outrageous to suppose that something like us was meant to be here. Ours is not just any old universe, but one that physicists describe as 'fine-tuned' for the possibility of life. Whatever its origin, our universe definitely could not appear more as if it had been designed to be this way.

We are not speaking here just of the universe's manifest order and intricacy. To be sure, life would be impossible were the universe not sufficiently ordered and intricate. Far more compelling, however, are all the delicate balances that physicists refer to collectively as the 'anthropic coincidences.'[8] In theory, the basic parameters of the universe – the force strengths and fundamental constants – could all have assumed values very different from what they actually are. Yet, were any of a great number of them even minutely different, say, by even less than one part in a hundred trillion, we would not be here.

The very existence of stars like our sun, for example, depends on certain very delicate balances. Were gravity only slightly weaker or electromagnetism only slightly stronger (each by even one part in 10^{40}, i.e. 10 followed by 40 zeros), all stars would be red dwarfs, too cold to support life.[9] With similarly slight changes in the other direction, all stars would be blue giants, exhausting their fuel in millions rather than billions of years – too soon to support life. The existence then of stars like our sun depends on an astonishing calibration of forces, one of which is 10^{39} times weaker than the other.[10]

We also would have ended up with either all red dwarfs or all blue giants if the electron–proton mass ratio differed only slightly. As it happens, the electron is about one ten thousandth as massive as the proton. An even slightly less massive electron would have produced all red dwarfs whereas an electron only slightly more massive would have produced all blue giants.[11] It is truly startling that something as gigantic as a star could depend on a balance between particles one trillionth of a centimetre in size. Yet, there are many other examples like this. The universe would contain none of the chemical building blocks of life if the neutron did not outweigh the proton by about 0.1 per cent, approximately the mass of two electrons.[12]

Any one of these coincidences is fantastically improbable. That they and many others all obtain simultaneously, by chance alone, is beyond belief. Thus, astronomer Fred Hoyle was prompted to describe the universe as 'a put-up job'. Similarly, in his autobiography, Nobel laureate Freeman Dyson writes, 'The more I examine the universe and study the details of its architecture, the more evidence I find that the universe in some sense must have known that we were coming.'[13]

The current consensus among physicists is that the anthropic coincidences of cosmology do require explanation. The apparent design of the universe is not a pseudo-problem.[14] Of course, most physicists resist any appeal to God. The best alternative explanation is that our universe is only one of an infinite number of others, each with different values of the basic parameters and force strengths. Only a very small percentage of these are capable of supporting life. Most are in a sense 'junk' universes, destined never to become conscious of themselves.

Yet, if the number of actual universes is truly infinite, there will always be some like our own that exhibit the perfect balances necessary for life to evolve. It is then no mystery why we find ourselves in a universe that appears fine-tuned. It is only in a fine-tuned universe that we could possibly find ourselves. The law of large numbers removes all the mystery from the apparent fine-tuning.

The theory of many-universes cannot be dismissed. Indeed, a quantum process called 'inflation' may explain at least some of the anthropic coincidences, and one possible by-product of inflation is an endless proliferation of universes.[15] At the moment, however, the postulation of many universes remains highly speculative and hardly less extravagant ontologically than believing in God.

Nor are God and the many-universe theory mutually exclusive. We have already observed that the immensity of our own universe may be an extravagance necessary to get intelligent life to appear even once. Perhaps endless junk universes are just a further extravagance towards that end. Such a view neatly coincides with the mysticism of the Kabbalah, according to which God attempted numerous abortive universes before embarking on this one.

Once we begin to take seriously the possibility that we were meant to be here, we can only be struck by the very fact that our universe has a history. The universe has not been static throughout eternity. Rather, over the course of 13 billion years, the universe has been going somewhere. As it turns out, it has been going somewhere specific.

Thus, when we return to the Heibrunn Cosmic Pathway, we again need not feel dwarfed into insignificance by the hair-width span of our own history. We may similarly view the enormous time preceding us as a great labour of preparation.

In truth, we could not have emerged much sooner than we did. Certainly, we could not have appeared during the first three minutes of the big bang, when the average temperature of the universe was a billion degrees and only the lightest nuclei were able to bind together. Up until a million years after the big bang, the universe was still too hot for atoms to form and was, moreover, so radiated by photonic pressure as to keep any matter from clustering sufficiently. It was only after several billion years that the universe had cooled sufficiently for stellar clouds to begin aggregating. These, too, took another several billion years to coalesce into the star clusters we know as galaxies.[16]

Nor could we have found ourselves circling one of the first generation of stars. For us to appear, hydrogen first had to be made into helium and helium into carbon and the other, organic building blocks of life. In the ultra-hot, dense cores of many stars like our sun, hydrogen is routinely converted into helium. That, however, is all that happens. Stars like our sun cannot also synthesise carbon. Carbon synthesis only happens in the cores of the red giants, and only then by virtue of a two–stage process that delicately depends on yet another anthropic coincidence – the double resonance of helium with beryllium and of beryllium with carbon.[17]

Eventually, the red giants go supernova, spewing out as debris their organic contents. As Carl Sagan has put it, we are literally star dust, for the debris of heavy metals and organic compounds eventually coalesces into new solar systems, now with planets containing the building blocks of life.

We emerged on one such planet of just the right size, and of continuously just the right distance from just the right kind of star, in one of just the right kind of spots of one of just the right kinds of galaxies.[18] Even this special planet too had first to be prepared. Among other things, it had to cool, and the atmosphere had to become just right. That could not happen immediately. Most likely, the earth's first atmosphere was blown into space from the impact of celestial collisions. After the collisions ceased, the second atmosphere was created by volcanic out-gasing, producing concentrations of water vapour and carbon dioxide. From the condensation of the water vapour, the first oceans formed.[19]

Once the oceans cooled, it took close to a billion years for the first life to form. Prokaryotes converted the carbon dioxide into oxygen, which first reacted chemically to reduce the ammonia and methane in the atmosphere. Only when these noxious gases had been largely eliminated did the atmosphere begin to accumulate the free oxygen on which more complex, animal life depends. It then took another three and a half billion years for evolution to generate us.[20]

We thus arrive at the hair-width moment of the present. Contrary to the impression conveyed by the Heibrunn Cosmic Pathway, during the preceding aeons, the universe had not been idly occupied with affairs having nothing to do with us. Whether by design or not, it had been at work on processes preparatory for our arrival.

Just as the history of the universe unfolded in just the way necessary to make intelligent life possible, the history of evolution unfolded in just such a way as to realise that possibility. When we finally do appear, we find that, lo, we have a history too. Is ours also going somewhere?

To speak of the histories of the universe, evolution and humanity as all going somewhere is to re-invoke the name of Hegel, the great German philosopher whom Marx avowedly turned on his head. Whereas Marx proposed a materialist account of history with a mechanism based on efficient causes, Hegel proposed a teleological account of history, motored by the Absolute Spirit.

Because, according to Hegel, all of reality is an attempt to realise a magnificent idea, the unfolding of reality is a creative process. It is creative in the expressive way a work of art or even a well-written essay is creative. A work of art or a piece of writing are not fully imagined in all their detail right from the start. It is not as if the sculpting, or the painting, or the writing are just rote copies in material form of an already graphic mental picture. Instead, the writer or artist does not even personally know fully what the driving idea is until it is actually materially expressed, until it is somehow articulated.[21]

Only when the idea is rightly materialised in stone, or paint, or words can the artist or writer step back and say, 'Yes, this was my idea all along'. Until then, the idea remains inchoate. The artist or writer can recognise what the idea is not. When a first attempt at articulation does not quite live up to the vision, the artist or writer can recognise this. The creative mind consequently attempts to wrestle the draft into a form that more truly matches what is not fully there to be matched against until it is successfully matched. Such creativity is a process of groping towards what one only fully recognises one is groping towards once it is reached. It is an anguished process in which one repeatedly pulls something up from one's guts and holds it out for inspection only to say, 'No, this is not quite what is down there; I need to try again'. It is Richard Dreyfuss in *Close Encounters of the Third Kind*, obsessively moulding and remoulding his mashed potatoes until they finally resemble the mountain he did not until then even know he was trying to represent.

This is the process of creative expression, always involving a dialectical contradiction between what has so far been materialised and what is actually sought. This also is how Hegel imagined the unfolding of reality. The Hegelian dialectic was not some mechanical formula with synthesis as a mathematical function of thesis and antithesis. If that triad often seems to fit the cases that Hegel describes, it is because it is from the contradiction between what is (thesis) and what is yet lacking (antithesis) that creativity pushes on to a higher synthesis.

For Hegel, the universe comes into being to express an idea, an inchoate idea but an idea nonetheless. In an unfolding history, the non-bionic universe comes into being. It is good, but not good enough. It is redrafted with an overlay of biological evolution. Better, but the driving idea is still not captured.

When humans appear on the scene, the Spirit's work slows to a human scale. Now, the pre-eminent society of each age simultaneously carries the Zeitgeist, the most advanced articulation of the driving idea. From the society's culture, the articulated idea is further expressed in social institutions. It is this causal connection between culture and material institutions that Marx eventually turned on its head, arguing instead that it is a society's material circumstances and institutions that give rise to its culture.

According to Hegel, human history is as governed as nature by the same idealist dialectic, the same contradiction between what has been actually articulated materially and what ultimately needs to be expressed. When the pre-eminent society of each age still fails fully to articulate the driving idea, that society is surpassed or transcended. It is transcended in a cumulative way that preserves as well as negates. Whatever element of the idea a society has managed to capture is preserved, but now in a form that also captures something of what was missing.

Although the end of the road for Hegel was multifaceted, it included the idea fully expressed. The idea fully expressed includes the self-recognition of the Absolute Spirit, now finally conscious of itself as such. In a sense, for Hegel, all of creation is the immanent, material struggle of the Godhead to become conscious of itself as the Godhead. It is the process that earlier in this book we refer to as *theosis*. Ultimately, *theosis* is brought to completion by us, socially, when we collectively come to represent the Absolute Spirit.

To be sure, there are many things to be said against this monumental system of Hegel's. It may offend some religious sensibilities to portray God as creating out of need, to fill a lack. It may further offend to portray God as not yet fully God until we arrive, and until then only groping and semiconscious. On the other hand, the need in this case is a noble one, and the idea of a struggling, groping, immanent God is fully coincident with contemporary process theology.

Many, both religious and secular, have been aghast at how Hegel treats human agency. Hegel's 'cunning of reason' seems too overtly to make human beings into unwitting tools. It is not just that too much happens behind our backs. The problem, rather, is that Hegel's Absolute Spirit is too heavy-handed, too much of a micro-manager. It is impossible to accept, for example, that Napoleon specifically was called up to answer the universe's special needs.

Such heavy-handedness, however, is not an intrinsic feature of teleology. God, or the Absolute Spirit, could work much more subtly – and we have already seen how. In particular, as parametric settings, the anthropic coincidences are only meta constraints on the cosmos. They are not intrusions at the level of specific cause and effect. Thus, they do not predetermine any definite outcome but only condition the possibilities in a certain direction. Perhaps this is better called by a weaker term than teleology such as teleonomy or entelechy.[22]

There apparently is also some evidence of teleonomy or entelechy in biological evolution as well, some remarkable elements that cannot fully be explained solely by the mechanism of blind variations and selective retention.[23] And perhaps there are such more subtle elements of teleonomy or entelechy even in human history. Let us, for example, follow a suggestion from Marx. Suppose it is a principle of history that unjust social systems are sooner or later bound towards instability and that, further, this tendency intensifies as history progresses. Such a principle would neither predetermine the specific outcomes of history nor remove the need for autonomous human agency. It would, however, bias the long sweep of history in a utopian direction.

There lies the contemporary rub – or at least the first of two. After we have only just evaded nuclear holocaust and while even now we are busy cooking the earth, it can seem outrageous to suggest a utopian bias to history. It thus needs to be said at the outset that even with a utopian bias, utopia is by no means assured. If collectively we indeed have been entrusted with a cosmic task, it still remains very uncertain whether we will pull it off.

In our postmodern era, any suggestion of progress is suspect. Yet, is it really so outrageous to see some moral progress in our history? Although it may persist in some places, the evilness of slavery is now almost universally taken for granted. Similarly, whether or not human rights and democracy are honoured more in the breech, these concepts have at least entered our shared, global consciousness. That there even is something of a shared, global consciousness – a kind of 'noosphere' – is itself a significant development.[24]

Francis Fukuyama to the contrary, we are hardly ready to declare the end of history. As Marx observed when writing *On the Jewish Question*, to make such an announcement now only confuses political emancipation with human emancipation. However triumphant the concept of democracy may be, when the 20 per cent of the world's population in the Northern hemisphere devours 80 per cent of the world's resources, human history is not ready to end. Especially, it cannot end with the nominal democracies in the Northern hemisphere still contributing so much to the maintenance of this very condition. It does not detract from the moral progress we have made to observe that the current world system remains a grossly distorted one. It is not a world we are ready to yield back to the Absolute Spirit as the mirror image of itself.

The global, neo-liberal order of consumer capitalism itself remains to be transcended. The question now before us is whether it is humanity's vocation to transcend it, to strive towards yet a better society. With that question, we confront a second, contemporary rub.

The second rub relates to 'ultimate concern', which theologian Paul Tillich considered to be the essence of religion. Our ultimate concern is that which ultimately concerns us, that to which our lives owe their ultimate allegiance and from which they receive their ultimate fulfilment in return.[25]

To speak of ultimate concern is to speak in terms of what Weber called *Wert* rationality, the rationality of values and final ends. Whereas instrumental rationality addresses the problem-oriented, technical matter of the best means to any given end, *Wert* rationality addresses what our ends ought to be in the first place.

To speak of a concern that is ultimate is to suggest that our ends are not all on the same level, that they form instead a hierarchy with lower-level ends subservient to ends that are more fundamental or encompassing. What should ultimately concern us, says Tillich, is fundamentally a religious question. It is always a form of idolatry, for example, to be ultimately concerned about anything that is not truly ultimate.

What is ultimate? This is a question about the meaning of life and as such explains why ultimate concern is a contemporary sore point. The meaning of life is a concern that the contemporary world seeks to evade. To be sure, we are quite willing to speak of multiple meanings of life, of our own myriad, personal meanings. Yet, we positively resist the imposition of any one, grand meaning that might objectively call into question the true ultimacy of our own personal meanings. There are no such grand meanings, we protest, there are no overarching meta narratives. The only tenable meanings now are local, individual and entirely subjective. In effect, postmodernity addresses the question of life's meaning by relegating it out of bounds.

Admittedly, there is a danger when we introduce talk of a single, grand, objective meta narrative. The danger is intolerance and coercion, the attempt to impose on others beliefs that they are not inclined to adopt on their own. Postmodernist thinkers have been right to warn against this. Yet the danger is avoidable. Postmodernism tends to conflate the contents of our claims with the postures with which we advance them. Just as modest claims too can be advanced in a totalising posture that brooks no dissent, so can even the grandest of claims be submitted in a modest way that invites correction.

The latter is the way of Haverim.[26] When we serve each other as Haverim, when we are ever-willing to have our own blind spots exposed in a shared, respectful spirit of enquiry, we need not refrain from reaching to name even the most exalted truths. We must simply remember that when our reach is long, the less firm is our grasp. It is only with Haverim that we should reach towards the meaning of life.

Less observed today is the fact that we also court danger if we fail to reach out. If we truly have a human vocation, then by keeping our gaze too close to the ground, we are apt to miss our calling. Too close to the ground is where our current gaze remains. One strong legacy of the Enlightenment is the continued hegemony of instrumental reason. Individually and collectively, we are proficient at matching means to ends. Yet neither individually nor collectively do we pause long to consider our ends themselves. This is the one-dimensional thinking against which the Frankfurt School railed.[27] If anything, by discouraging reflection on ultimate matters, postmodernist philosophy only abets this one-dimensional orientation.

The Eastern religious traditions have a name for this condition. They call it Avidya – our tendency to become so bedazzled by the goods closer to life's surface – be it possessions, status, family or even community – that we ignore the higher ends to which we are called.

Named during the 'axial age', in the millennium before the Common Era, the condition called Avidya has long been with us; the wise have ever been few. Today, however, Avidya is not just a metaphysical trait of the human predicament. Today, it is also a specific social condition. Capitalism is an economic system that not only thrives on Avidya. Because it is on Avidya that capitalism thrives, capitalism positively promotes Avidya. If anything, it produces surplus Avidya.

The contemporary world capitalist order is an order of desire. It promotes the very kinds of venal attachments from which Buddhism and Hinduism have long sought to free us. Capitalism encourages us to find our identities on the surface of life: in things, in sex, in status. Corporate capitalism defines us as market segments, and it is as market segments that we are content to identify ourselves. We are the driver of this or that SUV, the drinker of Coors or Michelob beer, the wearer of a Rolex or a Swatch. Our consumer niche becomes our identity. It is bad enough to become so, but the Siren song of capitalism persists, hypnotising us with what is lower, making us forget that we were ever – or meant to be – something higher. And all the while, the earth groans under our waste.

It is bad enough that capitalism operates so in the developed world. Worse is that it functions similarly in the Southern hemisphere on those who can less afford it. Under the 'demonstration effect' of the north, the leadership of the south is diverted from social justice to greed. The ever-globalising American culture of consumption is like Circe, magically transforming human beings into swine.

For humanity to have a vocation and ignore it is an alienation of the most profound sort. It is an alienation from the cosmos itself. It is an alienation from why we are here and who we are meant to be. As such, it is also an alienation from our authentic selves.

Today, talk of authentic selves is as suspect as talk of progress, truth and meta narratives. It is no accident that these suspects are all related. To speak of our authentic selves is to speak of an ontological or alethic truth. It is a truth related to still other alethic truths. In particular, our authentic self is that self that matches our true place in the universe. If humanity has a true place in the universe, that place is capturable by one or another, sufficiently inclusive meta narrative. That meta narrative in turn should be reflected in human history.

Do we really have authentic selves and a true place in the cosmos? It is quite possible that this exquisitely fine-tuned universe of ours was all just a meaningless accident of blind causality. The particular way the universe unfolded may have been accidental too. It may also have been accidental that intelligent life was generated by evolution. And it may be accidental that human history just happens to operate according to the principles of historical materialism. Conversely, such appearances of goal-direction in the universe may actually be important signs, signs that we truly were meant to be here.

The choice is between viewing ourselves as cosmically insignificant and viewing ourselves as cosmically important. According to theologians Hans Kung and David Tracy, the affirmation of God is in the first place an affirmation of meaning over meaninglessness.[28] Belief in God affirms that it is not just through causality that we find ourselves here. It affirms instead that we are also here for a reason.

Many religious people are content just believing that we are here for a reason. They do not trouble themselves too much to consider what that reason might be. Bourgeois religion tends to interpret the reason very individualistically. For bourgeois religion, we are here to work out our own, individual salvation. Others who are religious dimly sense that we do have some collective task to perform. They say that while here on earth, they want 'to make a difference', to leave the world better off than they found it. They stop short, however, from thinking too deeply about what a better world would be.

Whatever the reason is for our existence, it must match the grandeur of all that prepared for our arrival. That grandeur is not honoured by viewing the entire universe as just a launch pad to be discarded when after death we wing our way to heaven, having no further relation to this reality. This universe or multiverse is just too magnificent to bear no value in its own right.

Thus, whatever the reason for our existence, it must include somehow bringing the universe itself to completion. That is a collective not an individual project – although to be sure we each must participate in it individually. There are as many names for this project as there are religious traditions. In

Mahayana Buddhism, there is the tradition of the Bodhisattva, the enlightened one who, realising that enlightenment must be universal, refrains from passing over into Nirvana until the whole world is ready to make the same transition. In Judaism there is both the tradition of the Messianic age, which bespeaks a time of social justice and peace, and the Kabbalistic 'Tikkun Olam', which refers to our becoming co-creators with God in the task of healing a broken world.

Christianity too need not devolve into either bourgeois individualism or an exclusive preoccupation with sexual morality. Its main thrust reaches higher concerns. One of the most historically reliable things we know about Jesus is that he proclaimed the dawning reign of God, not just in heaven but already here on earth. He showed us, moreover, what this reign is like. It is a reign of open and inclusive commensality, in which ethnic enemies are greeted as neighbours and women too discourse on Torah; it is a reign opposed to the rule of Mammon in which people rather than profits come first, and in which money is lent not only without interest but also without expectation that it will even be repaid.[29] Jesus compared this reign to a mustard seed, which begins too imperceptibly to be noticed. He expected this seed to grow and so left his followers a world historical task.

Marx described religion as the 'heart of a heartless world, the soul of soulless conditions'. Religion is that, but it is also more. It is also humanity groping towards its vocation. That vocation always lies in a utopian direction, a direction that until the end always transcends the present. If ultimately we are to mirror something back to the Absolute Spirit, what else could it be than a collective existence that deserves to be called the reign of God.

Notes

1 Carl Sagan, *Cosmos*, Random House, New York, 1980, p. 7.
2 See Robert Rood and James Trefil, *Are We Alone?*, Charles Scribner's, New York, 1981. More recently, see Peter Ward and Donald Brownlee, *Rare Earth: Why Complex Life is Uncommon in the Universe*, Copernicus, New York, 2000.
3 Ward and Brownlee, *Rare Earth*.
4 Ward and Brownlee, *Rare Earth*.
5 Ward and Brownlee, *Rare Earth*.
6 Ward and Brownlee, *Rare Earth*, concede that mircrobial life may well be very plentiful in the universe.
7 Stephen Jay Gould, *Wonderful Life: The Burgess Shale and the Nature of History*, Norton, New York, 1989, pp. 48–52.
8 There is now a vast literature on this topic, from the highly technical to the more popular. For a range, see, for example, John Barrow and Frank Tippler, *The Anthropic Cosmological Principle* (Oxford University Press, Oxford, 1986); John Gribbin and Martin Rees, *Cosmic Coincidences: Dark Matter, Mankind, and Anthropic Cosmology* (Bantam, New York, 1989); Paul Davies, *The Accidental Universe* (Cambridge University Press, Cambridge, 1982); John Leslie, *Universes* (Routledge, London, 1989).

9 Davies, *Accidental Universe*, p. 73.

10 Davies, *Accidental Universe*, p. 73.

11 Davies, *Accidental Universe*, p. 73. See also Leslie, *Universes*, p. 5,

12 Leslie, *Universes*, pp. 39–41.

13 Freeman Dyson, *Disturbing the Universe*, Harper & Row, New York, 1979, p. 250. Hoyle's remark is quoted by Paul Davies in *Superforce* (Simon & Schuster, New York, 1984), p. 233.

14 At one time, Adoph Gruenbaum argued that the whole issue of anthropic coincidences was a pseudo-problem. That judgement, however, is belied not only by the seriousness with which physicists are considering it but also by the fact that it admits of solutions other than God. See Leslie, *Universes*, for the most decisive argument against Gruenbaum's position.

15 See Alan Guth, *The Inflationary Universe: The Quest for a New Theory of Cosmic Origins*, Jonathan Cape, London, 1997.

16 Barrow and Tipler, *Cosmological Principle*, pp. 369–372.

17 George Greenstein, *The Symbiotic Universe: Life and the Cosmos in Unity* (Quill, New York, 1988), pp. 33–45.

18 See Ward and Brownlee, *Rare Earth*, who further argue that a great many galaxies are as a whole incapable of supporting any life.

19 Ward and Brownlee, *Rare Earth*.

20 Ward and Brownlee, *Rare Earth*.

21 My reading of Hegel owes much to Charles Taylor's *Hegel* (Cambridge, Cambridge University Press, 1975).

22 For the concept of entelechy, I am indebted to my old teacher, Kyriakos Kontopoulos. He discusses this concept in his *Logics of Structuration* (Cambridge University Press, Cambridge, 1993).

23 See Michael Behe, *Darwin's Black Box*, Touchstone, New York, 1996.

24 The concept of a 'noosphere', or a layer of global consciousness, comes from Teilhard de Chardin, *The Phenomenon of Man*, Harper & Row, New York, 1959.

25 See Paul Tillich, *The Dynamics of Faith*, Harper & Brothers, New York, 1957.

26 For the concept of Haverim, see Clark Williamson, 'Doing Christian Theology with Jews: The Other, Boundaries, Questions', pp. 37–52 in Roger Badham (ed.), *Introduction to Christian Theology*, Westminster, Philadelphia, 1998.

27 See, for example, Herbert Marcuse, *One Dimensional Man*, Beacon, Boston, 1964.

28 See Hans Kung, *Does God Exist? An Answer for Today*, Doubleday, New York, 1980; and David Tracy, *Blessed Rage for Order*, Seabury Press, New York, 1975.

29 See John Dominic Crossan, *The Historical Jesus: The Life of a Mediterranean Jewish Peasant*, Harper, San Francisco, 1992.

12 Emancipation, social and spiritual

Andrew Collier

Critical realism started by doing philosophical underlabouring work for the sciences. In this way it arrived at the epistemological and ontological conclusions which are among the premises of this book. But it has also aspired to do underlabouring work for another practice, the – largely political – practice of human emancipation. More recently, some critical realists, including Roy Bhaskar and the authors of this book, have raised the issue of another kind of human emancipation, the spiritual emancipation which has traditionally been the work of religion. This is not just a matter of using the critical realist conception of science derived from Roy's earlier work in doing theology (which has also been done, for instance, by Alister McGrath).[1] It is a new subject matter for critical realist thought, widely referred to, in connection with Roy's version of it, as a 'spiritual turn'.

There are different views about the relations between these two kinds of putative emancipation. At one extreme, some religious radicals would simply identify the two. This identification usually looks like what other people would regard as political emancipation. In other words, spiritual liberation has in some measure been reduced to political liberation. At the other extreme, there are those who regard the two programmes of liberation as negatively related – as alternatives in fact. In the context of critical realism, those who think like this would generally be committed to the political programme of emancipation, to the exclusion of the spiritual. They would favour Marx's characterisation of religion as the opium of the people, or, in Graham Greene's paraphrase, the poor man's valium, the means whereby the oppressed reconcile themselves to their oppression. Third, there are those who regard the two programmes as mutually irreducible, but both worthwhile and important. Perhaps this view can be attributed to Karl Barth, who was a Christian and a socialist, but rejected the confusion of the two things in 'religious socialism'. I believe that this position is closer to the truth than the other two, but with the proviso that there is a positive correlation between the two. (There has also to be, I fear, a proviso to the proviso, that in particular instances there might also be a negative relation between the two, but not of such a nature that we have to reject one or the other. More of this later.) A final view, characteristic of some liberation theology, is the idea that spiritual liberation cannot occur until after social liberation has. But this has the disadvantage that it tells us nothing about how to live until the revolution – which, of course, may never happen.

I shall now look at some Christian ideas about spiritual liberation, before returning to discuss political liberation and the relation between the two. First let it be noted that the image of freedom in every age is different, according to what it is contrasted with. Hence for John Stuart Mill, in the Victorian age freedom contrasted with interference in one's intellectual or private life. For a modern Tory, it contrasts with taxation, which for Mill was not an issue of freedom at all. For anyone in the Roman Empire during the first century, freedom meant first of all not being a slave. Spiritual freedom was seen on analogy with this.

The New Testament talks about being free or being made free in two sorts of way. Sometimes absolutely: freedom is simply contrasted with bondage. Thus:

> Then said Jesus to those Jews which believed on him, 'If ye continue in my word, then are ye my disciples indeed; and ye shall know the truth, and the truth shall make you free.' They answered him, 'We be Abraham's seed, and were never in bondage to any man: how sayest thou, Ye shall be made free?' Jesus answered them, 'Verily, verily I say unto you, Whosoever committeth sin is the servant of sin. And the servant abideth not in the house for ever: but the Son abideth ever. If the Son therefore shall make you free, ye shall be free indeed.'
>
> (John 8.31–6)

Here we not only have the saying 'the truth shall make you free' – the charter for the ethical naturalism of explanatory critiques – but also a contrast between the way you are treated by (personified) sin, which treats you as slaves, and the Son (Jesus himself) who makes you free.

Yet, there is another way of talking about slavery and freedom (in the spiritual sense) which makes the two symmetrical. Thus Paul writes: 'when ye were the servants of sin, ye were free from righteousness . . . But now being made free from sin, and become servants to God' (Romans 6.20 and 22). One can be free from sin and a servant to God, or free from God and a servant to sin, but one cannot be free from both. We have become so used to thinking of freedom as indivisible and always good that this way of speaking grates on modern ears. Yet it is a simple fact of social and political life that every freedom excludes certain other freedoms. You can be free to use your car whenever you want, or free to breathe clean air, but not both; you can be free to do what you like with your property, or free to live in congenial surroundings, but not both. The difference between capitalism and socialism is not that one provides more freedom than the other, but that they provide different freedoms. Paul is saying that it is the same with spiritual freedom. You choose your master. This is echoed by Roy Bhaskar's idea of emancipation as wanted determinants in place of unwanted determinants (there being no option of no determinants at all). At the end of the passage in Romans, Paul does point out an asymmetry (using the New English Bible translation, which brings out this point better): 'For sin pays a wage, and the wage is death, but God gives freely, and his gift is eternal life, in union with Jesus Christ our Lord' (Romans 6.23). But the asymmetry is, so to speak, a second order one, as in Bhaskar's definition of emancipation.

With these points in mind, let us turn to Luther's formulation about Christian freedom, and Marcuse's critique of it as 'the specifically bourgeois concept of freedom'. Luther starts with two theses which he says seem to contradict each other:

'A Christian is a perfectly free lord of all, subject to none.
A Christian is a perfectly dutiful servant of all, subject to all.'[2]

As Marcuse rightly comments, Luther resolves the contradiction by saying that the first sentence refers to the spiritual person, the second to the outer person. However, we should not imagine that there is some sort of Cartesian dualism here, whereby what happens in the spirit has no effects in the world. Part of freedom for Luther, as for Paul, is freedom from legalistic ethics. The service which is owed to all, according to the second sentence, is not adherence to such ethics, but works motivated by love. It would not be forcing Luther's point too much to say that the inner freedom is freedom to love, and the outer bondage is to do the works of love. For it should be said that Luther is far from decrying good works; only he sees them as an effect of salvation, not a means to it.

Now this freedom to love and duty to do works of love does not look much like a specifically bourgeois concept of freedom, and indeed it is not. Even the restriction of freedom to something purely inner, which is counter-emancipatory and of which Luther is sometimes guilty, is not specifically bourgeois. On the contrary, bourgeois freedom is very much an outer freedom – freedom to do what one likes with one's own property. And Luther is not an ideologist of the bourgeoisie. Not because he sees beyond the time of the bourgeoisie to human emancipation in a social sense, he does not; but because he is thoroughly pre-bourgeois. In some ways this makes him better than a bourgeois ideologist – in his condemnation of usury, for instance. But in other ways it makes him worse than one – for instance, his advocacy of submission to the powers that be. However, this does not vitiate his account of spiritual freedom; it merely means that he has not drawn from it a conclusion which he should have, namely that since some works of love involve changing society, the spiritually free person may very well be a rebel politically. As Berdyaev says somewhere, bread for me is a material issue but bread for my neighbour is a spiritual issue. Being 'a servant of all, subject to all' is not the same as being an obedient subject of the king or emperor; it ought rather to mean first and foremost being a servant of the poorest and most oppressed of one's neighbours. Luther did not draw this conclusion, not because it was not supported by his premisses, but because his natural conservatism prevented him from being consistent.

Spiritual emancipation, so far from being an alternative to social emancipation, ought to provide a motive for it, namely love of one's neighbours. But it cannot tell you what is required for that emancipation in any given epoch. It will not be the same in the modern age as in those in which the Bible was written. It seems to me that emancipation in the modern age is best defined by Marx in his introduction to the programme of the French Workers' Party (*Parti Ouvrier Français*), where he states that workers can only be free if the means of production belong to them; that this can be either individual or collective ownership; and that modern industry makes the individual form impossible. Hence emancipation equals common ownership, and Marx holds that this emancipation 'involves all mankind, without distinction of sex or race'.[3] Clearly Marx is saying that oppression along the lines of race and sex is caused by class exploitation. I think he is right about this, but there is no space to argue it here. What is clear is that he does not *neglect* non-class forms of oppression.

Now this is obviously a programme which presupposes that modern industry exists, which it did not in Biblical times, but it is arguably the necessary modern application of the politics implicit in Judaeo-Christian religion. The most political part of the Bible dates from the time when Judah and Israel were independent or semi-independent states, and the prophets could have some hope of influencing the course of events. The pre-exilic prophets, and some of the later prophets who continue their witness, are consistent in what they regard as the truest service of God: to defend the poor, to share goods with them, to let the oppressed go free, to 'break every yoke'. They are scathing about specifically religious works: temple services, which the first Isaiah calls trampling the Lord's courts (Isaiah 1.12), or fasting, which the second Isaiah contrasts with the fast that the Lord has chosen, to let the oppressed go free and deal bread to the hungry (Isaiah 58.6–7). Their political programme is not of course socialist – that would be anachronistic for the reasons stated; it is for freedom of the workers through individual peasant proprietorship, in which everyone shall dwell under his own vine and fig tree (Micah 4.4). That this programme was in opposition to a nascent ruling class is clear from the denunciations of landowners who were extending their land at the peasants' expense, of judges who decided against the poor, and so on. The prophets were partisans of the oppressed in a class war. Alongside the demand for a classless peasant society, there are injunctions to protect those who, even in such a society, were least able to protect themselves (widows, orphans).

In New Testament times, any rational political practice was made impossible by the Roman Empire. One could of course foment nationalist rebellions against it, but they could only end in the slaughter of the rebels. Or one could collaborate with it, but that was not possible for those who refused to worship the Emperor. The alternative was to change what could be changed without confronting the state power, and prepare for the times to change. It is noteworthy what form this course of action took for the early Christians: voluntary communism. Of course, this 'communism of consumption' is not the same as the common ownership of the means of production, but it is worth saying that the phrase 'to each according to their need' (Marx's definition of communism) originates here (Acts 2.45). Regrettably, by the time the Empire became (nominally) Christian, this experiment had ceased. But its memory remained:

Rosa Luxemburg[4] quotes from three of the greatest Church Fathers: St Basil the Great (330–379), the founder of communal monasticism in the Eastern Church; St John Chrysostom (347–407), Patriarch of Byzantium; and St Gregory the Great (540–604), Pope of Rome; all three are among the 'Doctors of the Church'. Basil challenges the right of the rich to their wealth, saying 'How do the possessors become rich, if not by taking possession of things that belong to all?'; Chrysostom extols the good that would come if the Christians of his time would imitate the early Christians in freeing their slaves and sharing their goods; Gregory says that those who keep their wealth are murderers of those who starve in consequence, and that giving to the poor is 'not an act of pity, but the payment of a debt'. Unsurprisingly, these pleas for common ownership fell on deaf ears, and John Chrysostom died in exile.

How does all this compare with Roy Bhaskar's 'spiritual turn' and its relation to his politics? It should be clear by now that the present book is also part of a spiritual turn in critical realism, though different in some ways from Roy's. In part the difference is due to the fact that all three of the present authors are Christians. Roy's position in regard to religion is not the same in *From East to West*[5] as in the later 'meta-reality' books,[6] so there are in a sense two spiritual turns on Roy's part rather than one. *From East to West* is a frankly religious and theistic work, drawing perhaps mainly on the Hinduism of the *Bhagavad Gita*, but also on Judaism, Christianity, the Sufi tradition of Islam, Buddhism and Taoism. The meta-reality books are intended to be compatible with either theistic or secular positions; they still tell us about transcendence, but it is a much more immanent kind of transcendence. They also draw on a particular tradition of Hindu philosophy, *advaita*, or non-dualism. While the term 'the cosmic envelope' has replaced 'God', one is inevitably reminded of the idea of the identity of Brahman and Atman, the Deity underlying all reality and the individual soul. I do not have the space to discuss the whole theory, nor do I think I am qualified to do so, but I would like to discuss two of Roy's ideas, one of which I think is true and important, the other misleading.

First, Roy's insistence that, in order to exist and flourish, anything, including wholly or partly evil things, depends on good of some kind. Thus war, which is an evil – even an unjust war, which is unmitigatedly evil – depends on the courage, loyalty and comradeship of the soldiers. Capitalism can only work because of the creativity of the workers – that is why a 'work to rule' is effectively a form of strike. Capitalism also depends for the reproduction of labour power on the non-market relations that exist within the family. (Of course, the family can also be a site of oppression, but the non-market relations within it do provide a model for non-market relations in society at large as is witnessed by the fact that, however critical they are of the existing family, socialists, like Christians, address one another as brother and sister.) And as Plato's Socrates points out, a band of robbers will be more effective if it practises justice within its ranks.

I think this view of Roy's is profoundly true. To an extent, it is also true in the individual character. Every vice needs virtues if it is to be carried out effectively. Human potential, which is the condition for good and evil alike, is itself good. All this is implicit in St Augustine's teaching that being as being is good, since God is its author, and evil can only exist as a corruption of being – where 'corruption' is not just a synonym for evil, but a live metaphor from rust and rot. Though I agree with this view of Roy's that evil is unilaterally dependent on good, it should be said that it is not obvious, and that some have thought the opposite, that is, that good depends on evil for its existence. Adam Smith, Hegel and Nietzsche are cases in point, as is the fatuous slogan which I have seen on a student's t-shirt: 'peace through superior fire-power' (fatuous because it invites the question 'superior on whose part?').

However, I do not have space to refute these views, which would require very elaborate arguments. I simply want to register my agreement with Roy on this. But it does not follow that there is a good and free being fully formed inside each evil and enslaved one, just waiting to get out. Here we come to the view of Roy's which I think is misleading, and which I have called a nutcracker model of human liberation: the idea that the kernel of each individual (what Roy calls their 'ground-state') is already good and free and untainted by the evil in the shell, so that all we have to do is crack the nut and discard the shell. As against this I think that spiritual liberation is a work of transformation, which has its raw material (the existing character), its means of production (spiritual practices) and its end-product (a better, freer character). A secular writer would call this self-transformation, but for a Christian it is transformation of a willing agent by the grace of God. There is, I think, a difference between the Vedanta doctrine of the identity of Brahman and Atman – *tat tvam asi*, 'that thou art' – and the Christian doctrine of *theosis*, the becoming divine of the originally sinful person as a work of divine grace. This idea of *theosis* is emphasised more in the Orthodox Church than by Western Christians, but it originates with the Greek Fathers of the undivided Church, and so is perfectly orthodox (small 'o') for Catholics and Protestants too. Indeed, it forms part of the mystical tradition in Western Christianity too.

This makes spiritual liberation far more homologous to political liberation as understood by critical realists. According to the 'Transformational Model of Social Activity',[7] human agents, in the course of conscious and intentional actions, unconsciously and unintentionally reproduce social structures, which structures pre-exist each generation and constrain it to reproduce the structure by its actions which have quite other ends. Changing the intentional actions of human agents will not lead to a different structure; for that, an organised work of conflict and transformation is necessary. For instance, different work practices will not transform capitalism into socialism; equality of opportunity, and the breakdown of formalities between members of different classes, will not affect the class structure one jot. I would suggest that spiritual liberation, like political liberation, is a work of transformation of a bad structure (though one founded on goodness and with a potential for good) into a good structure, not a work of shedding veils which obscure an already existing good structure.

It should be stressed – and I do not think Roy would deny it – that spiritual liberation, even of a great many individuals, will not by itself bring political liberation. The individuals would need to become organised on a scale commensurate with the task of transforming concentrated power relations to do that. But it will strengthen rather than weaken the motivation for political liberation.

My contention that personal, spiritual liberation, like social liberation, is more of a work of transformation than of shedding is, I think, a real difference from Roy's position in the 'meta-reality series'. But I do not want to exaggerate this. The difference, and its limits, are expressed in his interview on 'The Philosophy of Meta-Reality'.[8] He is asked 'Your ground-state is already informed, inside you?' and he answers 'Absolutely'. But he goes on to say: 'It's not difficult for people to access the consciousness of their ground-state in meditation or some other state of rest, the difficulty is for them to take the ground-state and its consciousness . . . into activity.'[9] Thus, Roy is not denying that personal spiritual liberation, like social liberation, can be hard work. I think he is right that we can access the love that underlies our being through meditation. To anyone who finds it difficult to do so, I would recommend a Quaker meeting. I agree too that this is only the beginning of a work of transformation, not the end. But what is accessed is not a complete self that only has to be let out, but a resource for transforming what Roy calls your embodied personality.

Now I want to look at a problem which makes the issue of personal spiritual liberation crucial to social liberation, and at the same time gives grounds for qualified pessimism about the relation between the two, which is certainly not a relation of identity. Let me instance my own experience. For two six-year periods I was active on the left of the Labour Party, and for an eight-year period in between, I was active in the Socialist Workers' Party. I do not regret these periods of political activity; I believe that they were entirely appropriate to their time and place. But it was my experience that political struggle can seriously damage your (spiritual) health. This is so even though my own activity consisted only of selling papers, making speeches, going on demonstrations, organising strikers' support groups, and occasionally confronting fascist organisations. Even in these relatively non-violent struggles, a continuous state of anger and suspicion is induced, which it is very hard to combine with love. And of course no political struggle is non-violent in essence, even if it is in form, since in all politics the control of the state is at issue, and the state is by definition that which can dispose violence.

In periods of overt violence though – periods of revolution and civil war – the corrupting effect of politics on its agents is infinitely worse. Robespierre started off as a really nice guy, and ended by guillotining his old comrades. It has been said that of all the leading French Revolutionaries, only Grégoire (a radical Catholic bishop at the outset of the Revolution, and later the head of the Constitutional Church, which accepted the democratic church reorganisation imposed by the Republic) survived the whole Revolution without betraying a friend or a principle. It is perhaps significant that he was one of the few revolutionaries who did not have a secular world-view.

The Russian experience was the same. The Bolsheviks were not natural terrorists. On the morrow of the Revolution, they released the arrested members of the old Provisional Government on parole, which of course they broke. Nicholas Berdyaev, a Russian Orthodox Christian, was allowed to set up a Free Academy of Spiritual Culture in Moscow, and to criticise the Bolsheviks in his lectures. Yet within a few years – well before Stalin's time – the Bolshevik regime (or the Cheka acting in their name) was sending to Siberia or executing not only members of rival socialist groups but electricians who had blown a fuse and housewives who had bought a cup of sugar from a neighbour. Or consider the change wrought in Trotsky, the advocate of soviet democracy in 1917 and again in the 1930s against Stalin, but who at the end of the Civil War proposed the militarisation of labour and the governmentalisation of the trade unions.

There is no easy answer to these problems. It was not that the Revolution was wrong or the Bolsheviks deeply mistaken in their strategy (though of course there were mistakes). The Revolution was a genuine instance of human emancipation – perhaps the greatest in history – yet it deeply corrupted its agents. A spiritual dimension with a commitment to love of one's neighbours, even one's enemies, would have made struggle psychologically more difficult, but far more likely to lead to liberation. The problem is that while spiritual liberation gives a motive to struggle for political liberation, political liberation has adverse effects on spiritual liberation: it makes it far easier to hate than to love. Where the two kinds of liberation co-exist, there is necessarily a tension between them. But it is all the more important that both be maintained. One should have a deep sense of the value of each person as a child of God and as a brother or sister – even if they have to be faced across the barricades and perhaps killed. I think that this is recognised by Roy in connection with Krishna's advice to Arjuna in the *Bhagavad Gita*. But I feel that Krishna was also urging Arjuna to stop feeling the *tension* between his duty to wage a just war and his love for those he would have to kill. Yet if we let go of such tension and commit ourselves wholeheartedly either to just war or to peace at any price, we condemn ourselves either to become political gangsters or to become politically ineffective. It is entirely understandable that political revolutionaries tend to reject spiritual liberation and that those committed to spiritual liberation tend to keep out of politics, since these options avoid this tension. But it is entirely wrong. Even those who have combined great spiritual awareness with political action, like Mahatma Gandhi or Toyohiko Kagawa, have generally been pacifists in their style of work. And while they have certainly achieved a great deal, they have not and could not have dispossessed the possessing class.

In the wake of the collapse of the Eastern European regimes which called themselves Marxist, many people are claiming to find lacunae all over Marx's theories. I think most of these so-called lacunae turn out to be the strengths of Marxism – the freedom from utopianism, for instance, or the causal prioritisation of class over other types of oppression. But there is one great lacuna: the absence of a spiritual dimension, with its ethical corollary of unconditional love. I think Marxist critics of Roy's spiritual turn often find unconditional love – which must include love for one's class enemies – the hardest thing to swallow. In the long run it may be essential if any future movement for social liberation is not to be deflected into brutal power politics as happened to such movements in the past.

Notes

1 Alister E. McGrath, *A Scientific Theology*, Volume 2, 'Reality', T. & T. Clark/Continuum, Edinburgh and New York, 2002.
2 John Dillenberger (ed.) *Martin Luther: Selections from His Writings* Doubleday Anchor, New York, 1961, p. 53.
3 Karl Marx, *The First International and After*, Pelican, Harmondsworth, 1974, p. 377.
4 Rosa *Luxemburg Speaks*, (ed. M.-A. Waters), Pathfinder, New York, 1970, pp. 139–41.
5 Roy Bhaskar, *From East to West: Odyssey of a Soul*, Routledge, London, 2000.
6 Roy Bhaskar, *Meta-Reality: The Philosophy of Meta-Reality*, Volume 1, 'Creativity, Love and Freedom', Sage, London, 2002.
7 See Roy Bhaskar, *The Possibility of Naturalism*, Harvester Wheatsheaf, Hemel Hempstead, 1979, pp. 34–44.
8 Roy Bhaskar interviewed by Mervyn Hartwig, 'The Philosophy of Meta-Reality', *Journal of Critical Realism*, 2002, 1 (1): 67–93.
9 'The Philosophy of Meta-Reality', p. 74.

Index

15324366R00111

Printed in Poland
by Amazon Fulfillment
Poland Sp. z o.o., Wrocław